BASS NOTES

BASS NOTES

JAZZ IN AMERICAN CULTURE

A Personal View

Chuck Israels

Essex, Connecticut

Backbeat Books

An imprint of Globe Pequot, the trade division of
The Rowman & Littlefield Publishing Group, Inc.
4501 Forbes Blvd., Ste. 200
Lanham, MD 20706
www.rowman.com

Distributed by NATIONAL BOOK NETWORK

Copyright © 2023 by Chuck Israels

Every effort has been made to identify copyright holders and obtain their permission for the use of copyrighted material in this book. If you believe there has been an oversight in this regard, please be in touch directly with the publisher.

All rights reserved. No part of this book may be reproduced in any form or by any electronic or mechanical means, including information storage and retrieval systems, without written permission from the publisher, except by a reviewer who may quote passages in a review.

British Library Cataloguing in Publication Information available

Library of Congress Cataloging-in-Publication Data available
ISBN 978-1-4930-7484-6 (cloth : alk. paper)
ISBN 978-1-4930-7485-3 (electronic)

∞™ The paper used in this publication meets the minimum requirements of American National Standard for Information Sciences—Permanence of Paper for Printed Library Materials, ANSI/NISO Z39.48-1992

CONTENTS

INTRODUCTION: A Fateful Letter		1
1	Skripitching	7
2	The Right High School and Wrong University	19
3	A Pressure Case	33
4	Paris and Bud	53
5	Jazz Professional	67
6	Playing with Bill	87
7	An Interruption	111
8	A Brilliant Drummer	119
9	Bill Redux	131
10	Independence and Study	147
11	Name That Tune	161

12	Survival	169
13	The National Jazz Ensemble	177
14	Simple Isn't Easy	183
15	The Jazz Education Industrial Complex	199
16	Panning for Gold	207
EPILOGUE: The Last Gig with Bill		217
Index		221

Introduction
A Fateful Letter

The afternoon sun was shining in the cobblestoned market square in the center of Spoleto—old Roman buildings, no cars, a few people going about their errands. I was basking in contentment at an outdoor trattoria enjoying a leisurely lunch, smiling slyly to myself, not knowing why. Suddenly I remembered I'd gotten a letter from my friend, Paula Robison, a classical flutist who was just starting her freshman year at Juilliard. I'd hardly been gone for two weeks and there was communication from home. Someone missed me!

I'd spent the morning listening to Jorge Mester rehearse the Udine Symphony, the resident festival orchestra with which I was to play the jazz bass parts in Bob Prince's music for Jerome Robbins' *Ballets U.S.A.* They were preparing a performance of Strauss's *Salome*, and I was intent on taking advantage of the opportunity to hear the music. I'd put Paula's letter in my pocket, anticipating the pleasure of savoring it later when I'd have the time to concentrate and enjoy it.

Dear Chuck,

I'm sorry — this letter bears sadness. Scotty LaFaro was killed in a car accident last week . . .

2 / INTRODUCTION

A twenty-five-year-old had fallen asleep at the wheel driving home from a gig in Newport, Rhode Island, to Geneva, New York, and slammed into a tree. Hardly newsworthy to most of the world but earth-shattering to me. A friend had violently died, and I made the thinly supported assumption that the job playing bass with Bill Evans—the position that Scott LaFaro, a uniquely brilliant player, had occupied commandingly—would become mine. Only a few weeks earlier, I'd spent an afternoon at the Village Vanguard listening to Scotty play with Bill as the trio made music that was to become a classic recording.

Scotty was a dominating presence in Bill's music, sharing more improvisational space and responsibility than the bassist in any other jazz group. Israel Crosby played a significant and admirable role in Ahmad Jamal's music. His playing was masterful—beautifully featured and integrated in Jamal's trio. Charles Mingus and Oscar Pettiford composed music and led groups from the bass chair, but their roles within the music were more conventional—standard, time-keeping accompaniments

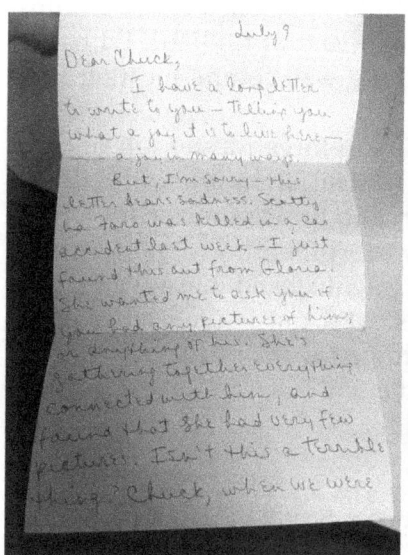 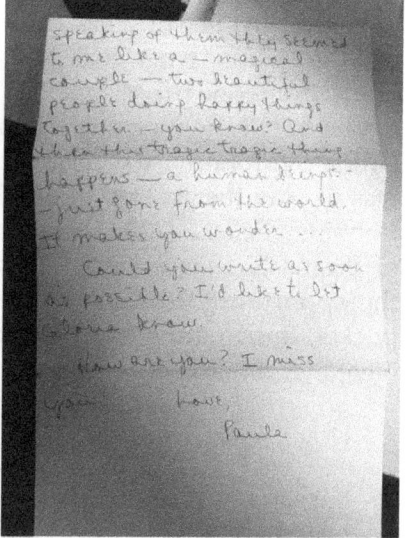

Letter from Paula Robison to the author with the tragic news of Scott LaFaro's death. Courtesy Paula Robison

with occasional brilliant solos. But it was still restricted compared to the way Scotty functioned within Bill's music.

There had been a development in rhythm section integration into jazz, perhaps the most significant stylistic advance since the development of bebop, and Scotty was an acknowledged master of this aesthetic progress. He'd developed a prodigious technique and used it assertively to respond freely to opportunities to make his accompaniments more creative and even to contribute aggressive, melodically competitive counterpoint to the piano's conventional lead voice. He wasn't the only bassist approaching music this way, but he was the strongest, the most justifiably confident, and clearly the best. I'd felt lucky to have been accepted into his friendship and held him in a position of admiration, even awe, tinged with a modicum of jealousy at the role he occupied in Bill's trio.

Bud Powell's music set the level for the sophisticated musical vocabulary and fluency to which all the bebop-oriented jazz pianists I knew and played with aspired. Bill Evans' playing sat on a foundation of Bud's—incorporating all the essential elements of that music we loved. It was clearly speaking the language of bebop—rhythmically, harmonically, and in its melodic contours. But it embraced other dimensions that were absent from the bebop template to which most everyone adhered. It had macro and micro dynamics, pianistic color, tone, and touch, occasional sensitively placed tempo changes, gorgeous, pianistically idiomatic rubato introductions and verses to standard songs, and an extraordinary rhythmic vocabulary—highly sophisticated, detailed, and immaculately played cross rhythms adapted from Lennie Tristano's pioneering work that provided unique surprise, tension, lift, and propulsion. Bill's music added all this to mastery of standard bebop. But even more important for a bass player, there was space. Bill's music breathed. It was full of definitive statements but allowed room for questions and responses. It was conversational.

Ahmad Jamal's relationship with Israel Crosby's bass playing was also conversational but more calculated. In Bill's music, the structure allowed the bass part, even invited it, further into the music's improvisational texture. Chord roots (conventionally assigned to the bass), present in Bill's solo playing, were omitted as soon as the bass entered, freeing up acoustic space. I'd played for a couple of months with Bud Powell in Paris a couple of years earlier. As much as there was to admire and love about his playing, he always played bass notes with his left hand—notes the bass player duplicated. And there was no conversational space. You accompanied Bud and waited your turn for your solo.

How could I not yearn to be participating in Bill's music—to be in Scotty's place? I imagined, hoped, I might someday be good enough, and lucky enough, to fill that spot. So, I read Paula's letter harboring intense conflicting emotions: sadness, loss, and ambitious anticipation of musical advancement—and a little guilt from how that last opportunistic thought had crept in.

I remember the street, the restaurant, the food, and the jacket I was wearing, but most of all, I remember the confused feelings. I didn't want to admit to opportunism, but it was there in a corner behind the sadness. I hadn't been responsible for Scotty's death—hadn't imagined him gone—but I wanted to be where he'd been.

Scott had been a towering presence—a handsome, charismatic, gifted, and disciplined musician—and he'd established himself in a powerful alliance with Bill Evans, the musician whose work represented my highest aspirations. I'd known Bill's music for five or six years, heard him in person and on recordings, and grown to love his playing. We'd met and played together a few years before while I was in college at Brandeis when Bill had been among a group of visiting musicians at a festival. Bill's way of making music resonated with me more than any other.

Bill had already established himself as one of a handful of jazz pianists in the highest echelon. He'd played and recorded with George Russell, Oliver Nelson, Chet Baker, Charles Mingus, and Miles Davis. He'd been instrumental in Miles's already explosively successful *Kind of Blue* recording—contributing his composition, "Blue in Green," as well as playing exquisite piano accompaniments and solos. Any jazz fan would have known of him by then and thought of him in the company of Red Garland, Tommy Flanagan, Barry Harris, Hank Jones, Sonny Clark, and any of the other well-known and respected active New York jazz pianists. And he'd made two well-received trio recordings for Riverside Records under his own name.

My jazz career was just beginning to take shape in New York. I'd played in George Russell's sextet opposite Ornette Coleman's Quartet at the Five Spot and had a few other prominent gigs. I was making progress and had reason to believe I'd have a career. But when I got Paula's letter in July of 1961, I was in Italy at the beginning of a four-month tour of Europe with Jerome Robbins' ballet company, buried in the pit orchestra with a few other jazz musicians. It was a good job but an anonymous one, and I had no reason to think that there was any chance I'd get to make the significant leap to playing with Bill until I read Paula's letter. I didn't think I was unquestionably deserving of the role; I just thought it was likely Bill would think of me as compatible. But I was too busy to dwell on the possibility—enjoying the travel to new countries, the company of my fellow musicians and some of the dancers, getting to know players in the orchestras we'd join in each new venue, and getting occasional local club gigs after we were through with the evening's ballet performance. There wasn't time to be obsessed with anticipation of hearing from Bill, but the thought was lurking, and so was the embarrassing feeling that I was glad Scotty was no longer in the place I wanted to be.

1

SKRIPITCHING

I was born on August 10, 1936. My parents divorced when I was four. I don't remember much before that, though there are photos of my younger sister Elizabeth (born March 29, 1939) and me, most likely in 1940, near our apartment at 79th and Riverside Drive. I do have vague memories of the first places we lived with our mother in Mount Vernon after the divorce. Our father, Carlos Lindner Israels, was a corporate lawyer, author of an important text on corporate law, and president of HIAS—the Hebrew Immigration Aid Society. His mother, Belle Lindner Moskowitz, about whom my sister would later write a fine biography—*Belle Moskowitz: Feminine Politics and the Exercise of Power in the Age of Alfred E. Smith*—was a social and political activist at the turn of the twentieth century, who worked on the investigations following the infamous Triangle Shirtwaist Factory fire. She was legendary New York governor Al Smith's most important political advisor and a friend of the Roosevelts.

My mother, Irma Commanday, was a smart and beautiful woman who gave a strong impression of being independent and liberated from patriarchal conventions at a time when that posture was far from the norm. Not long after living independently in Mount Vernon, which I imagine must have been a struggle, we moved in with my maternal grandparents, Frank and Betty Commanday. That's where my clear childhood memories begin.

Grandpa Frank had a printing company on Varick Street in the printing district in Lower Manhattan. He played the French horn and blew the shofar during high holy day services at Temple Emanuel in Yonkers. Betty was a doting grandmother, and my early memories are of being cared for and brought up by her, with my mother appearing at the end of the day after working in Manhattan as an editor for Armed Services Editions, a publishing house that prepared and sent paperback books to GIs in Europe during World War II. My mother acquired considerable editing skills working there under poet and anthologist Louis Untermeyer.

But it was Grandma Betty's daily care and attention that I remember from that idyllic period: the cozy stucco house on Ridge Road; visits to "Frank the butcher" down the hill on McLean Avenue, where Betty, imagining herself a favored customer, always demanded the best cuts; carefully prepared meals with the best ingredients, though mostly cooked with minimal flavorings, and always with three desserts; finding Betty in the kitchen making grape jelly, with grape juice dripping into bowls from cheesecloth bags hanging from light fixtures, or dripping drops of fudge mixture into a glass of cold water until it formed a ball that told her the fudge was ready to be beaten, and my sister and I scraping the remains of hardened fudge from the sides of the saucepan and thrilling to the sweet taste and perfect texture. We were cared for and loved, and Yonkers was a safe suburban environment, hardly exciting, but fine for growing kids.

And there were songs Betty sang to us and the popular songs on the radio we listened to daily—songs written by Irving Berlin, George and Ira Gershwin, Isham Jones, and Gus Kahn. That music, surrounding us with intelligently written melodies matched with a coherent harmonic language, instilled in us an understanding of, and appreciation for, the powerfully durable aesthetic values that shaped our musical future.

There was love and respect for other music in the house, too. Besides Frank's French horn, Uncle Robert, my mother's youngest brother, was a flutist. And the teenage girl living in the house next door practiced Chopin's Polonaise in A-flat major, Op. 53, with the windows open, pounding it out every afternoon until

I'd memorized every note. That was the atmosphere until my mother married Mordecai Bauman when I was seven. Mordy was a fine baritone at that time and was still in the army during WW II. They were married while he was on leave before he was shipped off to be stationed in France.

When the war was over and Mordy returned, employment opportunities for a classical singer were limited. So, in 1946, when he was offered a job directing the opera program at the Cleveland Institute of Music, he had to take it. We were uprooted, and our lives changed.

Now we lived in Cleveland Heights, my sister and I went to new schools that had flourishing music programs, and our house welcomed local musician friends and touring musicians passing through. I'd started studying the cello after not having had the nerve to tell my sophisticated, classical-music-oriented parents that I really liked the idea of playing the trombone.

My parents had asked the famous cellist Bernard Greenhouse if he'd take me on as a student. He'd asked if I was planning to be a professional as a condition for taking on a beginning student. I had no idea what a professional cellist might do besides playing solos and concertos, and that goal seemed unassailably daunting, maybe not even inviting. Ignorant of other possibilities, I said no, and so I had lessons with Robert Ripley, a good cellist with the Cleveland Orchestra.

I'd also started playing the guitar—figuring out simple chords and learning harmony by ear and the guitar fingerboard by deduction and fingering diagrams. I sang folk songs and occasionally ventured harmonically as far as a secondary dominant chord or a relative minor chord. In order to figure out these things, I sat for hours in my room doing what my mother called "skripitching" on the guitar. She made it clear that it annoyed her. But our home was full of music and musicians, and if there was a chance for my mother to show off my skills as a folk singer/guitarist, she'd insist that I perform for anyone she could get to sit still and listen.

The director of the middle school orchestra was a family friend, and when I was still in elementary school, in the sixth grade, he asked if I could learn the tenor banjo part to a Morton

Gould (also a friend of my stepfather) piece called "Corn Cob" that they'd programmed. I learned the part on a borrowed tenor banjo, figured out the necessary fingerings on an instrument tuned differently from the guitar, and enjoyed my first experience playing with an orchestra as a young, guest banjo soloist.

In the summer of 1948, our father sent my sister and me to camp in Vermont, where my skills as a twelve-year-old guitarist allowed me to stay up later than my bunk mates and play for the fourteen- to sixteen-year-old's square dances with counselor musicians. It seems likely that the early experience of playing on-the-beat rhythms for a room full of dancers led to an appreciation for, and an ability to keep, a steady beat.

Besides the classical music in our Cleveland Heights home, there were jazz recordings—78s of Louis Armstrong and the Hot Five and Hot Seven, Bix Beiderbecke playing "Jazz Me Blues" and "Riverboat Shuffle," and as soon as the LP was invented, we had an LP player and the recording of the 1938 Benny Goodman Carnegie Hall Concert. Why those recordings were in our home, I don't know. My parents showed no particular appreciation for jazz. But there they were, and I listened to them endlessly.

There were folk musicians who visited. Pete Seeger was a frequent guest, and when he became part of the wonderful Weavers group, some of them stayed in our home, and they all practiced there when they had an engagement at a club in Cleveland. Pete was an inspiring figure, spirited, smart, and dedicated to basic musical communication with as many people as possible. My parents loved him, and I remember being invited on stage somewhere to play the guitar and sing with him at the age of ten or eleven. Paul Robeson was another close friend of Mordy's, and he eventually became godfather to Joshua, the older of my two half-brothers from that family.

By the time I'd moved on to middle school and was playing the cello in the orchestra, musicians visiting our home were a normal occurrence. Pianist Arthur Loesser, composers Norman Dello Joio and Marc Blitzstein, Cleveland Orchestra principal bassist Jacques Possell, principal cellist Richard Kapuscinski, and pianist Seymour Lipkin were some of the regulars. As inspiring as this atmosphere could have been, and as much as it offered in the way of role models, it never crossed my early adolescent mind that I'd have a career as a musician.

I was more interested in science, fascinated by, and intuitively good at, physics and chemistry at the level they were being taught in the Cleveland Heights schools. And while my parents had at least one engineer friend, an early developer of the tape recorder, I wasn't confronted with a demonstration of professional engineering skills the way I was constantly exposed to the daunting accomplishments of professional musicians. So, I could imagine myself pursuing science and engineering as I grew up, and that path was accepted in the conventional wisdom of the time as likely to lead to economic and social success. My parents seemed to accept this as well and never openly advocated for a career in music.

My cello playing in the orchestra was fun and satisfying, and my accomplishments were reasonably good at a junior-high-school level, but I certainly understood I wasn't a prodigy. Lenore Kagan was the principal violinist in the school orchestra. She was smart and attractive and played far better than the rest of us. She also played the piano well and was studying with Leonard Shure. Lenore was the first contemporary whom I thought of as clearly more talented than I was. What I didn't understand was that she was also more disciplined and committed. Lenore *practiced*. I learned quickly what came easily, and that included enough technical security and agility to play the orchestra parts. I had little interest in working to achieve anything more demanding.

What I'd been doing while figuring out sounds and fingerings on the guitar was a kind of practice, but it was less an activity to achieve improvement or perfection of performance than an exploration of harmony and how it worked. It was more of an intellectual pursuit than a physical, kinetic one. I never learned the more demanding independent use of right-hand fingers and thumb that was needed for Pete Seeger's five-string banjo technique or the "Travis Picking" style of some of the more sophisticated folk guitarists. I didn't practice, I explored—making use of what I could find, doing what came easily, and instinctively avoiding other, more difficult challenges.

I thought everyone was like me—that those things came easily to others, and that they'd back off from meeting challenges—veering toward easily acquired things rather than pushing forward through the frustration of learning something that didn't come easily. Of course, I hadn't the perspective to analyze and express this point of view. I simply experienced things that way. I was inside a particular frame of reference—one where things came easily or weren't worth pursuing. And a lot of things came easily because, in fact, I had considerable ability—just no ability to confront difficulty. I had no experience with that and no context from which to imagine it existed for anyone else. So I interpreted greater ability and accomplishment as greater talent, not more dedication and work. These misguided perceptions were deeply embedded, and I operated under their influence for years.

The experience of being surrounded by a world of sophisticated music and politically active people as I was growing up in Cleveland Heights colored my thinking as I developed my own musical tastes. My parents were deeply committed to "European" classical music and American music created in that mold, and I acquired sensitivity to, and appreciation for, most of what I heard them listening to. My mother's new husband, Mordecai Bauman, was one of the first people to appreciate and sing Charles Ives songs, so I heard them often—compellingly rehearsed and performed. Those songs were quirky, adventurous, and distinctly different from the Duparc songs also in Mordy's repertoire, and I appreciated them as expressing an American point of view. Mordy also recorded 78 rpm albums of sea shanties, Shakespearean songs, and George M. Cohan songs, and my mother played those records often enough that the music played itself in my consciousness, even when the records weren't playing.

I heard rehearsals at home, recitals at the Cleveland Institute, performances by the Cleveland Orchestra, and had an identity at school as the first cellist in the school orchestra, where we played Dvorak's *New World Symphony* and Schubert's *Unfinished Symphony*. Classical music was all around, and musicians were in our home and often at other places we visited, but non-classical music was an equally influential part of my youth. I'd grown up hearing my grandmother sing indelible popular songs from the 1920s and 1930s. One of my earliest memories is hearing her sing, "You made me love you, I didn't wanna do it, I didn't wanna do it" teasingly, directly to my sister and me.

Songs by Isham Jones and Gus Kahn, Irving Berlin and the Gershwins were inescapable. And I loved Cole Porter's "Don't Fence Me In" long before I could understand and appreciate the more direct references to issues of adult romance in most of his other songs; "single entendres," my mother called them.

The presence of black folk and blues singers and the jazz records in the house offered some counterbalance to the Eurocentric orientation of my parents' taste. Leadbelly, the Duke of Iron, and Sonny Terry and Brownie McGhee spent hours in our living room rehearsing for the folk music concert of my parents' Popular Concert Attractions series at Severance Hall. Pete Seeger and Paul Robeson were friends, and their visits were more frequent and more engaged.

Paul was an enormous presence—a big man with a deep voice and penetrating intellect. He and Mordy loved each other, and Mordy revered Paul's voice and interpretations of spirituals. But the West African culture that created jazz flavor wasn't so evident in that music and didn't seem to occupy much family attention.

I don't want to assign too much weight to this seeming imbalance of my cultural background. I don't think it had much of anything to do with color—it was just how my parents' backgrounds led them to be sensitive to music that sounded more European, while I found a growing appreciation for more American jazz and discovered Fats Waller, Louis Jordan, Nat Cole, and Count Basie later on my own.

The one specifically black-oriented music that was revered in our home was Gershwin's opera *Porgy and Bess*—steeped in black culture as interpreted by a second-generation Eastern European Jew. It premiered in 1935, a year before my birth, and by the time it became appropriate for my mother to sing me a lullaby, the one I heard and absorbed in my infancy, and defined my conception of music, was "Summertime."

I'd been brought up well—specifically and notably to work against superficial prejudices of race, background, or economic class. At age thirteen, I'd been with my parents along with thousands of other people threatened with violence by angry mobs at an outdoor Paul Robeson concert in Peekskill, New York, in September of 1949, and seen FBI agents watching our home in Cleveland Heights when Robeson visited. My parents went to considerable lengths to educate us in what I thought of as enlightened cultural and political awareness, respect for, and lack of irrational fear of "others."

I had the sense that people like the Weavers, Paul Robeson, composer Marc Blitzstein, the union organizers, and left-wing political activists that were in our home in Cleveland Heights were admirable because of their ideals and unwillingness to compromise. The idea that the Weavers or Robeson might use their moderate level of success to lead them to record a commercial or do anything they didn't fully believe in was unthinkable. High-minded ideals were a nearly religious creed. Aesthetic or moral compromise was anathema. This was the value system I inherited: high-minded principles; no bigotry or intolerance (except toward those who opposed your values, or even just had other ones); dedication to durable, high-quality art; and opposition to activities designed solely for financial reward.

In 1951, as I was in my first year of high school, Mordy lost his job at the Cleveland Institute, most likely as a result of prevailing McCarthy-era political pressure. I don't know how long the idea had been in his mind, but as the job disappeared, Mordy began to work on realizing a dream of creating a summer arts camp for teenagers—a stimulating and educational environment for kids interested in music, visual art, theater, and dance.

Mordy had a friend, Joe Kruger, who had a successful boy's summer camp on Lake Mahkeenac, in Stockbridge, Massachusetts—only about a mile from Tanglewood in Lenox, where the Boston Symphony played in the summer.

Joe encouraged them to look for a place nearby, and there were a couple of beautiful old summer estates for sale. They found one called Oronoque, on Prospect Hill Road, in Stockbridge, formerly owned by the ambassador Norman Davis, and largely by borrowing from friends, they managed to pull together the money to buy it.

It was a large summer "cottage" with a separate barn, at once impressive, beautiful, and a little run down. I was only fifteen, with little idea of what my parents were taking on, but they said they were doing it for kids like my sister and me. I couldn't have been happy about being wrenched from what had been a comfortable life in Cleveland Heights, but I do remember being impressed with the multi-room mansion, the lovely grounds, picturesque Stockbridge village, and the cultural activity at The Berkshire Music Festival at Tanglewood, Jacob's Pillow Dance Festival, and theater at the Berkshire Playhouse.

My parents had some experience as entrepreneurs from having produced the Popular Concert Attractions series at Severance Hall in Cleveland in 1948—the series included some of the younger classical musicians in Cleveland at the time, like violinist Sidney Harth and pianist Seymour Lipkin; the folk music concert that included Leadbelly, Sonny Terry and Brownie McGee, Pete Seeger, and the Duke of Iron; and the two-performance presentation of Louis Armstrong's All Stars that gave me the chance to have dinner with the musicians between the Sunday afternoon and evening concerts. I don't have a lot of clear memories from that time, though the rehearsals at our home in Cleveland Heights certainly left an impression, especially the one during which the imposing folksinger Huddie "Leadbelly" Ledbetter consumed an entire chocolate cake and a whole bottle of muscatel.

I wasn't aware of the financial issues involved in these productions, but I know it couldn't have been without stress. My folks didn't discuss these things, except for my mother's continual complaint that my father didn't pay enough child support. I do remember that, although we never had much extra money to spend, we were always well fed, well clothed, and well housed, despite my mother's complaints about what she perceived as my father's stinginess, and that this had been possible while Mordy made his living as a singer and teacher. My mother supported him at home as a socially and politically engaged housewife, but the idea of starting what would turn out to be Indian Hill had to have been risky.

Indian Hill started in the summer of 1952. My sister and I were students at the camp, and we had the chance to enjoy the company of the thirty or so other kids my parents had managed to enroll for that first summer. The fee for eight weeks was $600, and there were scholarships for some who couldn't pay it all. Seymour Lipkin taught piano; Eve Gentry taught dance, and Eve's husband, Bruce, taught photography; Harold Aks, conductor of the Interracial Chorus in New York, directed the choir and madrigal group; Sidney and Teresa Harth taught violin, chamber music, and conducted the chamber orchestra; Dorothy Dehner taught art; Henry Cowell taught composition; Mordy taught the singers; and the whole camp attended Boston symphony concerts at nearby Tanglewood.

I remember many of the thirty or so people from the first year, some of whom remain friends: Jerry Rosen, who impressed us all with his ability at the age of twelve (allowed to attend Indian Hill at that "too young" age because of his exceptional playing, maturity, and intelligence), and who later became associate concertmaster of the Boston Symphony; David Berhman, son of the playwright S.N. Behrman, who became a composer and early advocate of computer music; Ruth Laredo (then Meckler), who became a renowned pianist specializing in Rachmaninoff's music; Ed Murray, who later taught music at Cornell; and others who went on to careers in various fields.

And I was still stuck with the same misguided perception that intrinsic ability determined everything.

I played cello in a string quartet in which Jerry Rosen played first violin. I was fifteen, and Jerry was twelve. I could get through the cello part of the Haydn quartet we played—maybe even expressively. Jerry could stand in front of the students at a recital and play a Bach unaccompanied violin sonata beautifully. Again, I thought Jerry was talented and I was not. It didn't occur to me he'd been practicing since he was three.

Practice and study were not friendly things; instead, they were frustrating ones; and for all I knew, frustration was to be avoided like poison. No one conspired to burden me with this paralyzing, wrongheaded conclusion I had arrived at it unconsciously by misreading my parents at an age when I was too vulnerable to make rational sense out of how my mother responded to me while I was "skripitching."

I didn't see the dedication and concentrated activity that went into achieving the artistic skills my family and friends exhibited. I don't remember Mordy practicing, although I know he did. My mother practically worshipped Mordy—as a singer and as an intellectual, but he didn't talk about how hard he'd had to work at it. I knew the famous French baritone Charles Panzéra and the affection Mordy and he shared as student and teacher, so I had to have known Mordy studied and worked at his art. But I didn't see it happening.

Pete Seeger was just "great!" I never saw him practice by himself, although I did see, enjoy, and appreciate the work the Weavers did as they rehearsed together in our home, staying with us partly for the company and camaraderie and partly because they weren't making enough money to be able to afford a good hotel.

Group practice was often on exhibit, one way or another, and it's always been an enjoyable activity for me—one I not only take for granted as part of the artistic process, but also one that brings the pleasures of social intimacy. Private practice was almost completely hidden, so I lacked the opportunity to assume it was normal. Paul Robeson seemed superhuman, an athlete, a scholar, and a powerful singer. It never occurred to me he'd been a student—that he'd had to work for his achievements.

2

THE RIGHT HIGH SCHOOL AND WRONG UNIVERSITY

After the first summer at Indian Hill in 1952, we moved back from Cleveland and were living with my grandparents back at their home on Ridge Road, in Yonkers. I was enrolled in my junior year at Roosevelt High School. I didn't know anyone, no one seemed interested in music, and I was isolated. It wasn't anywhere near where we lived. Yonkers High, where my mother had gone to school, was much closer, but my parents had heard that Roosevelt was a better school. I don't even remember how I managed the long bus rides from our house to the school in East Yonkers, a part of town I didn't know at all. I was miserable.

I'd tried to get into Music and Art High School in Manhattan, where some of the Indian Hill kids were enrolled, but they wouldn't take anyone after their sophomore year. A couple of Indian Hill dancers and pianist Morey Ritt were enrolled in the High School of Performing Arts on West 46th Street and seemed to like it. And the school needed cellists. They were happy to accept me, even a few weeks into the semester, as long as I used my father's address on Riverside Drive as my official residence.

Traveling from my father's apartment to school would have been easy, but I didn't live with him and didn't have enough of a relationship with him for anyone to consider it a possibility. There wasn't much room in his apartment, his new wife would have been unlikely to have welcomed me, and no one suggested it. So my long commute started—at least an hour and a half each way, no matter which of several equally inconvenient routes and modes of transportation you chose. I was traveling seventeen miles each way from Yonkers by an excruciating combination of busses and either commuter train to Grand Central and a long walk from there to the school or long rides from the Van Cortland Park terminal of the Broadway subway line. (At the time, the entire subway ride cost a nickel.) The commute was well worth being in the company of friends and like-minded kids during the day, but it put a serious crimp in after-school social life.

Performing Arts was full of talented kids: dancers Gigi Chazin and Tony Mordente, who went on to notable careers; Electa Arenal, then a fine dancer who later became a writer and scholar; actress Suzanne Pleshette; and quite a few talented musicians, like bassist Bill Salter, were my classmates. I played cello in the orchestra and guitar in the dance band. I was far from the best player in either of them, but I did well in music theory, as well as English, Math, Physics, and Chemistry without exerting much effort. So, I continued to be trapped in the perception of myself as not unusually gifted in music. Easy success in the other subjects—at the level they were being taught in a school oriented toward the arts—led me to think I had more ability in those areas.

I was assigned to physics teacher Irv Orfuss's homeroom and was sitting there the first period of the first day feeling new but not wholly alien when a girl came in with announcements from the principal's office. She was a vision in a cashmere sweater and a trim tweed skirt, had raven black hair, and made the announcements with utter poise and confidence, looking directly at me, a new face she didn't recognize. That was my introduction to Suzanne Pleshette, a budding actress later to perform in Broadway plays, Hitchcock films, and, eventually, to find stardom as the wife on Bob Newhart's television show. At sixteen, she looked stunning and carried herself with the grace and confidence of a sophisticated forty-year-old. It was a promising start.

As impressive as that moment was, it was the dancers who overwhelmed my sensibilities every day. As you entered the school through its unassuming doors on 46th Street, the first thing you saw was a large, mostly unadorned, room. At noon, during lunch hour, Latin music would be playing, and there'd be a sea of grace in front of you—dozens of dancers moving beautifully with a mesmerizing combination of control and abandon. The formal dance classes, both ballet and modern, and the school performances were really good. Of the three groups of students—the theater people, the musicians, and the dancers—the dancers were closest to approaching their prime, so they seemed the most professionally developed.

But it was what the dancers did informally, on their own, for the pure pleasure of it, that impressed me so deeply—not only because it was beautiful, but also because it demonstrated a sense of body that was foreign to me. Eve Gentry, the fine dancer who taught the dancers at Indian Hill, also held dance classes for the rest of us, and I had to participate. I felt out of control and incompetent. I had a fine sense of pulse, and I was a good enough square dancer at camp a few years before, but grace and what dancers call elevation—the movements that work against gravity and give the illusion of lift—eluded me. At least it felt that way to me, and I was too self-conscious to watch myself in the wall of mirrors to see how I was doing.

Later, groups of teenagers dancing became a cliché of afternoon television. But that was nothing like what was happening at my school. The TV kids danced to simple-minded rock music, and the movements were strictly repetitive, required little control, were relentlessly stuck to the simplest relationship to the beat—nothing syncopated or unexpected, and were largely graceless—clenched fists flailing mechanically at invisible punching bags. What I saw and envied daily at Performing Arts was a thing of youthful beauty. I only enjoyed it vicariously. I didn't have the courage to try joining the fun.

In the summer of 1953, the next year at Indian Hill, I played the cello part in Shubert's Trout quintet. Jerry played violin, and another young musician from Detroit, Ruth Meckler (later to marry violinist Jaime Laredo and become a virtuoso Rachmaninoff specialist), played the demanding piano part. Young Bill Rhein, from New Haven, played the bass part. Bill's father,

Sid, was the principal bassist in the New Haven Symphony, and Bill, at fifteen (later to become associate principal bassist in the Boston Symphony), could already play the difficult bass solo in the variation movement. I think I must have already shown some curiosity about the bass because I remember Bill showing me some of the similarities and differences compared to the cello and showing me how to hold the German bow.

It was difficult for my sister and me to recognize the depth of the experience we were having at Indian Hill. It was just family activity—what our parents did—a situation we were dropped into. The fact that our parents told us that Indian Hill was designed to enrich the lives of kids like us didn't necessarily make us aware that the salutary effects of that exposure were also intended to include us.

The intimacy gained in living together in such formative years, learning, making music and art, taking turns serving meals, playing sports, fumbling through naive attempts at relating to the opposite sex, and talking for an hour in the dark with your bunkmates before falling asleep, created powerful bonds. When I'm in touch with a couple of my contemporaries from Indian Hill's first year (1952), our conversations can be so fluid and warm, we almost seem to melt into one another. Indian Hill provided at least a partial antidote to life's loneliness for a lot of people. The sense of profound shared experience trumps awareness of death and having provided that for hundreds of young people was some accomplishment. It's no wonder that so many people remained attached to my parents for the rest of their lives.

I don't remember if the question came up as I entered Performing Arts in my junior year in 1953, but by the beginning of my senior year, I remember having conversations with my parents about where I might go to college. I talked with my mother and stepfather about this, and with my father, with whom I had a strained and awkward relationship, still colored by the unfairly ungenerous picture my mother painted of him.

There was no question I'd go to college. All my friends were planning to go to good schools, and they seemed assured they'd get in. Kids I'd befriended in the summers at Indian Hill were the children of doctors, lawyers, artists, or successful businesspeople, and they were mostly headed to Ivy League schools. I'd done well on my SAT tests, and there didn't seem to be much of an obstacle for me either. And my father was obligated to pay for college for my sister and me.

It didn't occur to me that I might succeed in music school. Everyone was focused on my mathematical and scientific interests and apparent skills, so the options were either liberal arts or science. I applied to Cornell, Swarthmore, Harvard, Amherst (my father's alma mater, where that connection was likely to guarantee admission), and MIT, where the provost, Walter Rosenblith, was a close friend of my parents and had carried me around the 1939 World's Fair on his shoulders when I was three. I was accepted at Cornell, Amherst, and MIT, put on Harvard's waiting list, and rejected at Swarthmore. Everyone, including my parents, bought into the conventional wisdom: I should go to MIT and pursue a career in science and engineering—a career that would guarantee the kind of security my father had as an attorney and that my mother and stepfather never had as musicians and educators. It seemed logical to me, and I thought there might be a path into electronics and acoustics, where my musical background would be useful.

So I enrolled at MIT and arrived on campus in the fall of 1954 to find an atmosphere unlike anything I'd yet experienced.

You are not coddled at MIT. You attend class, if you like it or not, as long as you show that you've learned what the curriculum requires. You don't even have to come up with the correct answer to a question on a quiz; you just have to show that you know how to find it. You buy a slide rule at the school coop, clip it to your belt in its leather case to demonstrate your membership in the club of those with technical sophistication, and begin to learn its mysteries. Some students thrived in that atmosphere. I was thrown by it—completely at sea.

I made friends. I liked the people I met in my dorm. We went to movies, ate at restaurants, and stayed up late in endless bull sessions. My supposedly stingy father, as required by the divorce agreement, was paying for all this.

I'd joined the MIT orchestra, expecting to play the cello, but I didn't have a decent cello, and the orchestra already had a dozen cellists and no bass players. The orchestra rehearsed in the beautiful Kresge Auditorium, where there was an instrument room with several good basses.

If you had to pick two instruments small enough for a young person to handle that would prepare him for playing the bass, those would be the ones I'd had some experience with: the cello, which requires the same basic technique and physical relationship to the instrument, and the guitar, whose four lowest strings are normally tuned to the same pitches as the bass. I just picked out a bass whose sound I liked and took on the orchestral parts.

It was easy. Bill Rhein had shown me some of the basics I needed back at Indian Hill a year or so earlier, and the bass parts were less demanding than the more active cello parts. And the attraction of being the only player on the bass part, instead of one of what would then have been thirteen cellists, was enticing.

Being in the MIT orchestra provided instrumental experience on the bass, and a growing interest in jazz led me to explore possibilities in the Boston jazz scene, a quarter of a mile up Memorial Drive and a bracing walk across the Massachusetts Avenue bridge, which put me out of the campus atmosphere and into urban Back Bay.

The Zebra Lounge was on Newbury Street, near the Boston University dorms. An enthusiastic musician there named Ray (so short that he played standing up behind a spinet) was friendly and introduced me to other places where we could hear music and meet other musicians. It was a dark club, decorated as it was named: black-and-white stripes with an occasional red accent. The music—secondary to selling liquor but an accepted part of the atmosphere—was the only attraction for me.

Jazz was then at the center of everyday popular music, and its rhythmic nuances acquired special meaning. Harmonies remained beyond all but my rudimentary understanding, but I started to remember some of the tunes, and the rhythms were indelible. Each musician had a recognizable rhythmic signature, and those timing inflections were fascinating and attractive. I became obsessed.

If I'd known only this alcohol-sales-driven side of the Boston jazz scene, I might have had more difficulty identifying with it. But there was another side with a different cast of characters. I met Herb Pomeroy, a Harvard-educated trumpet player whose intelligence and ability to inhabit a world outside the nightclub gloom provided a jazz model I could more easily relate to—a model where the music lived on its own merits independently of outside of nightclubs and bars.

A student organization hired me to perform in and produce a concert in MIT's famous lecture hall, Room 10-250, under the dome in the campus's central building. I don't remember why a piano was there, but MIT was a civilized place, with respect for the Science of the Arts, so it didn't seem unusual at the time.

I hired Herb and my pianist friend, Ray, from the Zebra Lounge. The rhythm section was drummer Jimmy Zitano and bassist John Neves. I played guitar, though with as little knowledge as I had then, it's hard to imagine how I avoided embarrassing myself, but I was paying attention to rhythmic subtleties—and playing for square dances at Camp Timberlake during the summers of 1948 and 1949 had left me with a healthy respect for a steady beat.

We played some standards, but a piece called "Ray's Idea" and Bud Powell's "Dance of the Infidels" were the intriguing ones; bebop became the language I wanted to learn. I didn't understand how that music was constructed, but I appreciated its angularity and impressive rhythmic and harmonic bite. The durable elements of form were there, recognizable as similar to the popular and classical music I knew, but also something else—a way of making music that struck me as compellingly timely and contemporary.

Of course, this style had been in development for over a decade, but I was unaware. I'd heard some of Gerry Mulligan's music and even Charles Mingus's bass playing. But Mulligan hid the bebop harmonic character beneath an exterior of swing rhythm, and I'd heard Mingus only in the context of Red Norvo Trio recordings, where the rhythms were a little stiffer than in Bud Powell's playing. The significance of these nuances was elusive, but I was aware it was there. I'd been bitten by things in the music that I could recognize but not yet name.

I had little idea of what to do about this. I belonged in college, and a few of the jazz musicians led lives with frighteningly mysterious aspects—rarely emerging into daylight, smoking strange stuff, and exhibiting covert, ritualistic behavior. Did I belong in the jazz scene there?

John Neves seemed to think so. Handsome in his Brooks Brothers suit, John didn't seem interested in the peripheral behavior of jazz musicians, only in the music. He carried himself with gracious elegance but no pretension, and he took an interest in me. I went to hear him in the Jazz Workshop at The Stable, a club in a part of Copley Square now occupied by air space above the broad trench created by the urban section of the Massachusetts Turnpike (Huntington Avenue then). John played in Vartan "Varty" Haritounian's quintet. Herb Pomeroy played trumpet and was the music director. Jimmy Zitano was the drummer, and Ray "Muzzy" Santisi played piano. Varty played tenor sax with some exaggerated mannerisms, but it was harmonically and rhythmically correct. The band was great.

Every night. If not the quintet, then a sextet, with the addition of Gene DiStasio, a dentist from Revere who was a fine trombonist. Sometimes Jaki Byard played piano or saxophone. For a while, Herb's big band played one night a week. All the regular guys were in it, along with other fine players like trumpeters Lennie Johnson, Everett Longstreth, and Joe Gordon, trombonists Joe Ciavardone and Bill Legan, and saxophonists Boots Mussulli, Bob Freedman, Jimmy Mosher, Deane Haskins, and Jimmy Durber.

It was Boston's jazz center. Everything happened through there. If you went two or three times a week, you saw every jazz musician in the city and heard many of them when they were invited to sit in with the band. Visiting musicians who played across the street in Storyville, where George Wein brought nationally known groups for a week or two at a time, came in to visit and play. Those of us who couldn't afford the cover charge at Storyville sometimes got to hear the same players in informal situations at the Jazz Workshop. But I'm getting ahead of myself, describing the atmosphere at a place I got to know well only over three or four years.

By now, I'd been playing the bass for a while in the MIT orchestra, and I must have talked about that with John. I modeled my posture, tone, rhythm—everything about my playing, on the way John played. I had no way of knowing then just how good he was. I was just lucky. Only John's shyness and under-the-surface social insecurity kept him from the wider recognition his playing deserved. Sometimes, when I was listening to the band at The Jazz Workshop, John would invite me to play. The band was tolerant, the musicians made it clear I was welcome, and John encouraged me. He told me about Steve Kuhn, a fine young jazz pianist from suburban Newton, and I started playing with Steve while he was still in high school and I was at MIT.

The music I was hearing in Boston was different from what I'd heard as I was growing up. My ears had become accustomed to the popular music of Victor Young, Irving Berlin, Jerome Kern, George Gershwin, Harold Arlen, Harry Warren, and Cole Porter. And even in a cultural climate that seemed only reluctantly to welcome black contributions, the songs of Ellington and Waller were irresistible.

World War II ended when I was nine. Black musicians returned from the war with an increased sense of belonging to their country, despite their less-than-warm reception, and a stronger style of jazz emerged—a style less beholden to the limits of music associated with entertainment, songs, and dancing—a style that embraced elements of twentieth-century classical music and a more robust and varied rhythmic language.

Of course, as a young musician, I wasn't even remotely aware of the cultural climate. It was just the world as I knew it—the only one I knew. So it was unremarkable to me that, as a kid in Yonkers, I could hear Bing Crosby, Rosemary Clooney, Nat Cole, and even Benny Goodman on the radio, or that jazz pianist Herman Chittison had a trio on the radio show *Casey, Crime Photographer*.

In Cleveland, I was too young to go to clubs, and the radio became less important as my school and social activity increased.

But when we moved back to Yonkers, and I started school at Performing Arts, we played some Gerry Mulligan charts in the "Dance" band, and I had a 45 rpm EP record on red vinyl of a Mulligan piece called "Bweebida Bobbida." That was the closest I got to hearing bebop.

Ironically, it was when I got to MIT in 1954 that I really got exposed to bop. Sometime during my first year at MIT, a friend told me there were jam sessions being held at the Harvard radio station in Cambridge hosted by a hip guy named Tom Wilson. I don't remember the exact occasion, but I know I went to at least one of those sessions, played, and became a quick friend of Tom's. Everyone I met respected Tom; I liked him, and he liked my playing. It was the beginning of what would later turn out to be an important friendship.

Tom told me about Donald Byrd, a young trumpet player from Detroit, who had taken Kenny Dorham's place in the Jazz Messengers with Art Blakey, Hank Mobley, and another young Detroiter Tom particularly liked, bassist Doug Watkins. Tom was planning to record that band at the Harvard radio station studio with Donald as the leader and our friend, Boston's brilliant trumpet player Joe Gordon, as an added soloist and asked me to be around to help.

Doug Watkins showed up at the studio with the fallen sound post of his bass having been jarred out of place moving it in and out of his car.

The post is just a pine dowel, about three-quarters of an inch in diameter, wedged between the front and back of the bass near one of the bridge feet. It supports the pressure of the strings on that side of the bridge and couples the front and back of the instrument acoustically. The sound post is called "the soul" of the instrument in French. Without it, the front collapses enough to mess up the relationship of the strings to the fingerboard. This substantially weakens the sound and structural integrity—making the bass virtually unplayable. It's a simple piece of wood that's part of all the instruments in the violin family.

There's a special, gently S-shaped tool that puts the post in place and adjusts it. You stick a chisel point on one end into the post to hold it while you maneuver it through the F-holes and then, once it's wedged approximately in place, use hook shapes on the other end to push and pull it into the exact position. Violin makers have sound post setters in three sizes: for violins and violas, cellos, and basses. Of course, we didn't.

I'd seen the operation done a few times. I loved to watch repairmen work on instruments, and basses come in such a variety of shapes and proportions that I find them endlessly fascinating. So there was Doug, stuck, and I had to try to help. We turned the bass over and rolled it around, lying on the floor, supporting it over our heads with our feet and hands while we tried to get the fallen sound post to roll close enough to an F-hole to grab it with our fingers and pull it out. They always just fit, so it isn't easy, but we got it.

Then I got a couple of wire coat hangers. I sharpened the end of one by smashing it with a hammer and bent the other into something that vaguely resembled the hook shapes in a real sound post setter. We were lucky. We managed to get the post jammed into an approximate position with the first hanger. By careful planning—moving the post through whichever F-hole was in a position that required us only to pull with the other hanger and never to push (the wire wasn't stiff enough for that)—we got it into position for the bass to play normally. Doug even thought it might be sounding better than before. I was a hero and had another friend.

As I went to clubs and sessions to hear music and play when I could, I got introduced to some older musicians on the Boston scene—some only slightly older, like pianist Dick Twardzik, trumpeter Joe Gordon, and saxophonists Boots Mussulli, Serge Chaloff, and Charlie Mariano—all of them modern players versed in the bebop language. And musicians from New York came to Storyville to play for a week at a time—organist Jimmy Smith, with the most remarkable drummer, Donald Bailey; Hampton Hawes, with Red Mitchell and Jim Hall; and Max Roach, with Clifford Brown. George Wein had Sunday afternoon sessions called the "Teenage Jazz Club," where young people, who were unable to get out at night or to be in bars where liquor was being served, could hear the visiting groups. Young musicians were sometimes invited to sit in with the professional musicians, and I remember playing guitar rather incompetently with Max Roach, Richie Powell, Clifford Brown, and Harold Land. I wasn't good, but there was something in my playing that interested Richie Powell, and I remember him asking me if I was picking every note. I wasn't. I had already adopted an approach to the guitar (that I later applied to the bass) I'd heard in Jim Hall and Red Mitchell's playing—a way of picking notes when I wanted an attack and playing others only with my left hand, striving for a more vocal quality.

Clubs and jam sessions were the only places a young musician could learn anything about jazz. Nothing specific to jazz was taught in schools. You could apply the principles of music theory you learned in college to the jazz language, but you had to translate those principles, and no one at school told you how to do that—or even suggested that would have any value. Jazz, as a method of making music, was largely ignored.

As much time and attention as I was giving to jazz outside of school, I still had to fulfill the responsibility of attending MIT. But classes were suddenly almost insurmountably hard. Physics and chemistry now involved advanced mathematical calculations, and the labs were technically demanding. Measurements had to be exact—lab technique cleaner and neater than I was inclined to be. I'd open the Sears and Zemansky physics book to read an assignment, get past a sentence or two, realize I didn't understand what I had just read, and rather than reread it, my eyes glazed over, and I only wanted to sleep. I was miserable and didn't understand what was happening. I felt stupid for the first time. I'd never had an experience like this.

It hadn't bothered me that I wasn't much of an athlete—that I couldn't play basketball and only managed minimal participation in softball games, but to find myself seemingly incompetent in the athletics of the mind was a shock, and I didn't know what was happening or why. I don't remember having any perspective, not even room to be conscious of blaming myself, though unconsciously, I know I was.

I just shut down and didn't want to recognize what was happening. I don't remember much about my classes—whether or not I went to them. I did spend hours, and learned something, building audio amplifiers in my dorm room where parts and wire clippings were scattered about. I was meeting jazz musicians and learning to play in Boston—that remained within reach, but I was unprepared to deal with anything I didn't understand quickly.

It's only in retrospect that I understand how this happened to me. I'd interpreted the signals I got from my upbringing to value those things I could do easily and to avoid concentrated work and anything frustrating, so I never learned to work hard at anything difficult. Life wasn't supposed to be difficult. I wasn't privy to the work my parents did to achieve what they'd accomplished; they just seemed to have arrived at where they were by some invisible, natural process. And I didn't see the work my friends were doing either. It was private.

My grades got worse, and I felt worse but didn't know what to do about it. I had no idea about consulting anyone for help. Help might have been there, but it wasn't advertised, and my friends didn't seem to need it. It didn't cross my mind that there might have been some kind of guidance that could have helped me. It didn't occur to me that I'd have been welcomed to talk more with our family friend, Provost Walter Rosenblith, who'd probably been instrumental in getting me into MIT in the first place. I thought I just didn't have the wherewithal to handle the challenges, so I pretended they weren't there and ignominiously flunked out after the first semester of my junior year.

I went home to my parents—then living in a small, rented house in Stockbridge, and they asked if I wanted to go to Juilliard. They didn't seem upset—they just thought maybe I'd been misdirected and might have more success studying music, something they were familiar with and where they thought I'd be at least competent.

The abstract idea of Juilliard intimidated me just as much as the reality of the experience at MIT had. I had no understanding that the only thing that I lacked was the ability to confront frustration and apply myself to something that required the ongoing application of effort and attention to whatever didn't come easily. I thought frustration was unbearable when, in fact,

I later figured out it's just the resistance you feel when moving forward.

Personal limitation was even more frightening in relation to studying music, where I'd have to compare my accomplishments with those of my stepfather, our family, friends, and kids I knew who played far better than I'd ever imagined I could. So I just said no and returned to Boston, rented a cheap room on Marlborough Street in Back Bay, and survived by working at Schirmer's music store filling mail orders, eventually finding a slightly better job building Dynakit amplifiers at The Listening Post, a fancy hi-fi store on Newbury Street.

I was miserable. Life was depressing, and I don't remember how I climbed out of that. I think I must have come back to Stockbridge in the summer and spent it at Indian Hill, but I also had to have been ashamed. This kind of thing didn't happen to kids like me. My friends were succeeding at places like Harvard, and I'd flunked out—hadn't even gotten started. I do remember talking with my parents about liberal arts education—something less challenging than MIT or Juilliard that wouldn't require a commitment to a long-term goal, and they were sympathetic to that. They didn't push me about music.

3

A Pressure Case

Brandeis University was a school with a good reputation, near Boston and Cambridge, where I felt at home and where I was making early inroads into the community of jazz musicians. Gigi Chazin, my high school prom date, was there in her sophomore year, so I had that connection. Maybe Brandeis would be a place where I'd manage to fit in well enough to get through the next few years.

I don't remember how I did it, but I arranged an interview with C. Ruggles Smith, an admissions officer who told me I'd committed academic suicide by flunking out of MIT, that I should go into the army, and they'd consider accepting me after I got out.

It was a summary dismissal, and I don't remember how Gigi found out about it. I may have told her, but I don't remember. What I do remember is getting a phone call from her a few days later, saying that she had a friend, another admissions officer, Phil Driscoll, whom she'd told of my experience with Smith. With Gigi's encouragement, he looked up the interview records and found no official record of my having seen Smith, so he was free to schedule an appointment with me without breaking protocol.

I don't know what inspired Gigi to feel so interested in and protective of me. We'd been friends, but to my regret, we were not close. And I harbored unrelieved embarrassment from the memory of having been reprimanded by her on our prom date for taking her into Manhattan from her home in Jamaica, Queens, on the subway, where she sat awkwardly in her yellow prom dress. It wasn't easy to create a situation in which Gigi showed discomfort. She was graceful, educated, thoughtful, and stunningly beautiful. If there's a stereotype of dancers developing only their bodies to the detriment of their minds, some of the dancers I knew at Performing Arts belied that stereotype, and Gigi was among them.

So I remember her at the beginning of our date, looking gorgeous with her red hair and yellow gown, letting me know I'd let her down by taking her on the subway, when her older brother would have been happy to drive us into town, if only I'd have thought to ask. It was an inauspicious beginning to an evening I remember being more embarrassed about than enjoying. I was certainly feeling lucky Gigi had accepted my invitation and also feeling seriously outclassed by her. I must have looked ridiculous, too—in my Uncle Robert's dinner jacket—at least three sizes too large. With that to remember, why had Gigi remained concerned enough about my well-being to call Phil Driscoll? Why had she bothered to remember me at all?

Phil was an entirely different sort of college administrator than Smith. Instead of a brusque dismissal, I found a sympathetic listener who decided to help make me what he called "a pressure case." Sometimes you just find people who want to help, empathetic people who understand that not everything in everyone's life goes in a straight line—people like Gigi Chazin and Phil Driscoll.

Phil asked whom I knew who might exert some influence on the admissions committee and suggested we contact my father. Again, someone who had no reason I could fathom to go out of his way to help stepped up. I'd had such a difficult relationship with my father—any possibility of mutual respect or understanding had been irredeemably undermined by my mother, and I don't remember ever having shown him gratitude or much affection for whatever role he'd played in my life up to that point. Nevertheless, he enlisted help from Judge Joseph Proskauer and

MRS. FRANKLIN D. ROOSEVELT
211 EAST 62ND STREET
NEW YORK 21, N. Y.

JUN 4 1956

May 29, 1956

Dear Dr. Sachar:

I don't know this boy about whom my friend, Mrs. Dorothy Brown, writes. She is, however, a very good judge of young people and I am therefore sending you her letter, not wanting to exert any influence which is the wrong kind. Mrs. Moskowitz, his grandmother, I knew well. She was an extremely able woman and if he has inherited any of her ability he will be, in the long run, a credit to any university.

I realize that you may be able to do nothing and I don't want to press against the best interests of the University. I simply want you to know of the situation and if you think it worthwhile, do as you think wise.

Mrs. Dorothy Brown is a daughter of old Dean Kirchwey and her husband is a well known lawyer in Boston. You can talk to Mrs. Brown on the telephone more fully if you wish to do so.

Very cordially yours,

Eleanor Roosevelt

Courtesy of the Robert D. Farber University Archives & Special Collections, Brandeis University

June 6, 1956

Mrs. Eleanor Roosevelt
211 East 62nd Street
New York, New York

Dear Mrs. Roosevelt:

I waited until the supporting data arrived on the application for admission of Charles Israels.

I am glad to tell you that he has been granted admission. It is a calculated risk but apparently he had been following an area of concentration which was of no interest to him. Now that he can start afresh, we share your hope that he will make good. He is fortunate to have your very warm recommendation.

                                        Cordially yours,

                                        A. L. Sachar

als/eb

cc: Smith

Courtesy of the Robert D. Farber University Archives & Special Collections, Brandeis University

Eleanor Roosevelt, two friends of his mother from her days as Governor Al Smith's campaign manager in his quest for the presidency. They both wrote letters on my behalf—two influential people who'd never met me. Support was accruing for me for no reason I could identify. I'd spent months in an emotionally and financially depressed state doing not much more than barely surviving, blaming myself for my circumstances without understanding quite how I'd gotten there, and self-protectively isolating myself from feeling anything too intensely, so I don't remember feeling much joy or appreciation for the support I was getting either. I was numb.

A few weeks later, I was accepted at Brandeis, where I hoped I'd be able to survive and maintain an acceptable college career. That was both a relief and a challenge I wasn't sure I'd be able to meet, but it did begin to lift me out of my feeling of helpless depression.

And that's what happened. I pursued a more-or-less normal liberal arts curriculum at Brandeis without working very hard at anything, played a little cello in a string quartet—still not practicing much, and through my own shortcomings, I failed to take much advantage of, or fully appreciate, the considerable opportunity a Brandeis education provided. I had access to wonderful professors and was afraid I'd fall short in relation to any of them. I still didn't know how to study or think I had the capacity to do it.

I did alright in music theory, although I look back on that with the understanding that my approach to doing theory assignments was also somewhat distorted. While my classmates did the assignments correctly—not that hard to do, there was something in me that looked for more complicated answers. I think I was directed by subconscious emotional motivation—that my personality would disappear if I just did what seemed to be correct. What seems strange in retrospect is that simply doing what occurred to me easily, playing what seemed to fit correctly, was exactly how I approached playing the bass in jazz groups. I was un-self-conscious because when you're in the throes of playing jazz, you don't have time to try to do much more than just function correctly. Originality, such as it is, has to take care of itself.

But I was learning to play jazz in Boston and Cambridge and had at least a little sense of the prestige my jazz life provided on campus. I may not have been much of a student, but I began to sense that people were paying attention to me and assigning me an aura of more hipness, sophistication, and importance than I actually had because of my extracurricular musical accomplishments.

It was the least-resistant path to some kind of success, and I was drawn to it because of that, long before I understood that it might be a deeply satisfying, lifetime pursuit.

In June of 1957, three jazz composers and three classical composers were commissioned to write pieces for an orchestra of jazz musicians who would come to Brandeis, spend a week or two rehearsing the material, and then perform it during an arts festival. My teacher, Harold Shapero, wrote "On Green Mountain," based on something by Monteverdi. Milton Babbitt wrote a twelve-tone piece called "All Set," with a complicated vibraphone part, and Gunther Schuller wrote "Transformation."

The jazz composers included George Russell, Charles Mingus, and Jimmy Giuffre. Art Farmer, Louis Mucci, Jimmy Knepper, Jimmy Buffington, John La Porta, Hal McKusick, Teddy Charles, Barry Galbraith, Joe Benjamin, and Bill Evans were all in the band, and Gunther Schuller was the conductor. I knew of all of them, but Bill was the most important to me. I'd heard him play at a club called The Composer, on a trip to New York a year or two earlier, and had been immediately taken with his playing.

I was able to listen to rehearsals and hang around with the musicians. Bill, probably the youngest of the group, was quiet but cheerful, with a sly smile and a hint of humor. And there was a palpable sense that all the musicians were impressed with him. Gunther, even with the responsibility of conducting and organizing everything, was accessible and friendly.

There was no nearby off-campus place for the players to eat between rehearsals, so they ended up at the student union's cafeteria and snack bar. There was a piano there, so I figured out when the musicians were likely to turn up and arranged for Steve Kuhn and Arnie Wise to be there playing with me. My bass playing was increasingly oriented toward playing with

JAZZ
ULLMAN AMPHITHEATRE
Thursday, June 6, 8:45 p.m. – Performance
Friday, June 7, 11 a.m. – Performance and Symposium

This program, which brings to the Brandeis Festival audience an evening of six premieres, marks the first time that a university has commissioned a program of jazz works. The uniqueness of this program is heightened by the fact that three of the composers whose works were commissioned are recognized composers in the jazz idiom while the other three are highly regarded composers of so-called "serious" music. Selection of the jazz composers was made by a committee consisting of jazz authority Nat Hentoff and composer Gunther Schuller, a major proponent of the concept of the correlation of the jazz and serious music forms. The selection of the "serious" composers was made by a committee of the Brandeis University Music Department.

Program
(not in order of performance)

All Set	MILTON BABBITT
Suspensions	JIMMY GIUFFRE
Revelations	CHARLES MINGUS
All About Rosie	GEORGE RUSSELL
Transformation	GUNTHER SCHULLER
On Green Mountain (Chaconne after Monteverdi)	HAROLD SHAPERO

* * *

In addition to the commissioned works, the program will include two jazz compositions which have influenced the development of the idiom: Duke Ellington's "Reminiscing in Tempo," written in 1935 (specially adapted for this concert by Gunther Schuller); and "Eronel," by the French critic, André Hodeir.

The program of Friday, June 7, consists of the six commissioned works followed by a symposium featuring the composers of these works. Reverend Norman O'Connor will act as chairman of the symposium and Nat Hentoff will serve as moderator of the discussion.

The jazz works are performed by a combo including Hal McKusick and John Laporta, saxes; Louis Mucci and Art Farmer, trumpets; Jimmy Knepper, trombone; Robert DiDomenica, flute; Manuel Zegler, bassoon; Bill Evans, piano; Teddy Charles, vibes; Joe Benjamin, bass; Margaret Ross, harp; James Buffington, French horn; Barry Galbraith, guitar; and Teddy Sommer, drums.

Program from the Jazz concert at the Brandeis Festival of the Arts, June 1957. Courtesy of the Robert D. Farber University Archives & Special Collections, Brandeis University

Steve and Arnie. Steve was a year younger than I, and he could really play. Even then he was an accomplished pianist, and he had the capriciously distributed musical gift of absolute pitch. That meant while he was able to hear and remember all the melodies and harmonies of the tunes we were playing, I was struggling to remember the right bass notes (fortunately fewer of them than melody notes, and usually more repetitive) along with where the next modulation was headed.

Despite the disparity in our musical abilities, Steve and I shared a lot. I was far behind in what I could do, but I listened to the same things and had a broad, sophisticated background. That gave me confidence to withstand being regularly shown my deficiencies as I played with Steve.

Steve studied piano with Margaret Chaloff, whose son, Serge, was a brilliant baritone saxophonist—famous as a musician and for his reputation as a heroin addict. Steve learned a lot from Mrs. Chaloff. He had prodigious technique and a beautiful sound. She told Steve that Red Garland's touch represented an ideal, and Steve responded by acquiring a similarly nuanced ability to control the pressure on each key to bring specific voices into proportion. And he could swing. Accompanying him was a pleasure; my solos, still in their formative stages, were always provided with attentive and beautiful piano accompaniments, though Steve was quick to let me know when my memory or my ear fell short of his expectations. His absolute pitch was a frightening pain in the neck, but he played better than any other musician regularly available to me, and I grew to prefer his music to that of the other Boston jazz pianists.

Arnie Wise was a young Englishman from the Golders Green neighborhood in London whose family had moved to Brookline. He was a talented artist and a student at the Massachusetts School of Art. I thought he played the drums like an angel. He had all the steadiness and jazz feel we needed, with such a subtle, beautiful sound you could sit right next to the drums all night and hear everything else going on in perfect clarity and proportion. Arnie played the same things other good jazz drummers played but softer. I think some musicians experienced that as being weak, but Steve and I loved it.

This was a time when there was virtually no jazz played by university students. I knew we were a good trio and thought the New York musicians would be surprised by the level of our playing. I knew it was important that they heard us. When they did, they stayed, listened intently, and nearly forgot to eat. It was the first time Bill Evans heard me play.

A few professional opportunities came up while we were still in school. Don Elliott, who played the vibes and mellophone, got a gig at Brandeis, and our trio was hired to accompany him. I got to play with Herman Autrey, a fine traditional jazz trumpeter, and Howard McGhee, one of the first bebop trumpeters, at The Crystal Room in Milford. Boots Mussulli ran monthly Sunday night concerts there. Stan Getz came to Brandeis, and we accompanied him. Coleman Hawkins came later. (When asked if he'd need a microphone, he said if Stan hadn't needed one, he certainly wouldn't.) Those were the first of many wonderful encounters with more experienced musicians. Though we were already playing at a professional level when jazz didn't exist in university settings, there was no expectation that three college kids playing in a student lounge could hold the attention of some of New York's best and most accomplished jazz musicians.

So the New York musicians were stunned—believing their ears but not their eyes. The music was professional and coming from students, barely twenty years old, and it astonished them. We had a fine trio—not only as individual musicians but also because we had already become an integrated ensemble that exhibited musical intimacy and sensitive interaction. Certainly, Bill Evans was paying attention. He even played a couple of tunes with Arnie and me, making it clear he was treating us as colleagues.

Sometime during my first year at Brandeis, my relationship with Tom Wilson, whom I'd met and started a friendship with while still at MIT, began to blossom and take up more of my time and attention. I'd drive to Cambridge to spend time with Tom, and we found many common interests that drew us together, jazz being the most important.

When Tom started his own record company, I spent countless hours, adding up to weeks and months, hanging out at his house helping with the fledgling Transition Records—writing liner notes, packing LPs into sleeves and covers, and being general factotum. I don't remember if I was paid for these services, but it didn't matter. I had Tom's friendship, and that was all I needed. Tom was a black Harvard graduate at a time when there weren't many of those. He was smart and intuitive, had a great sense for new directions in music that might turn out to be meaningful, and a poetic way of expressing things. He sported a herringbone jacket with a pattern that could be measured in inches instead of the usual half- or quarter-inch chevrons. He called it his "herringbone and a half." I was "Chucklet."

I adored Tom. I was naive and a little insecure; Tom was hip, terminally hip, and he liked me. I could sense genuine interest and respect, which Tom demonstrated to me over and over. I trusted him, his instincts, and his advice.

In early 1958, Tom asked if I'd go to New York with him to record with Cecil Taylor. He had convinced Cecil that I was the bass player for the job, and he'd hired Kenny Dorham to play trumpet. Louis Hayes would be the drummer, with John Coltrane on tenor.

Tom had been following Coltrane's work and may have been the first to record him as a leader some time before this. Certainly, the jazz public knew him through his playing in the Miles Davis Quintet. That had been his job for most of the preceding three years, but John Coltrane was not yet a household name, and he was far from being the jazz icon the world would make of him later. He was just one of several fine tenor players—the one Tom thought would make the best contribution to this session. Tom had even scheduled the date during spring break to make it easier for me to get away. I thought it would change my life.

I was going to be on a jazz record! Some recordings we'd made with our trio in a home studio on Beacon Hill had turned out well, but this was going to be released and distributed. I don't remember gloating, but though I had to acknowledge Steve Kuhn's superior musicianship, I was going to make a record first. And I was more than pleased with the level of acceptance that led Tom to include me in a group with known New York musicians who'd already been on recordings I'd bought and listened to incessantly. I knew Coltrane's playing a little. Kenny Dorham and Louis Hayes were well-established, and I looked forward to playing with them. Some of the players in Boston were just as good. Joe Gordon's trumpet playing was competitive with Kenny's, and Jimmy Zitano met the standards of respected New York drummers. I knew that. But there was still the added cachet of recording in New York with musicians who'd already made a significant mark, and that was a thrill. Only Cecil was relatively unknown, and it was Cecil's playing that particularly interested Tom.

We got to the studio, on an upper floor of a building on Broadway near 47th Street, around the corner from the High School of Performing Arts on 46th, where I'd been a student four years earlier. Kenny was sweet-natured. Louis was quiet, and John didn't say much that I remember. The mood was friendly, and no one made anything of the fact that I was the youngest in the room and looked different. We played a couple of standards that everyone knew, and it became apparent that four people were doing one thing, while Cecil was intent on doing something else. We went our way, he went his, and the two rhythmic conceptions never jelled.

Most musicians I knew had learned to reach toward a smooth meshing of pulsation that helped to center the rhythmic nuances and minor discrepancies that were inevitable in each player's personal time signature. Cecil cared not a whit for that. His playing bumped and lurched, landing askew of everyone else's placement. It was never far away, just erratic enough that you couldn't adjust to it. We could only ignore it and find a center for the four of us. That meant we didn't listen to him much. Since we had to shut that part out, Cecil's jagged melodies and purposefully clashing harmonies didn't have much effect on us either. We played the harmonies we knew and let the resulting juxtaposition create what it would. Some people find the results interesting, even intriguing. To me, it sounded like four against one. It's always boiled down to form, tempo, and unity of rhythmic accent for me. Without that agreement, it just feels too separate to qualify as an ensemble experience.

Musicians have different definitions of what it means to "play together." For some, being in the same county in the same month qualifies as "communication." Others have more stringent notions. Even among those whose ideas on this subject are relatively refined, there's room for varying points of view.

None of my misgivings, if they were shared by any of the other musicians, were expressed to Tom. We did the job. We each needed the $300, and musicians were not in the habit of turning down recording opportunities. I was thrilled to be there, and a little exercise in imitative counterpoint I'd been working on appealed to the horn players, who found it on my music stand and took for granted that it was material for the date. It was just three short, harmonically ambiguous motives, each appearing once over the harmonies of a twelve-measure blues but in different sequences in two versions of the line. If you played both lines together, you heard the same material appearing first in one voice and then in counterpoint in the other voice. It wasn't very sophisticated, and I thought it needed more refinement. (I almost always feel that way, until I've tried every combination of possibilities and adjusted everything I can think of.) But Kenny and John liked it, and that felt like real acceptance.

Another thing happened at that recording session that was to shape my playing from then on. We made an early take and stopped to listen to the playback of a tune that included a bass solo. Everything had gone well until a measure or two into my solo when I heard myself skittering ahead of the tempo, making the changes a little early, and expressing an unbearable amount of anxiety. It wasn't only that I hated it, which I certainly did, but that I recognized then I'd been dangerously ignorant of the problem while it was happening. My own nervousness was dictating reactions I needed to control. It's hard to see the picture from inside the frame, but the playback served as an unforgiving, severely objective mirror.

I describe my reaction now as if it had been a studied, intellectual response, partly because I've encountered the problem so many times since when working with student musicians and have to think about how to convey helpful solutions. But at the time, my reaction was just as emotionally driven as the problem itself. I simply hated the result, and I was going to do everything in my power to prevent it from happening again.

No one said anything, I think I must have grunted and looked dissatisfied; we agreed to do another take.

I had to adjust the way I was experiencing my music, but the motivation to avoid expressing panic was strong and forced me just to do it. My time already felt right in the accompanying parts. The solos had to be just as stable.

Some musically sound part of me understood that I'd been misinterpreting signals from my senses, making me think that I was late, when, in fact, we hadn't gotten to the moment yet. Anxiety rarely helps you slow down and take the measure of your experience, but that is what's needed to control the compulsion to rush. Part of your consciousness must live in a world that's slowed down enough to take the time to observe what's going on in real time. That phenomenon happens quickly. You jump out of your subjective reactions momentarily to hear what you are playing—like a third party to the action—check things out for an instant, make the necessary adjustment, and jump back in. Half of you plays, and half of you listens—not only to others but also to yourself as well. Otherwise, there's a serious risk of sounding horrendous.

The record came out on the Transition label, under Cecil's name, as *Hard Driving Jazz*, with a Formula One car photo on the cover. My tune was called "Double Clutching," and there was another blues number called "Shifting Down." It's since been re-released several times (as an LP and as a CD) under John Coltrane's name as "Coltrane Time." Though market-driven concession has undoubtedly sold many more copies than would have sold under Cecil's name, it has fostered the misconception that the decisions about who played and what happened were John's. In fact, they were neither John's nor entirely Cecil's but, instead, mostly Tom Wilson's. (Tom went on from there to become an important producer for Columbia Records, working with Simon and Garfunkel, Frank Zappa, and Bob Dylan.)

The session was a milepost, but it didn't change my life the way I thought it would. I was either hired or passed over for the same gigs, and girls didn't pay any more attention to me than they had before.

I spent most of my summers in idyllic Berkshire County, helping or hindering my parents in their efforts to provide a stimulating creative environment for teenagers interested in music, theater, dance, or art. Berkshire County, in the summer, is one of the few areas in the world where a person of essentially urban sensibilities can experience rural charms without feeling out of contact with other city people. They've all escaped to the same part of the country.

You could avoid the crowded concerts of old warhorses at The Berkshire Music Center at Tanglewood in favor of chamber music or a cornucopia of well-played twentieth-century pieces during the week devoted to that. And you could meet anyone: Aaron Copland schmoozed at the Red Lion Inn bar; Leonard Bernstein mounted his pop opera, *Trouble in Tahiti*, here; Lukas Foss needed extra people for his opera *Griffelkin*, and my sister got to dance in that production; and jazz pianist Randy Weston was at the Avaloch resort with a band every summer. At one time or another, so many instrumentalists, composers, conductors, dancers, actors, directors, and painters spent time in Berkshire County that it wasn't the least bit remarkable to run into actors such as Anne Bancroft or Lou Gossett Jr., playwrights Arthur Penn or William Gibson—or for my brother, Josh, to hitch a ride and get a lift from the young conductor Michael Tilson Thomas. Jazz flutist Hubert Laws had an accompanying role in one of the Berkshire Playhouse productions and kindly came a mile up the road to play piccolo and bass duets with me for the Indian Hill students.

It was into this already heady atmosphere that our friends Phil and Stephanie Barber, founders of the nearby Music Inn resort, decided to launch jazz concerts in a tent during the 1958 Tanglewood season. Since I was only a couple of miles away at Indian Hill, when it came time for Phil and Stephanie to find a rhythm section for a Billie Holiday concert with her accompanist Mal Waldron, they called me. I hired Jimmy Zitano to come out from Boston to play drums.

Dan Morgenstern, a jazz scholar and critic, was there. He'd graduated from Brandeis a year or two earlier and was beginning to pursue the interests that would become his profession. Dan has written about the concert and described where I showed consideration and courtesy to Billie. I'm glad to hear it, but I only remember how I had to concentrate on musical responsibilities to come through the evening unscathed. I don't remember which of her tunes I knew, but I couldn't have known many of them well enough to feel confident. Sadly, I don't know how she sang that night. I remember her music more from her records than I do from having played with her. Billie was graciously complimentary to Jimmy and me at the end of the evening and let the audience know that she'd been pleased by successful results with a couple of musicians unknown to her and that a potentially stressful situation had turned out well. She didn't look good that summer, and she died a year later.

The Barbers also founded The Lenox School of Jazz, a two-week, late-summer program modeled after what had existed for years at places like the Berkshire Music Center at Tanglewood and Marlboro Festival in Vermont. This was long before jazz education became a bloated industry, sunk by its own weight to its present depth.

Like Tanglewood and Marlboro, there were no "music teachers." Instruction was given by professional performers of the highest level. The years blur together in my memory, but over the school's 1957–1960 existence, the faculty boasted the enthusiastic presence of the Modern Jazz Quartet, Max Roach's Quintet (with Booker Little, George Coleman, Art Davis, and jazz tuba player, Ray Draper), Jimmy Giuffre, Jim Hall, George Russell, Bob Brookmeyer, Dick Katz, Gunther Schuller, violinist John Garvey, historian Martin Williams, and other significant people.

I didn't enroll as a student, and I was far too inexperienced to be considered faculty, but the student population was deficient in bass players, so I was simply invited by the Barbers to participate. Hod O'Brien was a student that first year; so was Bob Dorough, a tall, skinny guy from Texarkana who sang and played a quirky style of jazz piano. Enormous depths of creative talent and intelligence were hidden behind Bob's deceptively rural southern drawl. He later went on to compose the music for a clever and successful ABC television educational cartoon series called *Schoolhouse Rock!* It was really *Schoolhouse Jazz!*

I learned a lot that year. I got a chance to play with a string quartet performing a piece by Jim Hall. I knew Scotty LaFaro had recorded it, and I was proud to play his part. Gunther Schuller had written a piece based on John Lewis's "Django" for strings and rhythm, and I had to learn that part. Everything was fine until I got to a solo, where I had to improvise through a progression of dominant seventh chords that moved around the circle of fifths a little faster than I was used to. I wasn't doing all that well with it at the dress rehearsal on the afternoon before the evening performance, but Gunther gave up a sit-down dinner,

Chuck Israels, Steve Kuhn, and Arnie Wise playing at Adams House, Harvard ca. 1957

eating his supper from a paper plate so he could accompany me at the piano while I did my last-minute practicing.

I was in my senior year in 1958. A couple of Brandeis students—Paula Kelly and Joyce Kalina—opened a Harvard Square coffee house in a large space they rented at 47 Mount Auburn Street. For the better part of that year, our trio played Wednesday through Saturday nights at Mount Auburn 47. It was nearly ideal. Four nights on and three nights off is a perfect schedule. You have no chance to get tired of playing, and by the time you've been idle for three days, you're eager to get back to playing music you love. There was a nice piano and an appreciative audience.

Harvard Square denizens were an interesting bunch, not as jazz aware as those who frequented The Stable, but they recognized good music when they heard it. And they showed appreciation by filling the place often enough to keep Paula and Joyce in business and happy with us. One night when the job was no longer exclusively ours (John Neves and his pianist brother Paul were playing there), a fourteen-year-old came in with his family and set up drums to sit in for the evening. Tony Williams had been studying with Alan Dawson, and he sounded great.

There were occasional other notable musical experiences. Our trio got a job playing at a University of Pennsylvania fraternity house in Philadelphia one weekend, in a block with several fraternities. We could hear another band across the street, a jazz quintet with tenor and trumpet, and they sounded good . . . too good. They were local Philadelphia guys. Jimmy Garrison was the bass player, Odean Pope played tenor, and drummer Jimmy (later conductor James) DePriest (Marian Anderson's nephew) was the leader. I've forgotten the other two guys' names, but they were good too. Our bands were back and forth at each other's gigs for the rest of the weekend.

It was probably unusual for two fraternity houses on the same block to have first-rate, young, professional, real jazz bands on the same weekend, but it could and did happen. For the last thirty years, there has been periodic talk of a jazz revival, but you don't see this kind of thing. And it wasn't a jazz festival. It was just a college fraternity weekend, with all the usual distractions that suggests, and one was all-out, committed jazz.

Then there were the Latin bands that my high school bass player friend Bill Salter played in. On New York trips, I'd go with him to a place on River Avenue, across from Yankee Stadium. I think it was called The Riverside Plaza—a big dance hall that held about 3,000. What an experience. There was an undulating sea of graceful people, dancing, mostly from the waist down, hips gyrating, and shoulders seemingly suspended by invisible forces. The band leader was a robust-sounding tenor player named Hugo Dickens, and there was an impressive trumpet player named Vinnie McEwan. Barry Rogers, the trombone player, had an enormous sound and was a great improviser that a lot of jazz fans never got to hear because he spent almost his entire career in Latin bands. Eddie Diehl played wonderful guitar solos and knew all the pieces by heart. I don't think he was much of a reader, but that was no shortcoming in this situation; he knew the music. Rodgers Grant or Artie Jenkins on piano, with Bill Salter on bass, supplied the pitched part of the rhythm section. Then there were the percussionists, three or four guys playing with every imaginable nuance of Cuban rhythm, plus some unimaginable ones. I can still picture Phil Newsum, tall and good-looking and sounding exceptional, playing the timbales in front of the band. (In this kind of drum-intensive music, the percussion section is the front line.)

And there was Pete La Roca, recently graduated from the High School of Music & Art, handsome as a movie star, graceful as a cat, and playing the drum set like an angel or a demon—you didn't know which. Whatever he was, he was bewitching and magnetic. You couldn't be in the same room and take your eyes off him or ignore his playing for a second.

Some athletes are like that, mesmerizing in their work, riveting your attention on them as they rivet theirs on an immediate physical goal. This generation knows Michael Jordan and Michael Johnson. Gregory Hines had this quality, and I've heard some flamenco singers with the same power. It's one of the most intensely beautiful things—at once animal in its purposefulness and completely human in applying that attention to creative play and expression. Pete La Roca was the embodiment of that kind of intensity. He accomplished the same thing behind a jazz drum set, and few could escape being captivated by it.

Sometimes I went to Small's Paradise, or Minton's Uptown House in Harlem, usually to hear Hod O'Brien play with Oscar Pettiford. I was beginning to figure out that what Oscar was doing was not ordinary bass playing. His accompanying pulse and his note choices were impeccable, and his solos had a melodic arc that eluded most other bass players. I don't remember much about the tunes and arrangements. I don't think I had the space in my only partly developed musical consciousness to absorb all that along with what Oscar was playing. I was lucky such an advanced musician welcomed my attention.

Occasionally, I'd be invited to sessions in the homes of jazz lovers. Hod was involved with a wealthy woman who had a vast Park Avenue apartment where Oscar Pettiford would hang out and play. And there was a nice guy named Kenny Karpe who had a loft off lower 5th Avenue where there were sessions.

I heard Art Farmer, Kenny Burrell, Freddie Redd, and Lin Halliday, a talented young tenor player from Texas who disappeared from the scene before making his mark.

Arnie Wise and I sometimes worked at the Green Street Bar in Albany, driving across Massachusetts to the gig in his VW bug, drums jammed in the back and the bass over the seats, neck between Arnie and me, with the scroll barely missing the dashboard. There's a hill on Route 20 (the road you had to take before the Massachusetts Turnpike was built), in Rensselaer, just east of Albany; during one of those trips, on an icy night, we slid down the entire hill backward. The weight of the engine hanging out behind the back wheels was too unstable, and gravity took over. It all happened in slow motion, and we didn't hit anything, but we didn't breathe from the top of the hill until we crunched without harm to a stop in a small snowbank at the bottom.

The leader of those Green Street gigs was J.R. Montrose. Hod usually played piano, and Sal Amico was on trumpet. J.R. was a little guy from Utica who played swinging tenor and was fun to be around. He married a girl I knew from Pittsfield (near Stockbridge), so we ran into each other in the summers too. A couple of times, guitarist Rene Thomas drove down from Montreal to play with J.R.

Jake Hanna—a notable drummer with a simple traditional style (no cross-rhythms to speak of; just a good beat, good sound, and dynamics)—had a successful career playing for singers like Bing Crosby and Rosemary Clooney. He came from Boston and was living there at the same time. He called me for a week-long gig at Otto's in Latham Circle, just north of Albany. My friend Jay Migliori, the tenor player who had patiently taught me the basics of jazz harmony and modulation, was on the gig, so I took off a week from school to do it.

There are hundreds of Jake Hanna stories. He was wry and bitingly funny. Later, when Jake had moved to Los Angeles, someone asked, "What part of LA do you live in?" Jake responded, "L."

I was enjoying acceptance among Boston jazz musicians, learning more about the music and developing opinions and preferences, and gaining a little notoriety at school for my professional-level jazz activities. But I didn't think of myself as being in pursuit of a career as a jazz bassist. I was just doing what I was able to do that was fully engaging and fun—something that brought me deep, sensual, musical pleasure, the company of musicians I admired, and a little prestige among my student friends.

I was beginning to form a system of habits and opinions shaped by the prevailing values of my musical surroundings. An unerring commitment to the underlying pulse of the music was a principle held by all the musicians I admired. Everything had to swing. No idea you might have would be good enough to play if you couldn't play it in tempo. I held on to that idea as tightly as I could. And I was developing preferences for the styles of some of my colleagues over others. Some of those preferences seem superficial at this distance, but I was already forming a system of aesthetics. A few of my developing aesthetic leanings later led to unpopular opinions. But for the moment, I was enjoying acceptance in the society of Boston's professional jazz musicians.

4

Paris and Bud

Somehow, despite all the distractions, I survived my senior year, spending a lot of time with graduate student composer Alvin Lucier, but I was still far from ready to write anything more than what had almost incidentally gotten used on the Cecil Taylor recording and a few arrangements and tunes for the yearly student musical. I managed to pass all my courses, and I was finished with school, never having really studied anything.

I had $1,000 in savings bonds put aside by my father, a small fortune in 1959, and bought a ticket to Europe on the Holland America Line. Many of my contemporaries did things like that. We went to Europe to find ourselves—as if "ourselves" hadn't been living with us for the better part of a quarter century but had somehow been hiding out in the old countries of our ancestors. Trips like that do help you know yourself—they quickly reveal which parts of your personality are related to your immediate circumstances and which are part of your character, following wherever you go. But most of us didn't know that. We were genuinely curious about the romance of Europe and eager to get away from the influence of our families.

Though an ocean voyage sounded attractive, the North Atlantic, on a relatively small ship, proved cold and rough even in the summer. But the send-off had been exciting. And the seven days from New York harbor to landfall in Ireland at Cork passed quickly enough. My old college roommate, Paolo Lionni, met me in Le Havre and drove me to Paris, where he'd been living for the last few months.

I'd become close to Paulo and his sophisticated, artistic, European-American family. His father, Leo, was a famous artist, illustrator, writer of children's books and art director of *Fortune* magazine. I'd been welcomed on vacations in their Greenwich, Connecticut, home and enjoyed Nora Lionni's generous hospitality. They had a villa in Italy, and Paulo was a cosmopolitan, multi-lingual guy who was eager to introduce me to the pleasures of Europe.

Paolo wanted to make sure my first sight of Paris was sufficiently spectacular, so we drove up Avenue de la Grande Armée, L'Arc de Triomphe looming in front of us, around L'Étoile and down Champs-Élysées. I don't think I've seen a more beautiful city, before or since. I got installed in the Hotel de Londres on Rue Bonaparte, a couple of blocks toward the Seine from Boulevard Saint-Germain. Cheap hotel rooms in Paris were depressing, but everything else was enchanting, so you spent as little time as possible in the hotel. We sat at Les Deux Magots watching the passing scene and occasionally meeting other Americans.

By the second night in Paris, Paolo had wrangled an invitation to film director Roger Vadim's apartment on Rue Vielle du Temple, near Les Halles. I had brought my bass—the invitation was specifically directed to me as a jazz musician. We arrived to find movie cameras and lights and the stunning Annette Stroyberg, then Mrs. Vadim. And I was invited to play with Kenny Clarke and Bud Powell.

Bud's music had been the prototype for so much of what we played that I was awestruck at the idea. He was a legendary living fountainhead of our music, but it was Kenny Clarke I found most inspiring. His playing had the musical equivalent of what the dancers at Performing Arts called elevation: the illusion that laws of gravity were temporarily suspended. Kenny's beat made playing with him feel weightless. Of course, bass notes had to be played with solidity, and that required effort, but when Kenny played with you, he shared that effort in a way that lifted you. You could play chorus after chorus and not feel tired.

Bud, on the other hand, was so strange that I didn't know what to make of him. His playing lacked the strength I'd heard on his records, and he had a distracted grin that either stared past you or looked at you with only partial recognition. He seemed to be playing automatically, without the thoughtfully timed phrases and pauses in his improvisations I'd heard and appreciated on his recordings. But he was still the great Bud Powell, and the people respected his history.

Years earlier, Bud had been beaten in a fight and had several stays in mental hospitals where he'd been treated pretty badly. Now in Paris, Bud's wife, Buttercup Edwards, held him with a tight rein, and Bud seemed perpetually groggy and unfocused.

Buttercup did her best to keep him away from the cognac he'd try to get a fan to buy him that would make him even more morose. That was the shell of a man I met. Those films from July 1959 probably exist in some archive. I'd be curious to see if watching them now would recall the off-centeredness I felt in Bud's playing and the joy I experienced with Kenny Clarke.

Buttercup went everywhere with Bud. She was his manager and caretaker, and she was there at Vadim's that evening. She heard me, and within a couple days, she hired me to play with Bud at his regular Le Chat Qui Pêche gig; it was a cave on Rue de la Huchette, off Boulevard Saint-Michel in the Latin Quarter. Both more than I'd dared to expect and a profound disappointment, the gig paid 500 old francs a night (the equivalent of $10)—enough for the hotel room and meals.

The drummer was Granville "G.T." Hogan, a very good player in the Philly Joe Jones style. G.T. was a Texan whose expansive, friendly personality made it easier to deal with Bud's inability to make real social or musical contact. Our family friend, composer Marc Blitzstein, came through Paris and stopped by to hear me play with Bud, sending a photo back to my folks with a message about a skinny white kid playing in a dive with a fat black guy.

I was in Paris and playing almost every night with a jazz legend. I was ecstatic about that, and it should have been enough, but the music didn't seem very good to me. I made no bones about it, expressing dissatisfaction in my pretty-good French to the French musicians and Bud's adoring fans. I felt it was my duty to enlighten everyone about the shortcomings and failed to understand that this was going to make me unpopular with a lot of people.

In retrospect, I'm surprised I came away with any friends, so great was the French reverence for Bud's creative history. I don't know if they were imagining his former glory when they listened to what seemed to me to be the empty shell of his music or if they heard what, to me, was a hollow charade and simply didn't care. They always applauded and treated Bud with the respect his legacy deserved. There was one disturbing thing about the gig with Bud Powell: With all the protestations of reverence, the Le Chat Qui Pêche piano was an out-of-tune, broken-down upright—a fact that seemed not to disturb any of the rapt listeners. But I was frustrated. I saw the French audience as populated by people for whom anything with a remotely African component (unless it was Algerian) had a primitive advantage over the years of discipline and constraint in the European tradition. Maybe I wasn't entirely wrong, but my lack of restraint in expressing my point of view was a gross gaucherie.

Some French musicians tolerated my inconsiderate behavior. Bassist Michel Gaudry and his wife overcame the characteristic French reluctance to invite guests easily into their homes and invited me over for meals and long talks. Martial Solal, the Algerian pianist, had a wonderful quartet that played at Club Saint-Germain. Roger Guérin played trumpet. Bassist Paul Rovère and Swiss drummer Daniel Humair were the rhythm section. Daniel had amazing technical facility and ambidexterity. A few left-handed drummers reverse the standard procedure, but most play time on the ride cymbal with their right hand and accents on the snare with their left. Daniel could switch back and forth in the middle of a phrase with no discernible change in sound or rhythmic feeling and was great with the brushes. His memory for, and understanding of, music was prodigious.

The quartet played a long composition of Martial's "Suite En Ré Bemol" that I admired. It had a variety of orchestration, with each instrument playing unusual roles. Roger used mutes and open horns; not only were there sections in various tempos, but the end featured a perfectly controlled accelerando. I went to hear them play it as often as I could.

French television played short films of beautiful women undressing for bed as "sign-of" features late at night—intolerably sexist for our present-day mentality but attractively European risqué to a young American. Martial wrote the music for some of these and hired me to play.

Sometimes we went to the Blue Note, at 27 Rue D'Artois on the Right Bank, where Kenny Clarke had a trio with organist Lou Bennett and guitarist Jimmy Gourley. We got to hear other good French musicians, like pianists Rene Urtreger, George Arvanitas, and Raymond Fol. Paul Rovere's brother Bibi was also a good bassist. Pierre Michelot was a great bass player. Barney Wilen, the young tenor saxophonist who recorded the music for the crime film *L'Ascenseur pour L'Échafaud* with Miles Davis, had a uniquely beautiful tone that made an indelible impression on me. At one point, people were talking about a young tenor player from Pittsburgh playing with Raymond Fol at Club Louisiane, so I got to hear Stanley Turrentine. The Mars Club on the Right Bank featured Art Simmons, another American piano player, and Andy and the Bey Sisters sometimes worked there. Paris was jumping.

Quincy Jones had a band preparing to tour Europe that summer. They rehearsed in the Olympia Theater mezzanine, and I was invited to listen. It was a great band with some of Quincy's friends from Seattle, like Buddy Catlett and Patti Bown. Les Spann was the guitarist and played some flute solos. Jerome Richardson and Sahib Shihab were in the saxophone section, and Joe Harris played drums. I listened to several pieces with solos by various band members. It would be unfair to say that they were perfunctory, but later, when Phil Woods stood up from the lead alto chair to play his solo, the atmosphere changed. Phil played as if there were no tomorrow. The contrast was striking, and I have always remembered the impression it left—if you practice rehearsing, when the time comes to perform, you're ready to rehearse. Phil practiced performing.

Arnie Wise showed up on the same kind of exploratory trip I was on. So did Jon Mayer, a piano player from New York who'd been a student at Indian Hill. The job with Bud had ended, and we got offered a job in St. Tropez on the Riviera and thought it would be great to see the fishing village turned resort that had been made famous by Brigitte Bardot. The job didn't pan out as promised, but it was a beautiful place; we stayed a week or two and heard Don Byas play with a horrible Italian dance band at night.

Don was a fisherman, and at night he'd walk into this crowded, sweltering nightclub, wearing a baseball cap and bikini bathing suit, his sixty-year-old body rock-hard, looking like an athlete's. He'd take out his tenor and blast through the atmosphere for an hour, ignoring the incompetence of his accompaniment—obliterating even the electric guitars with the power of his sound. Then he'd leave, and the band would continue sounding just as horrible as before he'd come.

The only trip I've ever made to Africa happened late that summer of 1959. Lucky Thompson was in Paris, and he had an open-air concert in Mers El Kébir, near Oran, Algeria. He hired Martial Solal, G.T. Hogan, and me. I got to spend a night in Algeria and played with one of my favorite musicians. To this day, nobody I know plays with tone, timing, and invention quite like Lucky Thompson, and the jazz world is much the poorer for it.

I had moved from the Hôtel de Londres in Paris to the Hôtel Saint-André des Arts, across from Le Caméléon jazz discotheque and nightclub. Jon and Arnie stayed there, and Daniel Humair came by often. There were other Americans and a general atmosphere of artistic bohemia. We smoked hashish, ate steak frites, sat in cafes, and played pinball.

We spent wonderful hours talking about jazz and walking through a city that knows no equal for surprising vistas of all proportions. Every turn of a corner is a new wonder, every neighborhood a perfect mini-environment.

We encountered a dry period when there was little work in Paris, and my cushion of cash was running dangerously low. A Spaniard named Jean-Pierre Bourbon heard us play and offered a gig at a club he owned in Madrid. Clarinet player Perry Robinson (another friend from Indian Hill and son of an old family friend, composer Earl Robinson) came with us. We formed The New Blues Quartet.

The Whiskey Jazz Club was quite a change from Le Chat Qui Pêche, and Madrid was a world removed from Paris, where we'd lived and worked in old neighborhoods with narrow streets, mostly on the Left Bank. Here we were in central Madrid on Calle Marqués de Villamagna, off Paseo de Castellana, an avenue so wide that it was divided by not one but two tree-lined boulevards.

Buildings in this neighborhood were large and somewhat newer than what we'd been used to in Paris, occupied mostly by large apartments, private businesses, and government offices. You entered the club at #10 through an ancient, unmarked door of heavy planks held together by wrought-iron straps and hinges. Inside was a pleasantly decorated long room, with comfortable easy chairs and small couches clustered around low cocktail tables, a bandstand at the far end. We worked for the same fees as in Paris, about $10 a night, but despite the fact Spain was generally less expensive than France, somehow, our money went less far there. It felt like a sort of indentured servitude. You could only just survive. There was never anything left over.

Senor and Senora Bourbon were gracious enough employers, clearly from another class than the Le Chat Qui Pêche owner, who did her best to impersonate the French version of a Dickensian witch. Even Ben Benjamin, American owner of the Blue Note, friendly as he was, clearly had to be concerned about whether his club made money. For the Bourbons, the club seemed a pleasant social diversion. They could meet there as hosts to their friends and business acquaintances, where young American jazz musicians added a useful extra attraction—a cultural reason to come out, stay up late as Spaniards did, and drink.

A few other musicians came into the club. Belgian baritone saxophonist Jean-Pierre Gebler and Louis Sangarro (bongo player and son of a Spanish diplomat assigned to Portugal) were sometimes added to the group. Jazz singer Simone Chevalier (later Simone Ginibre, and George Wein's longtime partner in his European jazz festival ventures) would sit in. We lived in a hotel a few blocks away, sharing large rooms with several beds to save money. Jean-Pierre had a record player, and we listened with considerable interest to a new Ornette Coleman recording. The tunes were different and attractive, beautifully played by Ornette and Don Cherry. The nuances of pitch, dynamics, and timing were impressive; the ensemble's precision made it clear this was no accident. We appreciated the adventurousness of the solos, and it stimulated Perry to search for some of the same things in his playing, but by and large, it was the ensemble playing that intrigued us—how beautifully expressively and together Ornette and Don played the unison melodies.

Jean-Pierre also had a Brazilian record he liked, which was by João Gilberto. He understood Portuguese, which furthered his connection with Gilberto's songs, and he played the record often. For the first few times, it sounded like Hollywood soup to me. I didn't feel the power behind the gentle rhythms, and the subtleties of melodic contours and harmonies simply slipped by my ears without making a great impression. I thought it was a kind of Muzak.

The fourth or fifth time, without thinking I was paying any particular attention, it caught me. I was thunderstruck, though it wasn't quite thunder that knocked me over but rather a perfect musical feather. Antônio Carlos Jobim's "Desafinado" and "Chega de Saudade" had mesmerizing form that I was later to recognize owed a great debt to Cole Porter's compositional sensibilities. Certain pitches and harmonies were avoided . . . stored away to be brought into play at the precise moment they would have their most telling effect. João's singing was soft and without vibrato, reminiscent of Chet Baker, but with a little more rhythmic tension. Every word of that beautiful singing language was lovingly formed and timed to perfection. The accompaniment was in a gentle two-beat style—almost the antithesis of the way jazz bass players emphasize their half notes.

The arrangements were built around guitar chords played in hypnotic syncopated rhythms, the bass almost hidden, blended with bass notes played by the guitarist's right thumb. Other instruments played clear, expressive counter-lines when appropriate, or dropped in to add a momentary splash of color or emphasize a rhythm. The drum parts were also blended and subsidiary to the guitar. On top of this, João placed the rhythms of the words in perfect, swinging juxtaposition—sounding totally spontaneous but resulting in an effect that could be no other way. I was later to see him sit on the edge of a hotel room bed with his guitar, practicing one phrase over and over, placing the words differently and making minute adjustments until he got everything just the way he wanted it. He practiced meticulously, but you never sensed anything labored in his performances. As Red Mitchell once said, "There's nothing so prepared as a truly spontaneous performance." This was far from Muzak.

The audience at the club was generally appreciative and often consisted of Americans living or working in Madrid. Ava Gardner was there sometimes, and so was director Nick Ray, who was working on *King of Kings*. But the political atmosphere in Madrid was the antithesis of what we had experienced in Paris—a far cry from the freedom we'd been used to. On many street corners, and in front of every government building (there were plenty of them), were either army guards or armed Civil Guards. The uniforms were different, but everywhere you went, someone with a machine gun was watching you. They never stopped us, but the feeling was one of severe oppression. Women didn't walk alone on the streets unless they were prostitutes. I'm sure there was an underground of freedom in Madrid at that time, but we never found it, and the foreign community existed separately, as if under glass. We got a few gigs at the American Air Force base out at Torrejón.

We went to Barcelona, which was like a different country. Franco's presence was palpable in Madrid and almost absent in Barcelona, which felt then almost as it does today: partly a world unto itself and partly like any thriving seaport, free and connected to international commerce. Madrid sits in the middle of Spain, assigned its role as capital because it's in the center. Barcelona is planted into the country's geography, with hills and harbor dictating its reason for being.

We played in a jazz club and at a concert where the virtuoso Catalan pianist Tete Montoliu was part of the presentation, along with a fine Chilean tenor player, Fernando "Vicho" Vicenzio, with whom we became friendly.

Back in Madrid, we eked out a living without the excitement and sense of adventure that we'd had in Paris. Political repression, even if it seems to have no direct effect on your daily existence, takes a heavy toll on the social atmosphere. I imagine the reaction to repression is quite different if you're personally involved and fighting against it every day, but as visitors, we were in no position to do anything but observe. The Lincoln Brigade had long been defeated and gone, and the people we worked for were beneficiaries of that defeat. Memories of France looked good.

Nick Ray offered us work on his film, as extras or in small roles. That was an exciting idea. He knew we were in trouble, and in this way, he could pay us enough to be of substantial help. All we had to do was hang on for a couple weeks until the filming started. A sense of common political background attracted his interest in me. Jon Mayer, our pianist, who'd followed Jean-Pierre's lead and gotten sucked into drug trouble, for some reason went to Nick, though the relationship was with me. Maybe he was looking for an advance. In any case, he did something to anger Nick, and I found out about it. I've never been so openly angry with a friend. I read Jon the riot act, calling upon resources of expression I didn't know I had. I yelled a litany of invectives that must have lasted several minutes. Then—with the sense that it probably hadn't accomplished much for anyone but me—I called home for airfare and made plans for the quickest exit I could arrange. I'd had enough of living on subsistence wages in an oppressive political atmosphere. If friendships weren't going to be rewarding, and it was going to be weeks before any potential work would develop on the movie set, even playing jazz every night wasn't enough. I was leaving.

I had been using a borrowed bass in Spain. I'd left my instrument for some badly needed repair work with the fine luthier, Marcel Deloget, in Versailles. So I had to return to France for it before I could come home. Crossing the border into France on that train trip, I felt like kissing the ground for a lot of reasons—not all political. I was getting out of a personal situation that had deteriorated into what felt like a trap, leaving a country where I couldn't speak the language and entering one where I could. And it was the first significant step on the way home.

All these adventures in Europe were happening to an unfocused and undeveloped young man who had little relationship to professional responsibility or commitment. I had deeply held opinions and aesthetic points of view that, while they may well have been largely correct, had not yet been well earned.

Sure, I could play. Rhythm was my business, and if I had any advantage at all over most of my European counterparts, it was the training in Boston from listening almost nightly to John Neves's masterful playing, and in New York, from hearing the towering achievements of Oscar Pettiford. I'd learned to draw a "singing" quality from plucked strings by emulating Red Mitchell and Jim Hall, whose guitar playing had made a deep impression, and playing with Steve Kuhn hadn't done me any harm. I listened daily to the music that made our world real: Charlie Parker, Miles Davis, Horace Silver, Art Blakey, and the sorely missed Clifford Brown. I could no more have gone without that music than without food, as I maintained myself in the role of "jazz bass player." I had no idea of what else I'd do, but neither did I have any sense of permanence about the role. Someday, I'd have to get a job.

Not that I wanted one. But even in 1960, you couldn't sustain much of a lifestyle on $10 or $20 a day. If you were going to get realistic about adulthood, you needed a real job. On the other hand, guys with real jobs didn't have the fun I had making music with other people. It was communication in the most intimate way through this special code that, though it required some inside information, seemed universal in its ability to make people feel connected to each other and to you.

I headed back home to Boston, where I felt more secure, rather than New York. Already things were changing. Nothing much was going on at The Stable, and Storyville was closed or close to closing. The Mount Auburn 47 jazz coffee house now featured Harvard Square folkies. The people who'd been our audience two years earlier had been replaced by listeners who were listening intently to well-performed folk songs with three-chord accompaniments, minimal rhythmic interest, and lyrics that had little in common with the sophisticated language of Cole Porter, Lorenz Hart, Ira Gershwin, Frank Loesser, or Yip Harburg. Some of the more contemporary "folk" songs were about matters of social interest to the audience, but the ideas were approached in direct, unadorned language that didn't stretch the imagination any more than the simple musical style. If this was happening in Harvard Square, a neighborhood populated by some of the people with the highest educational aspirations, what might be happening in less ambitious environments? Something was beginning to happen to the population's willingness to spend the listening energy needed to reap the rewards of more sophisticated and layered music. People were paying attention to music that had occupied me in my early adolescence—music I'd outgrown. This was not a good omen. There was no jazz work, and I had to do something. Being a working jazz musician may have been romantic, but being an out-of-work jazz musician held little charm.

A friend of my folks, Harry Rubenstein (a musician they'd known in Stockbridge), had invested in Acoustic Research. Under Ed Villchur's brainy direction, the company had done ground-breaking loudspeaker design in a Cambridge industrial section behind the MIT campus. Harry worked there and, to help me out, got me a job at the plant. I rented a room on Ellery Street near Harvard Square and signed on at AR.

Most of what I did there was unbelievably boring or assumed technical knowledge I didn't have. Then, when I proudly improved a manufacturing process, making it more efficient, I expected recognition—a bonus. The AR people explained I hadn't earned that. They'd paid me for the work—all done on factory time. They were right, and my expectations were unjustified, but I was disappointed, irritated, and missed playing music. I quit.

I'd had enough, and summer was approaching. I could go back to Stockbridge and work for my folks at Indian Hill. But I'd been home six months, and the only music I'd played had been accompanying a beautiful folk singer named Joan Baez, who'd taken over the gig at Mount Auburn 47.

Joan was striking, of Mexican and Scottish descent; her father was a Harvard physicist. I was enthralled by Joan despite her music holding few challenges for a jazz musician. She was one of the few folk singers I had heard who could sing a strophic ballad like "The Copper Kettle" or "The Cruel Mother" and make each new verse sound different. The music was unchanging, so it was all in the delivery of the words. Joan had a clear, colorful soprano voice—always on pitch—and played the guitar very well. Her rhythm and general musicianship were so good that it was more fun to play folk music with her than to play mediocre jazz, which was all that was available then in Boston.

Joan used to say that working with a bass player made her feel dirty, as if it commercialized her performance, but I showed up undaunted, and she tolerated my presence and participation. The relationship was not without strain, but it was the best music available to me, and I must have needed it more than I realized. Joan was being courted by Columbia Records and by the Solomon brothers, who ran the much smaller Vanguard label. She talked about the situation and asked for advice from friends but decided to trust her gut and go with the guys she liked. Vanguard and Joan both benefitted from her instincts.

5
Jazz Professional

The early part of that 1960 summer in Stockbridge passed without memorable incident, and then I got a call from George Russell, the jazz composer who'd heard me play three years earlier when he'd been one of the Brandeis Festival's commissioned composers. He had formed a band in Indiana, and things were working well except for a conflict with the bass player. George was exploring the possibility of having me join. They were scheduled to arrive in a few weeks at the Lenox School of Jazz for final rehearsals before opening at the Five Spot in New York—opposite Ornette Coleman's Quartet. The engagement was scheduled to last several weeks.

If there was one identifiable moment when the idea of a professional career as a jazz bass player became a reality, this was it. The characteristics and shortcomings of my playing hadn't changed overnight, but this was an entry pass into the jazz world capital, and it was likely to attract attention. The fallow past six months had been an aberration, employment as a jazz musician was around the corner, and the promise of continuity seemed believable. I found a one-room apartment on West 88th Street off Riverside Drive. I could take this seriously.

We rehearsed during beautiful late August and early September days in the Music Inn tent, where I'd earlier practiced with Gunther Schuller and played with Billie Holiday. John

Lewis was there among the faculty, and when I told him how lucky I felt that George had asked me to be in his band, John said, "Nobody does you any favors."

It took me a while to understand that he meant I'd earned the position. The guys in the band seemed happy with my playing, and it was a pleasure to lock up the time with Joe Hunt's swinging and intelligent drumming. Some of the music was difficult, although more for the horn players than for me, but the bass line of "Stratusphunk," George's interestingly bent blues piece, was laced with unusually wide intervals; it was a challenge to play it smoothly and make it swing.

The piano parts were limited to a running commentary on what the rest of the band was doing. George could get around the keyboard pretty well, but he directed his playing toward a vocabulary of patterns unlike those of other ensemble pianists. It wasn't as disruptive as Cecil Taylor's ensemble style—you didn't have to tune it out entirely to keep playing your role, but it was designed to nudge you off your rhythmic and harmonic base, out of your comfort zone.

David Baker had the difficult trombone parts and played faster than we were used to hearing. He'd developed speed and agility but ignored fullness of tone or clearly focused pitch, so his playing, while startlingly fast, lost some of its potential impact. David Young played tenor well, and Alan Kiger was an insightful trumpet soloist with a good tone plus the ability to draw in listeners. There was a lot of ensemble structure in the book—most of which had been written by George, Dave Baker, and Carla Bley—with complex themes, backgrounds, and shout choruses. We didn't sound like any other band. We were self-consciously modern—we played Charlie Parker's blues theme, "Sippin' at Bells," at breakneck speed in three keys at once, obscuring the contour of the line by thickening it and making it uniformly dissonant.

George was committed to a particular way of hearing jazz harmony. He had studied a lot of music and derived some theories, which he'd hardened into a harmonic system based on the Lydian scale with its raised fourth degree. George's musical conclusions are supported by the fact his system lines up conveniently with the reality of the harmonic series. Resonating bodies operate in predictable physical ways, and George's choice substitutes the more consonant-raised fourth degree, which appears much earlier in the overtone series, for the philosophically less convenient, dissonant fourth degree of our conventional major scale. The trouble is the normal fourth-degree's dissonance serves a telling purpose in our conventional system of harmony and scales. George's system, reasonable as it might appear on the surface, leads inevitably to musical diversions that, though they might stimulate exploration, sometimes create trips from New York to Philadelphia by way of Cleveland. If a person is going to redefine the system created over centuries by consensus, that person better be Copernicus or Einstein.

The resulting music often sounded less perverse than this description might suggest, but there was always the risk that it could get unintentionally bent out of shape. If using such a system arises only from a desire to make music sound different from accepted vernacular, the outcome tends to sound stilted and stiff.

This band was looking for a way to create music that reconciled the available extremes, trying to inhabit an area between rote convention and avant-garde posturing. And as smartly played as it was, leaned so far in the direction of being recognizably modern that it wasn't as well-balanced nor as attentive to conventional beauty as most of the music that interested me—Charlie Parker and Bill Evans.

Sometimes I thought George's music worked, but I also thought it needed more time to develop, and that was prevented by our limited performance schedule. We worked on the music, rehearsing in George's apartment at 121 Bank Street in the Village and excitedly anticipated the Five Spot opening. Jazz clubs were doing well enough that double bills were normal. The bands would alternate hour-long sets from about 10 p.m. until 3 or 4 a.m., with the audience expected to stay for at least one set by each band.

We were going to play opposite Ornette Coleman at a time when his music was getting a lot of attention. Critics were bending over backward to avoid the mistakes made in dismissing

Charlie Parker's music when it emerged, drawing inexact parallels to the present situation.

Years before, the roots of bebop and the seeds of Parker's music had been hidden from the public thanks to a recording ban in place during its early development. The American Federation of Musicians, under James Petrillo's leadership, called a recording strike during 1942–1944 to force record companies to pay royalties. Live performances and radio broadcasts were unaffected, but because of the strike, bebop's beginnings remained largely unrecorded.

By the time the strike was settled, the music had evolved and seemed to jump out of a vacuum, an apparently revolutionary occurrence that wasn't nearly as sudden as it seemed. Those who'd been privy to the music in its early stages heard an evolutionary process—no more sudden or startling than many other historical shifts in artistic sensibility and style.

But when the ban was lifted and newer music became accessible to a wider audience, many critics were caught unaware. They were shocked by what they perceived as music that drastically loosened the ties to familiar rhythms, melodies, and harmonies. It disoriented them. They felt uncomfortable and excluded and relegated its characteristic rhythmic innovations, melodic jumps, and flurries of swirled notes to the realm of disorganized gibberish.

In time, critical sensibilities caught up with creative developments, and many were embarrassed by their earlier judgments. Once stung, twice shy, critics were afraid of being caught out again (at least reluctant to condemn what they weren't sure they understood) and therefore sometimes effusive in their praise—precisely because they thought they weren't understanding the music. Therefore, Ornette must be Charlie Parker all over again.

Musicians on the inside of the process heard plenty of attractive elements in Ornette's music. We were quick to acknowledge and appropriate the things we found useful. But the uncritical acclaim heaped on by many jazz writers was more disturbing than amusing. It called into question the discernment of their hearing, which threatened musicians who depended on critics' ability to recognize their degree of success in achieving musical goals.

Ornette's music was described as "beyond" Charlie Parker, and he reputedly could play Parker's music beautifully, despite evidence in his playing that this was unlikely. To someone who dirtied his hands daily in musical clay, Ornette sounded like a clever artist making the best of his limitations. There were many admirable things about that, but whether or not it was beyond Charlie Parker depended on the perspective. It didn't seem that way too many of us then and still doesn't.

It seemed Ornette had been encouraged to continue to abandon adherence to harmonic form and conventional melodic coherence by the laudatory attention of highly placed critics and some contemporary classical composers who were attracted by the release from traditional song-form restrictions his music promised. The essential question of whether this was a new open form, or too little form, was rarely asked.

Inescapable evidence of this came out in Ornette's later engagement at the Village Vanguard, where he favored us with his trumpet and violin playing. Ornette's approach to tone production on the violin had apparently started from scratch and gotten no further. It was not his strong suit. His quartet was instrumental in paving the way for conversationally inclusive bass and drum parts, expanding the way conventionally restricted accompanying parts could be more actively and freely engaged in the ensemble without losing the rhythm section's propulsion. That was an important and lasting contribution. Ornette's band wasn't alone in this, but it carried the practice further and with more spontaneous improvisation in the bass and drum parts than anything we'd heard before. Years earlier, Gerry Mulligan's quartet had abandoned the piano in order to leave more room for accompanying lines in the winds and more harmonic freedom. But nothing changed in the bass and drum parts. They remained rooted in conventional roles. Ornette's group provided a template that changed all that.

If jazz is, as Whitney Ballet described it, "the sound of surprise," then Ornette's music was, taken in toto, certainly surprising. What left me unconvinced and a little detached was that the solos were unrelated to any foundational structure. They weren't totally incoherent. There was some motivic development I could follow, but still, there was the sense that either the continuation of an idea or a change could happen at any time. It's hard to be surprised without the establishment of expectation. Seemingly random improvisation with insufficient recognizable form renders everything equally surprising—and ultimately not surprising at all.

The aesthetic balance between the predictable and the unexpected I'd absorbed from years of listening to Western music was largely abandoned in Ornette's band. The bass parts adhered to jazz rhythms but were folk-music-like in their lack of jazz harmonic complexity. The improvisations seemed to gravitate to resonance with the bass parts or pull away from them arbitrarily. There was an insufficient sense of formal expectation to create the power of musical coherence and drama I'd come to expect. Some "musical language" rules had been purposefully ignored, so I had the experience of listening to what sounded like people speaking in tongues. You could follow an emotional outline of some kind, and the sounds of the instruments as the band played them were attractive, nuanced, and expressive, but you couldn't understand the whole story. To my ears, there was too little of a recognizable relationship between the improvisations and the themes for me to follow the progress of the music. It was held together on some good levels—enough to intrigue me for a while and to attract considerable enthusiastic attention from some. But so much surprise, newness, and dissonance for its novelty, irregular rhythmic and harmonic phrasing, and lack of predictable formal moments, eventually vitiated the element of surprise. And the surprises that occurred didn't achieve the sense of retrospective inevitability I'd learned to appreciate by having that aesthetic model etched into my consciousness from years of listening to Beethoven. Too much seemingly unrelated variety ended up leaving me feeling I was hearing music that was disconnected from expectation and, therefore, lacking opportunity for surprise. Ultimately it ended up sounding too much the same to engage my full attention. But it sure was modern, like Bill de Kooning's paintings, and lots of folks were paying attention to it as representative of progress. That assured us that a lot of people were going to be at the Five Spot to hear our band too.

The Five Spot was on the Bowery at 5th Street in a low-rent district away from normal nighttime pedestrian traffic. Hundreds of people came there anyway, and we had good audiences. When I play in New York now, at the Blue Note or Village Vanguard, the one remaining bebop-era relic, the audience seems quite different. Of course, it looks younger, and that's partly a function of my chronological perspective, but it also looks at once more specialized and less knowledgably responsive.

Nightlife is much more expensive now; many who would gladly relinquish their remote control in favor of a little human contact, the warmth of a crowd, and the immediacy of a live performance can't afford it. Add to the cover charge and high minimums the price of a cab ride because the subway at night is too threatening, and the cost of live music becomes prohibitive for few besides the free-spending tourist or the executive on an expense account. Many in the audience are on foreign territory taking in local color unavailable at home, rather than people in their own neighborhoods sampling a weekly dose of the musical environment.

Jazz used to be the air we breathed. That's how it was in September 1960. The place was packed with New Yorkers. Besides the usual complement of jazz musicians, there was a representative mix of people from a broad cross-section of city life. Listening to live jazz was a normal activity for many folks, and you were likely to meet a lot of them throughout an evening: lawyers, reporters, businesspeople, dentists, actors, writers, students, advertising people, and even classical musicians. Jazz was probably as much a center of cultural focus as anything this country ever has been. Jazz musicians were connected, and the pull of that connection was hard to resist. I stopped toying with other possibilities and accepted re-entry into a flow I'd slipped out of when the flow disappeared from Boston.

By the time we played the Five Spot, the band sounded pretty good—the complicated ensembles were done well. The front line had to stand up to comparison with Ornette and Don, and the looser rhythm section style that Billy Higgins and Charlie Haden perfected was already in the air. Such developments are rarely the work of one or two people, and in this case, there were others who played that way, too. Joe Hunt and I were already leaning in that direction and found our own way to reconcile rhythm section variety with George's music.

We made a record for Orrin Keepnews' Riverside label the next month and two more in the next year for Decca. By the time of the second Decca date, Al Kiger had left the band to return home to Indiana, perhaps a little awed by Freddie Hubbard showing up on the scene with his overwhelming sound and technique. Freddie was about seventeen, also from Indiana, and already frighteningly good. Don Ellis, a trumpet player from Los Angeles whom I'd known when he was a student in Boston, took Al's place.

The George Russell Sextet had built-in problems that eventually proved insurmountable, and none of its music survives in general use today. One side of its personality, much the more attractive side, leaned toward the blues and a traditional bebop vocabulary.

Another side seemed afraid to rely on intuitive musical response and succumbed to the notion that following your intuition would always drive you away from being "modern" and "original." The results often didn't make the best of our abilities.

On the other hand, the writing, especially Carla Bley's evocative pieces, suggested a level of ensemble and solo space integration that held real promise. When that promise was unfulfilled, it was sometimes the result of young musicians trying too hard to make it happen. Then there was George's comping, often too high, in the same register as the soloist or higher. He played disruptive, repetitive rhythms and chords that obscured the harmony, disconnecting the bass line from the soloist's melody and the drum part from the soloist's rhythm. It was always competitive and interfering, compelling soloists to force their way through. They could rarely relax. Al Kiger handled it better than the rest of us.

It was George's band and his choice. No one could argue with something that was so personal and integral to how he wanted his music to sound, but it rubbed against the rhythmic grain, interfering with the swing. And it made hard work of musical elements I thought should have been easy. Then there was Don Ellis's preening attitude and his boasting that since he'd accomplished all that Dizzy and Miles had done, that he had to find something else to do. All this finally got irritating enough that I quit, having temporarily lost my appreciation of the fact that George had brought me to New York.

In early March of 1961, I got a call from Benny Goodman, and almost everything changed. The scene moved from a rough-hewn, thrown-together joint on the Bowery to a fancy club in the Lexington Hotel on East 54th Street, from an avant-garde jazz sextet to a ten-piece traditional swing band with a soloist and singers, from whatever suit you wanted to wear to tuxedos, and from loosely timed sets to precise showtimes. Everything changed but the money. Benny asked what I wanted, and I said, "I don't know—about $200 a week," roughly what I'd earned at the Five Spot, so Benny paid me $200 a week. I didn't think about the fact that he was rich—he was a jazz musician. If I'd asked him for five times that, he'd have paid it, and I'd have had less trouble with him. Benny didn't tell the more experienced players, all of whom were probably getting paid a lot more than I'd asked for, how to play. They had at least some respect from him, and some of that may have been earned by how much they insisted on being paid. If I'd known what some of those guys were getting and asked for similar pay, Benny might not have felt so free to give me playing instructions in the middle of a tune.

Benny hired Joe Hunt and me as his rhythm section. Joe didn't last long. Benny couldn't figure out any kind of drumming that wasn't heavily centered on the downbeats. It had nothing to do with whether the time was steady. Joe was plenty steady. Benny just couldn't feel it that way, so out went Joe and in came Dottie Dodgion—as heavily downbeat-oriented as you could find but not very steady.

The rest of the band was sensational. Buddy Childers played trumpet, and Carl Fontana was our trombonist. The sax section had Dottie's husband Jerry on lead alto, Zoot Sims on tenor, and Marv Holladay on baritone. Pianist John Bunch and guitarist Jimmy Wyble completed the rhythm section, with vibist Red Norvo as an added soloist. And there were two singers: Maria Marshall and the inimitable Jimmy Rushing, who took up a lot of room on the stage and sang like nobody's business. It was truly a great band.

But it was also a bizarre experience. Benny sometimes behaved as if in a fog and tended to act disturbed by what he heard coming from the rhythm section. Sometimes he would stop me from walking in quarter notes by glaring at me and holding up two fingers, indicating that he wanted me to play half notes, or perhaps to repeat quarter notes in a simple and less contrapuntal two roots, two-fifths pattern. Sure, Benny was the boss and a great clarinetist and jazz soloist, but he had a limited idea of what the rhythm section could, or should, do. He'd turn around to me in the middle of a tune and say, "No lines, just notes." This had a habit of happening in the middle of Zoot's second chorus—if Benny let him get that far. Zoot regularly generated such a level of joyful swing that attention was drawn away from Benny. Benny didn't seem to like that.

In the second week of the engagement, Benny replaced Dottie Dodgion with Mickey Sheen, who was no better, just as galumphingly wooden and heavy. A good drummer can't make a band all by himself, but a bad drummer can surely kill one. The band struggled for its life, swinging despite Mickey, and Benny continually intimidated me with his strange behavior and interference in the bass parts. As I said, I think if I'd charged him more, he'd have left me alone.

The band opposite us at Basin Street East was Kenny Burrell's trio, with drummer Al Harewood and Joe Benjamin (bassist from the Brandeis concerts four years earlier). Joe had taken a shine to me back then when we first met, and it was one of the nicest things that happened. He was kind-hearted and a great bass player. The job with Benny was coming to an end, and Joe had been offered a tour with Ballets U.S.A., a Jerome Robbins company that was going to tour Europe in the summer with some jazz musicians in the pit orchestra. Bob Prince had written two scores Jerry had choreographed that required a combo to play written parts within the orchestra. Joe couldn't take the job because of other commitments, and it became the first of several opportunities he turned my way. This was in the early spring, and the tour was a few months off.

Carnegie Hall was threatened with demolition, and on April 3, 1961, Isaac Stern organized a fund-raising concert, "A Salute to Jack Benny." I played in a sextet Benny Goodman formed from members of the band from the Basin Street East engagement on the program with Jack Benny, Stern, and the Philadelphia Orchestra under Eugene Ormandy. A lot of the amazing bass players in the symphony surprised me by saying they envied my position with Benny.

As exciting and encouraging as jobs with George Russell and Benny Goodman were, there were moments between glamorous jobs where I had to take whatever turned up. One of those pickup gigs was so memorable in its succession of difficulties and misadventures that I spent a few hours the next day writing about it:

> When Johnny White called me on Saturday morning and hired me to take an afternoon train to the Stamford Motor Hotel and accompany him and a singer, I didn't expect a musically rewarding evening, and I wasn't surprised as we rehearsed the first show with Jackie, the girl singer.
>
> John was one of those piano players who play solo cocktail lounge gigs because they have such a poor sense of time and no good musician tolerates playing with them easily. So, I gave up without a fight. "Just stand there with the bass and earn your thirty dollars. Look like a musician and play like a slob and everything will be cool," I told myself.

The beginning of the evening was uneventful, and I even had the promise of a ride back to Manhattan with Jackie, who was expecting her boyfriend to pick her up after the job.

The couple sitting on my right, an ad agency guy and his seemingly empty-headed and ungraceful young blonde Greenwich girlfriend, were carrying on the kind of sparring conversation the cocktail lounge atmosphere often provokes. Neither one believed a word the other said—maybe not anything they said either. She was naming girls they both knew and asking his opinion of each. "A man is more attractive if he thinks women that I think are attractive are attractive to him too. Don't you think that's right, Lionel?" "Hey! Play 'What's New.' You know that? Wha—at's Noooo? You know." I was stuck standing between the leader and the requestnik. "John, he wants, 'What's New.'"

We play it. Choruses vary from 31 ½ measures to 27 ¾ measures. The tempo varies—up. Lionel says, "Beautiful—fascinating to watch your fingers." We take a break, and I step outside for a breath of fresh evening air and relief from the stifling atmosphere.

When I return, Lionel and his girlfriend have been replaced by some middle-aged businessmen and their wives. One of them likes my playing, and in answer to his question, I tell him I've been playing recently with Benny Goodman. His eyes light up and leans over to me, "Hey, what's the inside dope? Is it true Benny's been going to a psychiatrist for the last twenty years, huh?"

"If he has, it's been the wrong one." I couldn't resist it, but it was wasted on this guy—didn't even register with him.

One of the women at the table seems annoyed the guy is paying attention to me and not her. She's jealous, so she throws pretzels at him—at her age!

A lawyer who knows of me through some mutual acquaintance comes in with a party of four. He likes me. He's Jewish, I'm Jewish, he's drunk, and he's a frustrated drummer. The last couple of tunes of the evening are spent accompanying the swizzle stick drumming of the lawyer and those at the table he can muster to join him. One o'clock comes, and my relief infinitely surpasses his disappointment.

Jackie's boyfriend has reluctantly agreed to drive me back to Manhattan with them, but my bass doesn't fit in his enormous Pontiac convertible. "See," he says. "I told you it wouldn't fit. I'll be glad to take you if you can fit it in." So, he's standing there while I struggle—maneuvering the bass every which way to no avail. "We can leave the window open—the neck only sticks out six inches," I suggest. "Oh no you don't—I'll get a ticket, and it's not my car," he says, in a *who-do-you-think-you-are-anyway* tone. "I'd be glad to take you if you could get it in," he repeats with unsurpassed charity. So, I try the open-window suggestion once more, and he gets salty. "No—not a chance. I refuse to drive like that." "Okay, I've got my return ticket, and I'll take the train. Just forget the whole thing. Thanks a lot."

I split without even saying goodbye to Jackie. By now I'm annoyed about the incident myself. I call a taxi, and the maniac drives down the parkway at 75 MPH, and I'm already so keyed up it scares me stiff. I'm in no hurry, the next train doesn't come for an hour, but it's his last call of the night, and he's tired and wants to go home. Christ, tired at 75 MPH.

So, I get to the station with an hour to wait for the train, and there's a sharply dressed black man and a tweedy post-graduate type, so drunk he's reeling but refusing to pass out.

"I'm George mumble-mumble some white protestant name, an' I wan' you to meet my frien' here," referring to me standing there with my bass. "My frien' plunk the banjo m—yeah mmm —It'sh quite obvious. My frien'— mmm— plunk mmm—dum dum dooms the banjo or whatever this ish m—perfeckly obvious. I wan' you to meet my frien' here. C'mon shake hands."

The drunk's forehead is cut, and his hand is bloody. He's pulling me by the clean sleeve of my raincoat, and I'm trying to protect my bass, keep him from smearing the blood all over me and humor him all at once. The humoring turns out to be a poor idea. He gets friendlier—puts his arm around the black man, who brushes him away brusquely, so he reels over to me. "Don't you think you ought to sit down?" I suggest.

"I'm a newspaper man, y'know. I can write more damned headlines. Where's my hat? I had a hat. Hat? I haaad my haaat," he sings.

"Sit down man."

Pianissimo, "I haaad . . . m—my hat. Where is my hat, oh where, oh where?"

He wanders over to the black man, who says, "Keep your hands to yourself, buster. Now sit down 'fore I bust you. Come on you drunken bastard, sit down."

The drunk reporter is a glutton for punishment and finally provokes the black man into roughing him up.

"Take it easy. Don't hurt him. It's not worth it," I suggest, hoping for de-escalation.

In comes a dilapidated showgirl type, a club-date musician returning to New York, and the MC from the club the girl worked in. She looks like a beat-up stripper. An eighth-inch of make-up, out-of-shape figure, and bleached hair frizzing out, fan-like, behind her. The MC stops the black man from hurting the drunk just as a police captain walks into the waiting room with his jacket open—tells the drunk to sit down and wanders out to the platform ignoring the threatening atmosphere.

The MC doesn't believe there's a 2:10 train. I tell him there is, and he says to the sad showgirl, good-naturedly, "Not waiting after that. If the train doesn't come soon, I might as well take you home with me."

"To your wife, sure," she grins.

"I'll catch hell for being out so late anyway, so what's the difference?"

Fat old club-date Sam points out the rather obvious lipstick print on the MC's cheek.

"I put it there!" says the girl possessively. "I like him."

Only five more minutes and the train should be here, thank God.

In walks a thin, tired young black mother carrying one sleepy child and dragging another.

"Doyouse togensona train?" she asks me.

"Pardon me, ma'am, what did you say?"

"Does the train take togens?"

Finally, I understand. "No, no tokens. You can buy a ticket on the train."

"How much to Mount Vernon?"

"Oh, about a dollar."

"A dollar! Humph."

She sneers at me as if it were my fault, but she can't hide the fear in her eyes, and it's clear that it's truly a lot of money to her.

The train is late. By this time, the drunk is annoying the show business trio and the MC is showing off by manhandling him. The police captain is ignoring it all while others straggle in to watch and the MC calls the cop names through the open door to the platform.

"Whatsa matter, I'm supposed to folla you around? I got nothin' better to do?"

"Follow me around? I'm sitting down, for Christ's sake. Whyn't you do your job?"

Stamford's finest turns its lawful back.

A slick operator tries to hype us into taking his taxi to NY. No deal.

Finally, the train—the drunk gets on too. Every place I sit down, he follows me and sits next to me—and I'm struggling with the bass. I succeed in losing him. He sings, "Dear Old Southland" to the black man. "I wish the South had won the war—best part of the country," he mumbles. The black man tries to ignore him unsuccessfully, and I try to smile sympathetically at the black guy.

The conductor, obviously experienced in such matters, handles the drunk expertly, talking to him in a stern voice, letting him look for his ticket and finally getting the money from him.

"I could've sworn I gave ya the ticket. Where's my hat, oh where, oh where? Dear Old Southlan . . . I'm a newspaper man, and we work like bastards—oh—we work at the weaver's tray—ayed—Dear Old Southland."

I sleep through till Penn Station. At the station, three suspicious-looking characters try to guide me to the 7th Avenue Subway.

"Where ya goin'? He'll show ya the way. Hey mac, show this guy where 7th Avenue is." He points the wrong way.

"That's okay, Dad, I know where I'm going."

He follows me, but I stall him by stopping to look at a magazine stand, and he finally leaves.

As I climb the stairs to the central express platform, a thin old black man is zipping up his fly after urinating in a phone booth. I pass him, and he shouts after me. Good God, no more of this, please—enough is enough. I walk briskly away.

"Hey wait, I ain't gonna touch you! My name's Monk Guzzy. Doncha reckanize me? I played with all the greats. I played with Jimmy Lunceford an' Erskine Hawkins."

I haven't the heart to walk away from him, so I let him corner me.

"My name's Monk Guzzy—Andrew Guzzy, but they call me Monk. M, O, N, K: Monk Guzzy. I played with all the greats."

"What're you doing now?" I ask, so exhausted by the events of the evening I can't hold back the cruelty of the question.

"Wha'dya mean? Why'dya ask that?" He looks hurt. "I do what I want. Wha'dya mean anyway? I come from Carolina. I'm a Tarheel, but don't hold that against me. Are you prejudiced against the negro people? Were there negro people in your school? Where'dja go to school? Doncha reckanize me?"

Anyway, here comes a local. I turn my back on him, wiping his spit from my face where he slobbered it and run full tilt, with my bass on my back, down the stairs and up to the local platform—knowing all the while that it's a hopeless race. The local pulls out before I get up the stairs, and I drag myself back to the express platform. So, I'll have to walk from 96th Street.

Fifteen more minutes. The express is full of parading gay men and drunks. At Times Square, a quartet of beastly looking women gets on. There are three seats opposite me and one on my left, crowded by the bass. The woman who sits directly across the car has a face to turn you to stone, so I try to focus on her rhinestone jewelry instead, but I'm simultaneously fascinated and horrified by her hopeless unattractiveness. The three I can see have carefully applied their lipstick with the bizarre result that they look as if they're constantly and uncomfortably puckered. The one on the right is sad-looking, with a single rhinestone sticking out of the middle of her every-which-way hairdo looking like a dead third eye. She sits with eyes as expressionless as the rhinestone, while the one I can't see on my left chews bubble gum

```
in my ear. Pop . . . pop . . . crack . . .
click . . . tsh . . . tsh . . . smash . . .
pop . . . pop . . . Bang!
   I carry the bass home from 96th Street
and Broadway to 88th and Riverside Drive
at 4:00 a.m. and fall into bed. It's 6:30
before I can fall asleep.
```

A few years later, when I showed Gunther Schuller something I'd written about how I perceived the endangered state of jazz at the time, he dismissed the article and its arguments. Gunther had been the conductor at the Brandeis Festival in June of 1957, when I'd met Bill Evans, Joe Benjamin, George Russell, and all the other New York musicians. Gunther was already a respected composer, conductor, and scholar, and he'd played the French horn on some of the famous *Birth of the Cool* recordings with Miles Davis. He was unassuming and accessible, and we began a warm friendship that lasted until the end of his life. Gunther loved jazz, studied it, supported it, conducted it, and wrote pieces that didn't sound anything like jazz but that included parts for jazz improvisation. He appreciated jazz but from the outside. He didn't play it or live inside it. So, when I was inside of it, feeling its life breath as part of my existence, I sensed the beginning of a changed environment for jazz before Gunther did. He didn't experience the changes I felt, so my article failed to register with him. But when I showed him this story, he liked it.

6
Playing with Bill

Around the time I was working with Benny Goodman, I developed a friendship with Don Freidman, a good pianist who'd recently moved to New York from Los Angeles. Don had a recording contract with Riverside Records, and he asked Joe Hunt and me to record with him. Don was friendly with Scotty LaFaro, the brilliant bass player from Geneva, New York, whose career would later have a deep effect on mine. Scotty had spent time in LA, where he and Don had met. I'd heard Scotty sometime before in Boston and tried to engage him in conversation, only to be brushed off with disinterest. More recently, I'd heard him in a trio with Bill Evans and Paul Motian at an upstairs club in the Village across from where the Blue Note now stands. It was simply the most personally meaningful music I'd heard.

Bill's playing was extraordinarily rhythmic—forceful and precise—swinging like crazy and, at the same time, colored with dynamic gradations and nuances of touch, tone, and articulation. It spoke to me in more ways than other jazz pianists did. Tatum was superhuman and full of variety, but Bill's playing was more developmental, less decorative. Erroll Garner was joyful and endlessly inventive, but as fulfilling as his music was, it was all about the piano part. Bass and drums were only accompaniment—the music would be the same without them. There were other bebop pianists whose music I loved. Horace

Silver made bold, percussive music with clear development and charming directness, but it lacked pianistic nuance, and it was always loud. Monk's unique approach to the piano, even more percussive than Horace's, seemed so excessive that the monumental genius of his music eluded me at the time.

I'd have been proud to have played with Red Garland, Hank Jones, Barry Harris, Sonny Clark, or Tommy Flanagan. Their music had countless qualities I valued, but it didn't have the breadth of Bill's. Bill had absorbed more classical piano literature. Elements of Chopin, Scriabin, and who knows what else were integrated into his music—flowing through it, inside it, fully part of it without self-conscious pastiche. And his style in trio-playing omitted bass notes in the piano, leaving space for the bass part to be heard and to have more effect on the music. How could I not think this was where I wanted to be?

Hearing that music expanded my conception of what a jazz piano trio could do. Bill's playing had romantic elements of impressionistic harmony while retaining the clarity, beauty of sound, nuance of touch, and extraordinary rhythmic variety I already knew to expect. And Scotty was playing an integrated, even competitive role, abandoning conventional bass parts for several choruses at a time—engaging in melodic counterpoint with Bill and doing it with blazing speed and pinpoint accuracy. The idea of a piano trio was re-balanced with a more varied role for the bass player.

Ahmad Jamal had featured bassist Israel Crosby's virtuosity and melodic invention in his influential trio recordings from Chicago a couple of years earlier. There were well-developed roles for the bass and drums in that music too. But it was carefully controlled, and its arranged quality was part of its attraction. What Bill and Scotty were doing (with Paul Motian's helpful drumming) was more varied. Organization was always there, but it remained hidden under a veneer of considerable improvisatory freedom. What Bill's music may have lacked in obvious structure, it gained in exciting, even dangerous, spontaneity.

I admired Scotty greatly and envied his job with Bill. He was a virtuoso bassist and an extraordinary musician. I wanted to know him. At the record date with Don, Scotty showed up to visit and heard me play a couple of tunes. The old cool-to-nonexistent reception I'd gotten when first meeting him sometime before turned instantly warm, and we communicated quickly and easily in a way that people who share similar musical sensibilities can. I was accepted by Scotty as someone who, though not as accomplished as he, was clearly heading in the same direction. If we'd have had more time together, we'd have become better friends. Fate robbed us of a deeper and more complete connection. I know his music, but we didn't have enough time together for me to have known him well.

My stepfather's piano accompanist, Lucy Brown, lived on West End Avenue, around the corner from my apartment on 88th Street. Her niece, Paula Robison, later to develop into an outstanding soloist and important member of several of the best chamber music ensembles, was coming to New York to be a flute student at the Juilliard School and needed a place to live for the summer. Paula was an attractive, smart, talented girl and already an extraordinary flutist.

I was going to be in Europe with the ballet company—the job Joe Benjamin had sent my way—so Paula would sublet my apartment. She'd landed a summer job in the orchestra at the Jones Beach Guy Lombardo Theater, where Scotty's girlfriend, Gloria, was a dancer. Before long, we were all friends, and I left a small society of Scotty, Gloria, and Paula when I went to Spoleto in late June.

Just before I left, Bill's trio had a live recording session scheduled at the Village Vanguard, and I went to hear them play. Most serious jazz fans know what I heard.

Bill Evans' *Sunday at the Village Vanguard* is deservedly one of the best-known piano trio records. I was thrilled by the music and overwhelmed by Scotty's virtuosity. I thought I could do it, too, though not with his speed.

I didn't think I'd get the chance anytime soon, but I knew there were elements in Bill's playing that lined up with more things I knew and felt about music than anything else I'd heard. There had to be possibilities to develop there. Playing together back at the Brandeis student union when Bill sat in with Arnie

Wise and me had felt great. Arnie and I had already developed the beginnings of a reliable, interactive rhythm-section style I knew Bill had to have appreciated. But it was just a wishful fantasy. Scotty had that locked up.

Before I left for the European tour with the ballet, I rehearsed with the band and dancers I'd be traveling with for almost four months. There were three other jazz musicians: drummer Bobby Thomas, a Juilliard student friend of Paula Robison's who had been playing with Wes Montgomery; Frank Perowsky on tenor; and George Barrow, who had played tenor with Charles Mingus and baritone on Oliver Nelson's *The Blues and the Abstract Truth* recording. Two other guys in the band could read well and interpret music in the correct style: alto sax virtuoso Vic Morosco and trumpet player Fred Mills. Werner Torkanowsky, from the New Orleans Symphony, was the conductor.

The music was well written and full of variety—so much so that, for musicians used to settling into a groove for the better part of a whole piece, it changed moods too often to satisfy our jazz appetites. But it was good for the ballet, and everyone played well. Bobby Thomas was especially adept at integrating perfect jazz drumming with the written music.

We flew to Rome in June and took the train to Spoleto, a charming town in the hills of Umbria.

Gian Carlo Menotti's music festival had transformed this sleepy village into a cosmopolitan music magnet. Ben Shahn and Alexander Calder were on hand to supervise the construction of the sets and mobiles they'd designed, and the symphony orchestra from Udine had been contracted to serve in a variety of capacities. Singer Shirley Verrett and conductor Jorge Mester were there, along with many other musicians involved in a series of opera and chamber music performances. It was an Italian version of the summer atmosphere in Berkshire County—city folk in country surroundings and another easy place to love. We were in Spoleto for at least three weeks of preparation and performances. There was time to get used to the place, to hear some other music, and to sit in cafes and read letters from home—including the fateful one from Paula.

I'd pocketed Paula's letter with a warm feeling of anticipation. We'd been connected by our families. Paula was seventeen, a lovely girl, and marvelously accomplished. It seemed fatefully serendipitous that I'd be leaving my apartment for the summer so Paula could use it while she got acclimated to New York. I was already established enough to have a place to live and professional work. There were a lot of ways Paula had already surpassed my musical accomplishments, but I was the New York professional, and I'd been a welcoming and appreciative host to her. So I was pleased and gently curious about getting mail from her, without an inkling of devastating fateful news—no idea that reading the letter would stir complex, conflicting emotions or become a life-changing turning point. We'd all lost a towering musician. I lost a model and potential friend and dared to imagine that there was now an opportunity to be playing with Bill.

I was way too busy to dwell on the possibility of playing with Bill Evans. Things were happening in Spoleto. The understanding company manager arranged a $1,000 advance so I could buy a wonderful old Italian bass from Bruno Martinelli, one of the players in the Udine Symphony.

We played a week in Venice and one at the Staatstheater am Gärtnerplatz in Munich. London was next, where we played a two-week run at a theater on Shaftesbury Avenue. The musicians in the London Orchestra were both extraordinary players and friendly people. It was a great time, and we recorded Bob Prince's music with those fine musicians in Kingsway Hall, a place famous for the quality of its recording acoustics.

We went on to Amsterdam and Paris, where Rudolf Nureyev caused a stir by defecting to our ballet company. By this time, I had favorite dances, and dancers, that I watched when I wasn't playing. I remember Lee Becker and Glen Tetley, and I loved watching Erin Martin turn herself into a Kafka-esque bug in "The Cage," choreographed to the Stravinsky "Violin Concerto in D major."

It was August, and most French people take vacations in August, no matter what. Pierre Sim was playing at Club Saint-Germain with Martial Solal, and he hired me to sub for him while he went on holiday. I had a theater job from 7:30 to 9:00 and a jazz gig from 10:00 until 2:00 in the morning. Paris was again wonderful.

Berlin was still a strange walled city in 1961, but we had an interesting week there and then a week or two in Copenhagen. Eric Dolphy had a concert engagement in Copenhagen during our stay. I had known Eric a little just from being on the New York scene. I may have heard him play with Charles Mingus at some point. Eric was such a nice guy that I wasn't going to pass up a chance to see him while we were both in Copenhagen, so I went to the Riddersalen after our piece was finished at the theater and arrived at his concert intermission. Eric saw me as he was returning to the stage and called me up to play a couple duets with him. Eric Moseholm was kind enough to lend me his bass, and someone recorded the concert. When the record was released some years later, I did receive a check, unlike some other experiences I've had with pirated recordings. Because of that recording, some people assume I had a more extensive relationship with Eric. It's another association that, like the one with Coltrane, invites people to ascribe more significance than I think it deserves. My relationships with John and Eric were both friendly and rewarding but were no more than tangential encounters for any of us.

Early in October, after a week in Stockholm (a city even more strikingly beautiful than Copenhagen), we returned to New York. Paula said there'd been a couple of phone messages from Bill and that I was to call as soon as I got my bearings. In New York, you can get anything on a twenty-four-hour basis, even bearings.

Between the time I'd met Bill at Brandeis in 1957 and the moment in Spoleto when I read Paula's letter, I'd developed and maintained a professional career, and Bill must have been aware of some of my more noticeable jobs.

As far as I was concerned, a call from Bill had been at least likely, and maybe inevitable, since July. I knew Bill was too much of a musician to stop playing for long, no matter how much he'd loved Scotty, and he was too strong a musician to have depended so much on anyone to shore up his musical spirit that he wouldn't have found a way to go on. I was simply one of two logical choices, and I didn't think Bill knew about Steve Swallow, though there's no question he could have done the job as well. I was as prepared for this in many respects as anyone I knew.

The three most important things in music are rhythm, rhythm, and rhythm—in that order.

No two musicians feel and express rhythm in the same way, but some are more compatible than others. On the strength of this issue alone, I thought Bill would like my playing. This is a sensual thing, and Bill's music just felt right when I'd played with him four years earlier. When Bill wound up and took aim at a point seven or eight measures ahead, superimposing complex cross-rhythms on the meter until he landed securely in an intelligible place, I knew what was happening on the deepest, most intuitive level.

I'd been particularly moved by an improvisation Bill had recorded for his record *Everybody Digs Bill Evans*. It was a piece that had developed spontaneously in the studio as he started to play the gently rocking ostinato figure he'd used as part of the accompaniment to Bernstein's "Some Other Time." That spontaneous moment in the studio was released as "Peace Piece," and it became an iconic representation of what a great jazz improviser and extraordinary pianist could accomplish without a rhythm section, improvising in one mood, using the simplest of materials as an anchor, and developing a piece of music as expansive and advanced as anything classical composers had written.

And he'd done it in one take—an outpouring of musical expression driven by the feeling of the moment—with no apparent calculation, no second thought, no editing. There was the unmistakable presence of the rhythmic nuances and accents of jazz that spoke to its American heritage and spoke to me as a sensitive listener to the combination of musical elements flowing through Bill his experience with Chopin and Scriabin, filtered through the depth of his commitment to the language of Bud Powell.

I'd already heard Bill play at The Composer in 1956 and again at the Brandeis concert a year later, and I knew *New Jazz Conceptions*, his first recording as a leader. I'd been immediately taken by the music. Bill's composition "Five" had particularly thrilled me. A couple of years later, Dave Brubeck recorded an album of jazz tunes written in unusual time signatures, sticking to those rhythms in obvious ways, lining up the music directly with the underlying time signature so that everything was stuck to the beat. It had its charm, and "Take Five" was done so obviously and so simply that it became a hit.

When I heard Brubeck's "Take Five," I knew what was going on. It was as if a flashing neon sign said, "Listen to this, we're playing jazz in 5/4." But Bill's music had far more sophisticated juxtapositions of rhythms, odd time divisions played unerringly against a swinging 4/4 pulse so that the listener didn't need to know that five notes were being equally spaced against four notes, or that four notes were being spaced across three notes (in 4/4 time!), to feel the rhythms making bank shots, ricocheting and hitting targets, pulling apart and coming together in fascinating syncopation. Bill didn't separate a 5/4 meter like Brubeck did, to write a tune in an obvious alternating 3/4, 2/4 pattern that added up to 5, and stick the melody to that from beginning to end. He was so comfortable in juxtaposing rhythms that, feeling one division of pulses in proportion to another, he was able to integrate those cross-rhythms into his music without having to restrict a particular passage to one meter or another in order to keep his place.

I wasn't even aware of what the underlying cross-rhythms in Bill's music were; I could just feel them and intuitively keep track of where they'd resolve. The timing conflicts didn't disturb me because I had confidence that Bill was in control and would resolve them in ways that would turn out to have been logical in retrospect. I wasn't thinking about that consciously, either. I just felt the thrill of the rhythms and was able to align my pleasure in the timing of the music with them. It was swinging in the most subtle and varied way, and it intrigued me and attracted me deeply. I couldn't have analyzed it or duplicated it consistently or accurately at the time, but I could hear it and feel it with Bill and thought I could play it with him. More than any other of the many extraordinary elements of Bill's music, it was how he felt and used rhythm that closed the deal.

If you'd asked me about the pitches, or the harmonies in Bill's music, I'd have been making educated guesses that might have been right more often than wrong, but I'd have had no reason to be as secure as I was about the rhythm. I just felt the rhythm as Bill did, and I knew it. I also knew that true compatibility communicated itself—if I knew it, Bill had to know it too. No question. I recognized the potential for a partnership, and I thought Bill would come to the same conclusion. If I was scared, I repressed it and didn't think about it. In retrospect, I can understand how that came across as arrogance.

We had one rehearsal, if you could call it that. Actually, it was an audition. I went to Bill's apartment on 106th Street, between the north end of West End Avenue and Riverside Drive. Paul Motian was there, and we played a few things. I remember Bill was quiet but not unfriendly. No one had a lot to say. When I was around Bill, I had the impression that the best way to communicate was through playing music. I know others who later spoke with Bill about his work and theirs. But I thought it was my responsibility to take care of that independently of him. I don't know where I got that idea, but it prevailed throughout our relationship, and the tone was set at this early encounter.

Paul was chattier, but both were clearly in judgmental audition mode, and I needed to pass, so I concentrated on myself rather than them. But when we were playing, I'd be as open and receptive to what they were doing as I could manage.

There was a dichotomy in my behavior—social self-centeredness and musical open-hearted empathy/generosity. I don't know why I behaved that way, but that's how I remember it. In my self-involvement, focused on being accepted into the trio, I don't recall discussing Scotty's death—it could be that my burning desire to communicate in the music blotted out all the rest, or maybe the poignant loss couldn't be brought to words by any of us.

After mistiming a rubato ending, I asked if Bill would nod to indicate the changing tempo. That's what I was used to from watching the first violinist in string quartets back in my cello-playing days. Bill said, "No, just listen." He was right. There's an inherent logic to appropriate changes of speed in music, and if you listen, you know. Visual indicators are mostly superfluous in good ensembles. I tried it. It worked perfectly then and for the better part of the next six years.

I remember that we played Bill's signature theme, "Five," the piece with the fascinating rhythms I'd heard on his first trio recording. It's tricky, based on the chords of "I Got Rhythm," overlaying quintuplets every four beats in the A sections and quadruplets over every three beats in the bridge. That's complicated, and I couldn't have told you what it was at the time. I'd have a hard time reading it now, but I could hear it and play it then—in a New York minute. That was the stuff that counted. I didn't know enough tunes, or enough about harmony, and certainly not enough of Bill's highly developed way of treating the harmonies of standard tunes. All that could come later. It was the rhythm that mattered.

After the audition, Bill told me he had some gigs lined up and wanted me to join the trio.

Bill's record producer, Orrin Keepnews, has described my demeanor at this time as arrogant. I didn't experience it that way, but I understand how insecurity can cause behavior that looks like arrogance. And I was harboring conflicting feelings of insecurity and confidence, neither of which were fully justified.

Another thing Orrin said was that I pulled Bill out of his slump and got him back into playing. No such thing. Bill got himself out of whatever condition he had been in after Scotty's passing. He had to get back to playing. If I hadn't been there, he'd have found someone else. It was just lucky for me the timing was right.

Our first gig was at a club in the black section of Syracuse. There was an upright piano, painted white, and we stayed in a hotel above the Trailways bus depot. I think it was Bill's idea of a place to hide out while we pulled the music together. There were bookings for the next few months: a long run at the Hickory

House and a couple of weeks at the Village Vanguard opposite the Modern Jazz Quartet.

Something happened at the hotel before the first night that set the tone for part of my relationship with Bill: He invited me into his room, where he and his wife Ellaine were shooting heroin.

It was a grisly scene. A belt around Bill's upper arm to make the veins stand out, a hypodermic needle in his forearm and an eyedropper in place of a syringe, squeezing blood in and out of his vein.

To Bill, it seemed a normal part of his life and nothing to hide from me. To me, it was morbidly fascinating but even more frightening. I said I'd rather not see that again if it could be avoided, and in all the years I knew Bill, I never did.

I didn't think about what I said—telling Bill I didn't want to see him shoot up. It wasn't a thoughtful choice—it was an instinctive, self-protective reaction. I was avoiding exposure to something I perceived as threatening and dangerous, but my rejection of what Bill might have been seeing as unguarded intimacy may have distanced the rest of our relationship—a relationship in which overtures of other kinds of communication and inclusiveness didn't come from Bill.

Chemical dependencies of various kinds became an inescapable fact of Bill's life. He told me that the only recording he ever made that wasn't under the influence of drugs was his first one. I'd met him first around 1955–1956, when he was playing at an East Side jazz club called The Composer and again at Brandeis in 1957—both were times before he had started using drugs. He was intelligent, with a wry sense of humor. His intellect and the beauty in his music never left him, but some of the humor slipped away, and as Bill's life became increasingly cloaked in a cocoon of opiates, his emotional contact with the world—and eventually even his music—became more remote. No one knows how much Bill's experience of the external world was changed by drugs, but careful listening to his music reveals how certain energies slowly ebbed from the expression of his inner world.

You can hear something happening to his music if you compare the recordings he made before 1961 to those that came after.

There are some positive developments, of course, but there is also a creeping increase in introspection. There are momentary exceptions, but generally, there is gradually less effort to reach outward to the listener.

Bill was a fascinating personality, at first only a little shy, then increasingly withdrawn. He was always articulate and insightful with words as well as music and brilliant when using words to describe music. His speech was as direct and unflowery as his playing—avoiding unnecessary elaboration of simple ideas. When obstinately probed about what his secret improvising method might be during a radio interview (with a musician who ought to have known better), he had to answer three times that all he was doing was expressing the form of the tune as he heard it. The interviewer was reluctant to let go of the question, and Bill, cordial as he usually was, didn't step out of his role to supply a new answer. He just kept answering what he had been asked until the interviewer relented. He demonstrated his process by playing. Though he could have talked a lot about what he was doing, the musical example was sufficiently eloquent to render talk superfluous.

Bill Evans and I had a close working relationship of about six and a half years in which we seldom had conversations, except for a few words on the bandstand or what was necessary to make musical decisions in recording studios and concerts. I respected and admired Bill not only for his musical acumen but also as a man who was both profoundly intellectual and extraordinarily able to express his ideas in spoken and written language. So, what kept me from talking with him and having that kind of access to his brilliance? I was afraid of him, and that fear existed on a few different planes.

Bill may have lacked the kind of conviction and self-confidence that would have allowed him to withstand the pressures and stay in Miles Davis' band, but he didn't show doubts about how he operated with his own trio. He was prepared and confident, and he was my employer.

I don't remember feeling immediately threatened—that I might be at risk of losing the job (I didn't even experience it as a job—more of some kind of dream calling)—but he controlled so much of what was important to me that I must have been afraid of challenging the situation, of disturbing it in any way.

A big part of the fear was the recognition that he'd done so much more work than I had in preparing himself to be fully musically expressive, that I didn't want to expose my ignorance—not so much to Bill, who must have been aware of the abyss between us, but to myself. I worked on learning in the ways I could and at the pace that was natural to me, given my reluctance to confront my limitations head-on. Without much conscious attention, I absorbed an understanding of the consistencies in Bill's harmonic system. Pretty quickly, I learned to expect certain kinds of harmonic movement in relation to the melodies of the pieces we played and could often anticipate the kinds of solutions Bill would be likely to apply to new pieces: where contrary motion would be likely to show up in the bass line, where a pedal tone might provide momentary static contrast to harmonic activity, where the harmonic motion might speed up or slow down, where an irregular chordal rhythm might provide interest (especially between phrases), where a predictably useful pattern might show up to move the music from one harmonic area to another, and how each of these choices was always made in direct and intimate relationship with the melody we were playing.

I never asked Bill about any of these things—asked him to talk about how he thought about them. I just learned them by playing the music and looking at the lead sheets he'd write out when he'd add a new piece to our repertoire. I was studying, but I wasn't assigning time to the activity. It was just happening in real time as we played things I knew or tried out new ones. Keeping up with the musical demands was pretty absorbing. I was working to gain understanding and fluency, but I didn't think of it as studying, and a lot of it took place on the bandstand.

In most cases, playing without discussion of the music—relying on Bill's minimalistic chord charts and my own intuition—got results that seemed to satisfy both of us. I never asked Bill if he liked what I'd played or if he'd found problems with it, and I only remember a couple of times I thought I made less than good choices in how I interpreted what little written or verbal information Bill provided.

When we recorded Bill's piece "Re: Person I Knew" (an anagram on producer Orrin Keepnews' name), playing it for my first time on our first trio recording date, Bill wrote out the chord symbols for the short sixteen-measure form and pointed out that the entire piece revolved around a C pedal.

I interpreted that to mean that all the harmonies were meant to be heard over a low C bass note. The expression "pedal tone" originally referred to sustained low notes organists played on the organ's foot pedals, so my assumption was historically logical. We recorded the piece, and Bill's playing is at its usual high level. But as I listen to my part, it feels excessively bogged down by reiterative low Cs—as if the piece is dragging an anchor. What I didn't understand, and what Bill didn't explain clearly, is that all the harmonies revolved around a C common tone and that that was best expressed with an awareness of that common tone in either the middle or high register, while the bass notes changed according to the actual roots of the chords.

If what I experience in retrospect as a less-than-fortuitous choice on my part bothered Bill at the time, he didn't say anything, and it didn't seem to affect the quality or freedom of his playing. Over time, I began to figure it out—to understand how to play the piece, and by the time we played it three years later for a video broadcast in London, I'd abandoned the anchoring pedal tone during Bill's improvised choruses, although I still held on to it during part of the opening chorus.

I made a similarly less-than-ideal choice in interpreting the chord symbols Bill wrote for John Carisi's tune "Israel." The chord symbols indicate a voice starting on the fifth of the first minor chord and rising it by a half step to the raised fifth, sixth, and, finally, the seventh of the chord. This happens while the root of the chord remains the same. I saw the symbols indicating the moving voice and mistakenly chose to include those notes in my bass line.

There's nothing wrong with including that harmonic movement if it's done in the right register. It's useful to find opportunities to express rising harmonic lines since harmonies resolve downward so often. If you can find an important inner voice that moves upward, that can help balance the melodic contour. What I failed to consider was that by playing that line in too low a register, it would have a disturbing effect on the smoothness of the harmonic progression.

This is simply the result of the physics of acoustics and human hearing. Low notes contain overtones heard subliminally in the range in which human hearing is most sensitive. A low A contains overtones that we subconsciously hear as an A major chord. So if a line that's perfectly appropriate in a middle-register inner voice appears in a bass part, it can be too low and affect an unwanted change in the harmony.

Bill wrote a chord sheet that contained information useful to him and to a melodic improviser—useful to me in creating a bass solo that would be securely linked to Bill's version of the tune but also some information I'd have done well to ignore when playing an accompanying bass part. It took me a long time to figure that out. When Ellington was asked what he wrote for his bass players, he said, "As little as possible."

But these instances of shortcomings in the non-verbal communication between Bill and me seemed rare, and most of the music flowed easily with a kind of balanced interplay. It just felt good to play a freely interpreted bass part to whatever Bill was playing. The sounds came in through my ears into my whole consciousness. It was a full-body, sensual experience that left me feeling deeply connected to Bill and to everyone who listened through whatever common understanding we had of this abstract language of musical structure and expression. I felt that way even at the early stages of our development as an ensemble.

Except for these outlying examples, the communication satisfied me, and I assumed it satisfied Bill. Bill, Paul, and maybe some listeners may have felt Scotty's absence, but I was so enveloped in the music I had no time to give that any thought. And some of the results of that first recording, like the interplay of the bass part with Bill's playing on "Polka Dots and Moonbeams," have been interesting enough for musicians to have transcribed for study. They've withstood the test of time.

I don't know if I thought that discussing any of this with Bill would or would not have been welcomed, or if I thought it might break some mysterious subliminal communication that allowed me to stay in the musical relationship. I just didn't go there.

Then there was the powerful element of the way I saw Bill's personal life. I had no understanding of what addiction to heroin might mean except that I thought it made Bill into a kind of person to whom I couldn't, maybe didn't dare, relate in any intimate way.

After the first exposure to Bill and Ellaine shooting up in the hotel before our first gig, I never saw it again. It had frightened and repelled me. I could only imagine that pulling blood into an eyedropper, mixing it up with some certainly impure and unregulated powder you'd just cooked up in a bottle cap over a lighter, tightening a belt around your arm, squeezing the mixture back into your vein, and releasing the belt so it rushed to your heart must result in a profound change in your senses and your real well-being—must change who you are. I don't remember Bill nodding out or showing an external change, but I assumed there must have been an internal one, and it frightened me. I couldn't imagine accepting that behavior as normal—poking around, sticking needles in your veins, and injecting God knows what to feel some way that you didn't already feel. How could it possibly be better? Different, I could understand, but not better.

Bill was frank about his habits. He was admittedly using or, during rare short periods where he'd cleaned up, not. But I still felt a kind of estrangement, even in those brief periods of knowing he was clean. They were unlikely to last.

Sometimes some people would naively ask me why I didn't try to dissuade Bill from his drug habit. My mother used to call that the rescue fantasy, when some Indian Hill kids would get overly involved in trying to help a troubled friend. She thought the rescuers were ill-equipped to help and were more likely to get pulled down by the attempt than to do any good. I guess I must have accepted that point of view because I never thought anything I could say or do would have the slightest effect on how Bill chose to behave.

I'd heard a story that Scott LaFaro, who'd had a far more powerful place in Bill's life than I, had skin-popped some heroin (injected it into flesh rather than mainlined it into a vein) to demonstrate to Bill that he knew what it was and what it did and still condemned its use, and it had had no effect on Bill. So what was I supposed to do?

I couldn't imagine what might drive me to use heroin. It took me years of being around casual marijuana smokers before I thought it might be okay to try. And while I spent a good deal of my twenty-second year enjoying getting mildly high, I figured out that it sapped my energy, and it lost a lot of its appeal. I was aware that my perceptions and thinking were changed under its influence, and I didn't always like everything about those changes. Sometimes they were fun, and sometimes they presented obstacles. And I don't drink alcohol, not from any moral antipathy—it just doesn't make me feel good. I may even be allergic to it.

It never occurred to me for a moment that whatever marijuana did for me, that I couldn't do without it. So what I knew about heroin—that many people became quickly addicted and couldn't live without it—needed it many times a day—put it in a different category, one I mostly understood to be dangerous, maybe seductive, but far too dangerous to be worth the risk. So I couldn't understand why this brilliant man was behaving this way—giving in to a demanding drug that controlled so much of his life, his relationships, his work, and his money.

Bill would show up scant minutes before we were scheduled to play, sit at the piano without saying anything, and start to play. Between sets, he was mostly quiet. After the gig, he was gone. Few strangers approached him, and that seemed fine with him. When we were in Paris for a prestigious and well-attended performance at the French Radio and Television concert hall in 1965, staying at the classy, five-star Hotel de La Trémoille, near L'Etoile, Larry Bunker and I took every opportunity to enjoy Paris. Bill and Ellaine drew the heavy curtains on the windows, blacking out the room, stayed inside until the concert, and returned to their cave as soon as we were done playing.

What was I going to say to a guy who lived enclosed in what I imagined to be a dominating veil (jail) of heroin? I didn't see the otherwise normal aspects of the man, things I know, in retrospect, to have at least approached attitudes I considered to be normal—wanting a family life, having material ambitions, things like that.

A relationship that seemed full of unrestricted beauty and communication in the music seemed otherwise closed. It wasn't entirely, but that was how I'd experienced it. And I contributed to its closure. I closed it myself—probably out of different kinds of fear—fear of exposing my shortcomings and the fear and revulsion of staring into the gaping wound of heroin addiction. I never thought I'd be tempted, and no one ever tempted me. Self-preservation kept me away.

I do remember the dichotomy of being afraid to get close to Bill and still trusting him completely on the bandstand and even sitting, carefree, in his car as he drove with complete confidence and control at seventy miles an hour. I can't go back, and regrets are useless, but there remains some sense of loss on my part that I couldn't have handled my conflicting feelings better, known and understood the brilliant and basically decent guy that Bill was (maybe except for how he treated some of the women in his life), and learned more from him in more direct ways.

A gig at The Hickory House was our New York debut, and lots of people showed up. The bandstand was in the middle of a large oval bar, in the center of a high-ceilinged room with tables and wooden booths around the perimeter. But it wasn't really a listening room like the Five Spot or Village Vanguard. Since there was no cover charge, people felt free to pay attention, or not, as the spirit moved them. In this atmosphere, it was possible to play long tunes, stringing out more choruses than usual without attracting much attention to the practice. So we worked out the music—practicing on the bandstand. I paid particular attention to improving my intonation as I moved through chorus after chorus of repetitive bass lines.

There are many romantic misconceptions about the way jazz is created. Since not much is written down and so much is made of its improvisatory nature, many think each performance is all made up new. That this defies logic does not deter some people from holding on to the idea.

In fact, harmonically functional bass lines are fairly well-restricted. Each piece has a particular set of low-register pitches that form the basis for its harmonic progression. Because of the power in these low notes, a peculiarity of their relationship to the sensitivities of human hearing, changing their sequence can wreak havoc on the integrity of a song's harmony. This restriction is not nearly so true of melodic solo voices, usually appearing in higher registers, so those voices have more freedom to explore different note choices. As the surface melody notes change, they occupy most of the listener's attention, so few people notice that this chorus's bass line is just about identical to the last one. You can change rhythms, nudge things this way or that, approach a target note from above or below, arpeggiate chords, or string notes in scale fragments. But you've got to hit the right ones at the right time, or you obscure the form and confuse the other players.

It's not a boring job if the other musicians relate creatively to the bass, but the bass player is uniquely dependent on the rest of the band for satisfaction in fulfilling that role. Just one player who misuses the bass part—ignoring it, or worse, leaning on it to extract rhythmic propulsion that isn't there in his or her own playing—can ruin your night. Amplifiers that allow the bassist to play loud enough to overpower the opposition do not solve the problem. The bass part is still the bass part, and bloating it accomplishes nothing good.

Of course, Bill and Paul were not only not a burden—they built superstructures on the foundation of my part that made it continually rewarding to play. So I practiced playing the bass lines as beautifully as I could and made my solo contributions as they were called for. I'm sure there were plenty of bass solos—there always were in Bill's trios. Yet it was concentration on the accompanying parts that I remember most from the Hickory House job.

A lot of people asked me then how it felt to replace Scotty. It didn't feel like anything; I never replaced him. And I was too busy responding to the joy of making music with Bill to be thinking what Scotty might have done. Many didn't understand that response, but if you were a man with a chance to be with Marilyn Monroe, would you waste time thinking about Joe DiMaggio or Arthur Miller?

From my perspective, there were significant differences in our abilities and the way we approached integrating our music with Bill's. I never confused what I was doing with what Scotty did in the same position. Scotty was much faster technically and in mastery of harmonic vocabulary. He played more accurately in the high register and had command of practiced melodic patterns that went well beyond what I could do. I couldn't compete with that.

Scotty maintained a kind of separate presence in the trio, sometimes even when playing a simple accompaniment. I insinuated myself into the atmosphere of Bill's playing. Scotty's solos burst into the available musical space in marked contrast to Bill's; I tried to continue Bill's musical thoughts and feelings. Scotty was a stronger individual presence; I tried to cement a more strongly bonded trio.

Bill's relationship with Scotty had been complicated by competition and some aesthetic disagreements. Ours seemed more smoothly symbiotic. I was content to blend accompaniments to his playing, to become a second—a lower left hand to his piano, functioning with just enough independence to keep the music interesting but rarely so much as to provoke a substantial change in what Bill was up to. I wanted my solos to flow seamlessly in and out of his.

This is how it worked: Bill would study a piece. He'd spend whatever time it took to find the harmonic nooks and crannies that let him express his personal way of hearing the tune. He had his own set of rules for doing this, and though they provided a degree of flexibility, there was a solid set of guiding principles:

- Leave the main cadence points of the tune intact.
- Don't do anything bizarre at those parts of the tune.
- Approach those main cadence points from interesting, usually chromatic directions.

- Use suspensions and resolutions to delay the final dominant seventh chord as long as possible.
- Harmonize available passing notes in the bass lines with passing chords where appropriate (thicken the bass line).
- Look for complementary motion, often contrary motion, in the bass lines first, and then if those possibilities are limited, put the motion in an inner voice.
- Move the harmony most when the melody is static.
- Find opportunities to include harmonically based cross-rhythms, putting three chords where there'd been two and five or six where four had been.
- Most important—make the harmony accommodate the melody.

It's cheating to change the melody to rationalize a clever harmony. Bill cheated once, but it improved Ann Ronell's already lovely "Willow Weep for Me." In the key of G, there are six high Ds in the melody. Bill changed the fifth one to a bluesy D flat, harmonizing it with an out-of-key E flat 9th chord, adding a hint of spice to what was already good and making it even better.

This was all accomplished in private. I never observed the process or participated in it, but the results made the principles increasingly clear, and I did begin to absorb them. Bill wrote down the results of his introspection in chord symbols, with occasional indications of bass notes where that would clarify the rhythm or direction of the line. It was nonverbal—discussion unnecessary. I looked at these little sheets of paper (often from a three-inch-by-five-inch music notebook), memorized them quickly—organizing the music by recognizable bass line patterns and successive key centers rather than chord by chord—and interpreted them as best I could on the bandstand during the next set. As long as I could digest the material quickly enough, the method worked.

I loved to play those bass lines. They were designed to be the most perfect counterpoint possible to the melodies of tunes I knew and cherished. Once they were in my part, Bill left them entirely out of his, molding everything he played around them, making them necessary and integral but leaving me free to realize that element with my own expressive nuances. Then those would affect Bill's playing, and I, in turn, would be affected by his reaction. It was the same intimacy of communication through special code that I had experienced among the players and the audience as I was first learning the music, but it was especially subtle, detailed, and personal.

Paul Motian's time was flawless. His interpretations of Bill's rhythmic subdivisions and his own contributions to the rhythmic textures always meshed. There were no count-offs ever. We simply started pieces, with or without musical introductions, and never a verbal one to either the trio or the audience. Establishing tempo was as easy as crossing a street to join a friend and falling into step with them—just as natural and instinctive. Geometry: two points establish a line. Music: two beats establish a tempo. No counting, and no discussion. Talking on the bandstand seemed as if it might break musical concentration, so we just didn't do it.

And the sound! What came out of Bill's hands at the keyboard was beautiful and personal. I've never heard anyone get more superb shading from a piano. Classical pianists spend years honing their touch, refining their sensitivities to the responses of the piano's mechanism.

Considering the convoluted design of levers, weights, and hammers, the piano is an amazingly sensitive instrument. Subtle nuances can be transmitted through this mechanism and translated into expressive variations in dynamics, articulation, and timbre. The piano's brilliantly conceived mechanical action amplifies the minute gradations of the player's touch and helps them reach the strings. Bill had a natural affinity for taking advantage of these characteristics. He had to study it, too, but he got more out of his experience than many classical piano specialists. He practiced Bach, Chopin, Liszt, Rachmaninoff, Debussy, and Scriabin with passionate concentration. It astonishes me when some jazz pianists who want to lay claim to Bill's heritage seem to imagine they can effectively do so without following the path he took to achieve this control. Bill loved the piano and its literature, and he played it for all it was worth.

Chuck Israels—don't know where this was taken. It must be sometime around 1965. kpa / Alamy Stock Photo

Subtleties in the bass part's touch, dynamics, and articulation emerged as integral to the trio's music, and I could do one thing Bill couldn't: I could shade pitches. It wasn't a calculated effort, but I found more of this expressive characteristic coming out in my music.

The plucked bass violin is essentially a left-handed instrument. The right hand mostly starts and stops the sounds and controls the notes' relative loudness, but the left-hand controls more of the expressive range. Pitches can be shaded or bent, notes sounded with or without vibrato, hammered on or plucked with left-hand fingers, and carried by glissandi from one spot on the fingerboard all, or part of the way, to another spot.

I had learned characteristic bebop melodic shapes, and a good part of the way I expressed the pulse of the music, from Oscar Pettiford, Percy Heath, and Paul Chambers. Some came from the beauty and power of Ray Brown's playing too. But the way of making the bass sing, that was from Red Mitchell—and Jim Hall, who did the same thing on guitar.

All these musicians were older than I was, although Paul not by much—just enough to distinguish a difference in generational style. No one could fail to be impressed by Scotty, but I was not so much influenced by him as I was part of the same shift in viewpoint. Scotty, Charlie Haden, Steve Swallow, and Albert Stinson were all in it. We listened to our immediate predecessors and loved their music. We just didn't restrict ourselves to traditional half notes and quarter notes to the same extent they did.

Attentive listening to recordings of Scotty, or Steve, or any of us, will reveal that we play plenty of half notes and quarter notes, with as much enthusiasm and joy as we can muster, just as we heard Oscar, Ray, Paul, Leroy Vinnegar, and Percy Heath do. But we also let our ears respond to the rhythmic density of the music we were playing and used other note values as well when they added contrapuntal variety. Many drummers were doing similar things, adding a great deal to the rhythmic palette. We hadn't stopped playing time as some believed, we just expressed it with a wider variety of note values.

7

An Interruption

Sometime late in 1963, Bill signed a management deal with Helen Keane, who'd been influential in the careers of Harry Belafonte and Carol Burnett. Helen quickly arranged a lucrative recording deal with producer Creed Taylor and Verve Records. A debut recording on the new label to be called "Trio 64" was planned, and the virtuoso bassist Gary Peacock was hired to play. No one had said anything to me—neither Helen nor Bill. I was simply, unceremoniously, dropped from the trio. I wasn't fired; I was just gone. Maybe the thought was that Gary's speed and virtuosity would be reminiscent of the musical relationship Bill had had with Scott LaFaro. The similarities between Gary's playing and Scotty's were superficial, but I can understand how some people might have thought there was reason to try out the comparison. Obviously, it occurred to Helen and Bill to try it.

I don't remember being bothered by the news, although it's hard to imagine that I wouldn't have been. I know I must have understood then, as I do now, that if Bill wanted to be playing with Gary, if that approach was what he wanted, then he didn't want mine. Part of what kept me from being preoccupied with having been summarily replaced in Bill's trio was the sheer volume of available work. I was among a handful of young bass players in New York who were getting attention and jazz gigs.

Soon enough, I was back at Basin Street East playing with Stan Getz, guitarist Jimmy Raney, and drummer Al Harewood. Tommy Williams, a wonderful bassist from Brooklyn I'd known for years, had suddenly quit the band, and I jumped in. I admired Tommy's playing deeply. It was rooted in bebop and as elegantly organic as the best soloists on front-line instruments. When he played in the Jazztet with Art Farmer and Benny Golson, his solos set such a standard of beauty and coherence that both Art and Benny preferred not to play their solos after Tommy. Benny said Tommy put horn players to shame.

By this time, my playing, because of common rhythmic tendencies inherent in the way we all approached ensemble playing, was being associated with, and compared to, Scott LaFaro, Steve Swallow, and Charlie Haden. That was certainly logical, and I admired them and many others, though I wasn't preoccupied with only being influenced by Scotty or any other single model. But if the devil had offered me the ability to play like Tommy Williams, I'd have made a Faustian bargain. Although Tommy retired from playing early, and few people know his music, from my perspective, I was, again, stepping into big shoes.

Shortly after I joined Stan's quartet, Jimmy and Al, having had enough of Stan's difficult behavior, quit, and Stan asked me to form a band for him. He was comfortable with the idea of trusting me, partly because his daughter, Pamela, had spent a summer with my parents at Indian Hill.

This was a timely opportunity. Stan was a great player, but he was clueless as an organizer of music. He always had a sideman who was the de facto leader. Bob Brookmeyer had gotten his start in that role, and Jimmy Raney had also filled it to advantage. It worked well for everyone.

Stan got someone to select repertoire and organize arrangements, and the musician in the cockpit got to try out his wings while Stan took most of the risk. Joe Hunt, the drummer from George Russell's band, was still in town and looking for work. That was natural, but I couldn't think of a suitable piano player. I had been spoiled by playing with Bill.

I didn't know any guitar players either, but I'd met vibraphonist Gary Burton. He was a fan of Bill's music, an intelligent person with taste in music and stimulating company. I suggested him to Stan. Skeptical at first, Stan's attitude changed after our first rehearsal at his palatial house in Irvington. Gary was impressive, and Stan saw a chance to do something that would sound quite different from anything else he'd done.

From the perspective of the right thing to do for Stan (and for Gary), it was a smart idea, but I'd outsmarted myself.

I wanted responsibility for designing the music, but I expected to be able to learn how to do that successfully a little at a time, at Stan's expense. I didn't walk into the situation prepared. I had little material selected, and almost none written, and I was far from fast at producing anything. Gary, on the other hand, was everything I was not in that department. He was quick and slick and had material ready to go. Anything he didn't have, he was able to produce overnight, and as needy as I was for the kind of relationship one could have with Stan, Gary was needier. They were magnetized to each other. Gary and I were friends, good friends, but once again, I was just the bass player.

Still, there was a lot of work. Stan was still riding the crest of the Bossa Nova craze, and João Gilberto's wife, Astrud, was singing what had been João's repertoire with the band. She made home run hits of things that João could hardly get to first base with because she sang in English while João resolutely stuck to Portuguese. He was so obstinate that he refused to use one word of English in any conversation. He simply repeated things in Portuguese—saying things in as many ways as he could think of until he made himself understood. He didn't learn much English that way, but I learned a good deal of Portuguese.

We had gigs on the road (one in Montreal was especially fun) and a run at the Café Au Go Go on Bleecker Street in the Village, opposite comedians George Carlin and Richard Pryor; both of them were just getting started.

I loved Stan's playing, but he was a complicated guy, and I could feel myself getting sucked in by his neurotic behavior. Neurosis is a communicable disease of the first order, most easily communicated to other neurotics, and I certainly was susceptible. Self-preservation suggested that I look for an exit. It came in the form of a call from Bill.

Things hadn't worked out as he'd hoped with Gary Peacock. Would I consider coming back to work for him?

I was about to go from being the bass player in a famous quartet where I had hoped I would have a more important role (only to be displaced by a vibraphone player better prepared for the gig) to being the bass player who'd been displaced in the most visible trio job in the world by another bass player, whom I was now being asked to displace.

The decision was a no-brainer. But no explanation would satisfy Stan, and he felt betrayed. He thought I didn't like his playing. I loved it.

But I didn't trust him or my own vulnerability to his manipulative habits. Stan was angry, and I considered myself lucky to have been able to slip out of that psycho-turmoil relatively unscathed. I was going from being less than a quarter of a quartet back to more than a third of a trio.

In 1966, long after I'd left Stan to rejoin Bill's trio, the phone rang one day, and it was Gary Burton. Stan Getz was in a jam and didn't dare call me himself, having made it clear when I'd left the band that he was not only displeased but personally hurt by my defection. Gary explained that Stan had a call from the White House for a command overseas performance. Steve Swallow, who had eventually replaced me in that group (much to Stan's delight), was too sick with the flu to make the trip to Thailand for the performance. Would I go in his place?

A command performance is just that. You don't turn it down even if you have other work. Lyndon Johnson's social secretary was responding to a request from the King of Thailand for Stan Getz, and the White House didn't want to disappoint its Far East host.

Stan remained angry at me for leaving his band, and he didn't like the idea of asking me for what he perceived to be a favor. But I knew the music, and there were only a few days before departure. He was stuck, and he was irritated. Stan had work booked in the States and in Europe, and some of it would have to be canceled or postponed. On top of this, command performances are not paid engagements. The performers' expenses are taken care of, usually royally, but there is no fee. But Stan still had to pay his sidemen, so he was losing income from engagements he couldn't fulfill.

Besides Stan and Gary, Roy Haynes was playing drums, and Stan's wife, Monica, the beautiful daughter of a Swedish diplomat, was coming on the trip. We were all to be escorted by Charlie Bourgeois, an old friend from Boston who worked for George Wein.

The six of us headed for an Air India flight to Bangkok by way of London, Geneva, Cairo, Mumbai (then Bombay), and Kolkata (then Calcutta). We were in the air, up and down, for about thirty-two hours—in a first-class lounge with free liquor. Stan took advantage of the bar and tried to ignore his irritation, but it kept getting the better of him; it wasn't pleasant for Gary or me. Stan was afraid of Roy and wouldn't bother him, but he was incessantly on Gary's case about something. And when Stan found ways to attack me, Gary felt responsible for it because he had gotten me into this.

Arriving in tropical Bangkok, we were hustled to a sumptuous hotel—too exhausted to think about seeing anything. We were to be there for a week, and the next evening, we would play for a Southeast Asia Treaty Organization (SEATO) meeting at the palace, attended by heads of state and military leaders. I had a tuxedo, but there was a last-minute change to white dinner jackets, and an excessively large one was found for me—reminding me of my embarrassment at having to wear my uncle's dinner jacket on my high school prom date.

Just before we were to get on the small stage, Stan said he'd been asked if we'd be willing to go play for the troops in Vietnam. No pressure, mind you, but the State Department had asked. I don't know what Roy thought, but neither Gary nor I were enthusiastic about the idea of getting close to a war, despite our sympathy for the soldiers who were forced to be there.

As we expressed our reluctance to come up with a quick yes, Stan became increasingly abusive—especially to Gary, whom he called a "Commie fag." When Stan was unhappy, he couldn't stand it unless he made everyone else miserable too. Everyone but Roy, who managed to stay out of the way.

When we played, the only real audience interest came surprisingly from King Bhumibol. President Johnson, seated directly in front of Stan, was dozing off—not just looking sleepy but really falling asleep.

Stan was beside himself and burst out: "Well, Mr. President, if you didn't like that, maybe we can come up with something you'll understand. You know, some square dance music, a hoedown. You can understand that!" I wanted to be anywhere else. Stan was drunk, and there was no controlling him. We played an Oliver Nelson piece called "Hoe-Down." There's nothing wrong with the song, and the performance was good, but the damage was done. No one said anything about it, but I just wanted to disappear.

We'd finally agreed that since the State Department had brought us so far at taxpayer expense, we ought to do something for the troops, so we spent a day flying to air bases in Thailand and playing half-hour shows at each.

We flew on to Germany, where Stan was picking up gigs in the middle of the interrupted tour. During preparations for the trip, Stan started having furtive, whispered conversations with Gary. Eventually, Gary told me Stan had received calls from Steve Swallow, saying he was now well enough to travel and ready to rejoin the band. Stan had been afraid of confronting me with this, so he'd arranged for Steve to meet the group in Rotterdam for the next concert without telling me. It was a fait accompli, so I couldn't have argued. Stan could be so childish and stupid that there was no way of reconciling his social behavior with his music. Zoot Sims described him as "a nice bunch of guys."

I didn't care. I was subbing for as long as I was needed and willing to cede the chair to Steve as soon as he was ready. Stan couldn't understand that, so he was defending against nonexistent demons. He was convinced everyone was against him and didn't believe me when I told him I'd be happy to go home. He continued to glower and scheme about how this exchange could be forced to take place if I didn't cooperate. It was finally arranged that I would fly to London from Dusseldorf Airport, where the band was to take a connecting flight to Rotterdam.

I'd spend a couple of days in London and continue home from there.

Didn't I think it was wonderful that Steve was so loyal? He so wanted to be with Stan that he'd get out of his sick bed and fly across the Atlantic to do his job. Wasn't that an example of an ideal band member? "Yes, yes, Stan, Steve is a great guy and a great musician. Now pay me what you owe me."

Well, there was the rub. We arrived at Dusseldorf with about an hour between flights, and Stan had yet to settle with me. He was still upset about my having left him two years earlier, irritated with himself for being in a position where he needed me, and angry about having to pay me for work he hadn't been paid for.

I looked for Stan in the bar where Monica said he'd be. When I found him, he said Monica had the money and I should see her. When I found her in the gift shop, she said, "No, Stan has the money. He's getting something to eat in the restaurant. Go find him." I was starting to get worried. Stan wasn't in the restaurant. When I found him, he started in with, "What are you going to do if I don't pay you, take me to the union?" Now I was really a little afraid that I'd be left high and dry, but instinct told me not to show it. I faked it: "Stan, you're going to pay me. What is this routine anyway? You know I won't have to take you to the union. You're going to give me my money, so what's your problem?"

"I don't have the money, Monica has it."

"Where's Monica?"

"I don't know. Maybe in the post office. You'll have to find her. She's got the cash."

This charade went on for a while, but I became more confident that I'd get my money simply by acting confident. The dance of the imbeciles must have been choreographed in advance because Stan and Monica both knew their steps, and I was the fall guy.

I began to recognize the routine for what it was—just Stan's way of dealing with his internal frustration, and I figured he would pay me at the last possible moment. I played out my clown part and eventually got my money. A year later, when concerts rescheduled because of the command performance were about to take place, Stan expected me to drop what I was doing and play for free because he'd had to pay me for the no-fee Thailand performance. I failed to see the logic and said no.

It's unfortunate that encounters with conflicted personalities like Stan's and Benny Goodman's create such specific, indelible memories. The details of these sad moments stand out in greater relief than any of the thousands of hours spent with wonderful people having great conversations and making great music.

8

A Brilliant Drummer

I was back in Bill's trio, but Bill had a Los Angeles booking he was going to do alone, and Paul Motian took the occasion to leave the group. Looking back on the situation, and from things Paul had said, it may have been partly because he wasn't enamored of my playing. That never occurred to me then—I thought of Bill's playing as so powerful that it would outweigh whatever negative qualities my shortcomings might have had for Paul.

To keep working, I joined a group led by Paul Winter, a young alto saxophonist from Altoona, Pennsylvania. He'd been noticed by John Hammond, a record producer with a great history of finding and developing jazz talent, who also brought me in to that group. I got to write some of my first arrangements for a date that involved Paul Winter, trumpet player Dick Whitsell, the more experienced baritone player Jay Cameron, and pianist Warren Bernhardt. Paul had put together a tour for the band, and drummer Ben Riley and I went along as the rhythm section. There was an experience gap between Ben, Jay, and me on the one hand and the rest of the band on the other; it made things less creative and fun than most other recent playing experiences. One good thing came out of our tour—we ended in Denver, closer to Bill in LA, and that inspired me to give him a call.

I called Shelly's Manne-Hole in Hollywood, where he was playing, and asked to speak with Bill, who responded warmly to my suggestion that I fly out from Denver. He'd been at Shelly's club with Red Mitchell, and it wasn't feeling right to him.

Bill paid for the flight, and I got my first glimpse of Hollywood culture. There were lots of things about it that I liked: good food, good weather, and the feeling of being connected with power that comes from knowing whatever happens there gets instantly distributed to the rest of the world. I never did find out what it was about Red's playing that didn't suit Bill, but we all remained friends and spent time at Red's house. I played Red's bass, he played mine, and Bill said we sounded like ourselves on either instrument.

We'd started the first week as a duo, enjoying the freedom of phrasing and dynamics the absence of a drummer allows, though we missed a good drummer's bite and propulsion. Composer/arranger Clare Fischer came to hear Bill; he insisted the dapper, elegantly bearded man listening intently to Bill's playing was the most sensitive possible drummer for us and said I should persuade Bill to invite him to sit in.

To say this first experience of playing with Larry Bunker was a revelation would be only half the story. It was a joy and an inspiration. Larry was as complete a musician as any drummer I know. He had an unerring sense for an infectious swinging beat, and his touch and dynamic control were exemplary. He knew all the music and made masterful contributions, adding things that weren't in the duo sound, prodding and informing our playing without inhibiting the freedom.

I wrote liner notes for an album we recorded during that engagement (Bill Evans Trio at Shelly's Manne-Hole, Hollywood, California): "If there were jazz musicians living in Southern California during those weeks in May of 1963 who didn't come to hear Bill Evans play . . . then they were conspicuous by their absence . . . People were rapt, trying to drink it all in. They followed every nuance, every shadowy feint, every broad gesture . . . (theirs) was an active engagement, at once involving, stimulating, and thrilling. . ."

This was an even better situation for me than I'd had with Paul and Bill because the sound was more transparent and the nuances more effective. If the music got strong, so did Larry's part. If it needed clarity and quiet for subtle aspects of the music to come out, Larry adjusted his sound and was energetically propulsive at a whisper. It was great for me and a little embarrassing because Larry knew more about harmony than I did. He had great ears, could play some of Bill's music at the piano, and sing the melody while singing important harmony parts between melody notes.

Larry Bunker abandoned his lucrative studio work as a percussionist and mallet instrument player to continue with the trio. He said he'd try it for a year. After all, if he was good enough to deserve the studio work he was getting, it would be there for him when he returned. If not, he didn't want it just because he was there in the rotation. It was a gutsy move. He stayed with Bill for the better part of two years and walked right back into the work he'd left in the studios when he'd had enough of the experience with Bill. After his return to studio work, he played the tympani on innumerable LA recording sessions.

Larry Bunker was a musician apparently less interested in personal recognition than I and whose accomplishments exceeded mine. He'd come early to the gig, sit at the piano playing excerpts of what he'd heard Bill play, and ask me if they were right. I was embarrassed not to know for sure, although it always sounded good to me. I couldn't do the same thing. I was afraid of the piano and afraid of confronting my limitations. Study was not a friendly thing; it was a frustrating one; and for all I knew, frustration was something I should avoid.

No one conspired to burden me with this paralyzing, wrongheaded conclusion. I had arrived at it unconsciously by misreading my parents at an age when I was too vulnerable to make rational sense out of what they did—how they responded to me. I don't want to make too much of their role in this because no matter what parents do, other things in children's lives modify parental input. But in retrospect, I can see performance got attention and practice was an annoyance. Furthermore, practice, being private, removed me from social contact. Carrying this unconscious childish viewpoint is an obstacle to the hard work that produces progress. Add to this enough natural skill to get by, and lots of experience avoiding difficulty rather than at overcoming it, and you have a twisted, balled-up string of reactions that needs a lot of unraveling.

I was perfectly capable of evaluating what I could do well, and I could appreciate the reality of certain accomplishments—the things that had come easily. I had a pretty balanced aesthetic understanding, but I knew there were things others could do that I couldn't.

A person with my pretensions to sound artistic principles had no business holding anyone else responsible for things I couldn't accomplish. I did, however, hold others responsible. My judgment was sound enough to observe my own shortcomings; I just wasn't prepared to do anything about them.

Since everything I could do had been relatively easy, I could only assume other people's skills must also have been easily acquired. They simply had stuff I didn't—or didn't have stuff I had. I was cursed with the need to defend an aesthetic value system that took in what everybody was doing. Most of that system held up to later experience and scrutiny, which did nothing to alleviate the problem of coming to grips with my own imperfect place in it. It was convoluted. It was also a fascinating subject for discussion. I talked endlessly and productively about music with other musicians without coming much closer to knowing what to do about my own shortcomings.

There is the powerful element of expectations. Who we become is, in large part, a result of who we expect ourselves to be, and that, in turn, is part of our emotional inheritance. I'd interpreted my mother's signals to mean she expected me to be Leonard Bernstein. If I could play the bass part to this music, in the company of artists of this caliber, why was I not creating more of this music myself, independently of others? I thought I was supposed to make a more significant contribution. I waited impatiently for a creative spurt to simply happen to me. I waited, and thought, and was prevented from further progress by personal musical hurdles—mostly inexperience with growth through effort.

Through all this, with all the attention I was getting as "Bill's bass player," I wanted more. I wanted the personal accomplishment and the individual recognition, and I didn't understand how to get either of them. Besides, I was sick and tired of my New York friends coming up to me on the street, greeting me with a warm handshake, looking me in the eye, and blurting, "Hey, man. How's Bill?"

These personal reservations are obvious only in retrospect. They'd have driven me nuts if I'd fully realized them at the time—they poked themselves out in moments of lonely introspection, only to be shoved into the background by another immediate musical challenge I had to handle. The dissatisfactions I had with my own work, or with the limitations of the kind of attention I was getting, were mitigated by the great pleasure of being in the music with Bill and bathing in my share of the spotlight.

One summer, between jobs with Bill, I was back in Stockbridge. Jazz at the Potting Shed had been replaced with young folk music acts. I needed to be doing something, and I was busy teaching and helping my parents in the daytime at Indian Hill, so I worked at night with the folk musicians.

Carly and Lucy Simon were there for a couple weeks as the Simon Sisters, as was Don McLean, a good singer/songwriter. I was interested in his work, but he didn't return the sentiment.

I had fun with The Tarriers, a folk trio of great musicians who were also intelligent, spirited guys. Marshall Brickman—who played guitar, banjo, violin, and bass—was sharp and witty. He was a fan of Woody Allen's humor and was creative in similar ways. Eric Weissberg was the strongest instrumentalist, a virtuoso on the five-string banjo, guitar, violin, and bass, which he had studied with Stuart Sankey at Juilliard. Clarence Cooper sang well and played guitar. I spent as much time as I could hanging out with them, playing ping-pong and laughing.

They had a different attitude toward music than the jazz musicians I knew. They were great at it and plenty serious about doing it well, but it was just something they did. They weren't obsessed.

It was the start of a working relationship that lasted some months. Whenever they had a good paying gig, in New York or on the road, I went with them, played bass, and had a fantastic time—even recorded with them. Their managers were Jack Rollins and Charles Joffe, who also managed Woody Allen and Bill Cosby, so there were always interesting people around the office. Marshall went on to write for *The New Yorker*, films, and Broadway and married Nina Feinberg, a beautiful, smart girl who spent a summer at Indian Hill. (I see Nina's name from time to time listed as a television producer.) Eric made a big reputation through music for the film Deliverance (with guitarist Steve Mandell) and playing all those instruments mentioned above, along with the pedal steel guitar, on innumerable recording dates. Few commercial music jobs I've had have been as much fun as working with The Tarriers.

It didn't occur to me to miss playing jazz that summer. It was only a matter of eight or ten weeks and I'd associated the jazz I loved with urban experience—jazz was city music, and I was in the country.

Marshall and Eric were people of intelligence and wit, whose conversation and humor depended on deep understanding of context to be appreciated. The comparison with Woody Allen is apt not only because of the association through Marshall's interest and the common management but also because, like Woody, these guys are quintessential New Yorkers. In many ways, they're just the kind you'd expect to be interested in the sophisticated musical communication inherent in jazz. I had as much in common with them as with most of the jazz musicians I knew, but they were devoted to the Appalachian music of Lester Flatt and Earl Scruggs, not the urban music of Parker and Monk.

If Hispanic-American music garnered their interest, it was manifested in a soft Caribbean folk song, not in Cuban dance music. As much as we had in common, the African component that seems inextricable from urban American culture didn't take to them as it did with me—not even with Clarence, who was black. Neither the propulsion of the rhythms nor blues inflections caught their attention.

There were lots of people like these guys, and the Berkshire County audiences seemed increasingly attracted to lightweight popular music. I couldn't put my finger on what it was about the

Tarriers that removed them from sensitivity to jazz, or what it was about jazz that kept it from resonating with them.

A split was beginning to show itself. The world was moving from jazz to folk. The new audiences didn't seem to recognize the coded information in jazz, not the way those at The Stable in Boston or the Five Spot in New York often did. Anyway, there was so little sub-code in this new folk music that it was inconsequential.

The Tarriers' material had elements of sophistication and was always musically literate, beautifully performed, and technically embellished in the simpler idioms it used, but the audiences didn't seem to differentiate between their work and the Simon Sisters', which had no rhythmic interest, and their harmonies moved weakly, like a sentence with too many adjectives and no verb. There was no question that they sang well, but they were composing songs using the musical equivalent of childish stick figures in which the arms and legs might not show up in the right spots, yet they got and held people's attention. What could a musical gourmet cook do if the audience was accepting pabulum? What was happening to people's digestive abilities and their taste?

These would have been pertinent questions, but what concerned me at the time was whether there was a useful bass-playing role. It didn't occur to me to be worried that the dominance of jazz as a basis for popular music might be threatened. I was just between jobs with Bill Evans.

I made recordings with the excellent trombonist and arranger J.J. Johnson (J.J.'s Broadway, March 12, 1963) and some others, including with Herbie Hancock and Donald Byrd (*My Point of View*, March 19, 1963) and Gary Burton and Jim Hall (*Something's Coming*, August 14–16, 1963). Gigs on the road with J.J. gave me the chance to work with Herbie Hancock, Walter Bishop Jr., Mickey Roker, and Roy Haynes.

During a drive to J.J.'s home in New Jersey for a rehearsal, he mentioned thinking it was a shame that anyone who could write music didn't do so. I took that as encouragement. J.J. was always clear. I recall him commenting, "I never want anyone to say I wonder what that guy was trying to play." Everything he played was as if designed for the trombone.

I was still finding consistent gigs in New York City, often at the Half Note Club. An inviting place run by the Canterino family, folks who loved jazz and were unfailingly open-hearted in their embrace of the musicians who worked for them. Few folks went out of their way to get to the Half Note unless they loved the music. The neighborhood was deserted at night, a block away from the printing district on Varick Street (where my grandfather used to run the Commanday-Roth Company).

Al, the waiter, was a skinny old guy whose sacred duty was to light any patron's cigarette before he or she could light it. It didn't matter if the customer was on the opposite side of the club, around the bar, and on the upper level. If a cigarette appeared, Al would be there like a shot. I never saw it happen, but I've often wondered, with Al Cohn's and Zoot Sims's sense of humor, and as often as they worked there, if they ever conspired to have a bunch of people take out cigarettes at a prearranged signal just to watch Al's reaction. Maybe they were afraid he'd explode. I had great times at that place working with Al and Zoot as well as Lennie Tristano. Thirty years later, although they hadn't had a club for many years, if I played at the Village Vanguard with Barry Harris, Sonny Canterino would come in to listen and say hello.

But I spent more time working at the Vanguard than any other place in New York. There were a couple of years when I must have been there for twenty weeks. I often played with Bill. I recall a long engagement with pianist Dave Mackay and drummer Arnie Wise opposite comedian/philosopher Lenny Bruce. But the Vanguard never evoked the open-hearted feeling that the Canterinos had created at the Half Note. A good part of that is because the Village Vanguard is more like a French cave than what one might expect in New York. It is really a hole in the ground, and about as uncomfortable a place as one can tolerate. You can hear well in the club; you just can't move or breathe well and would more likely die in a fire rather than be able to escape to safety.

There were also good times at Art D'Lugoff's Village Gate; I played there a couple of times with Bill's trio. Café Au Go Go was around the corner on Bleecker Street; besides the gigs there with Stan Getz and Bill, there were a few interesting weeks with singer Oscar Brown Jr., who'd written songs to the words of black poets. The poems were wonderful, and Oscar sang them with deep feeling for their content, but I don't think he realized most of his songs were in the same minor key and had the same conventional descending bass line. The accompaniments were a convenience, so he'd have something behind the melodies and texts of his songs. It didn't matter to him if they were all the same, but it did get old for me. Nevertheless, I enjoyed Oscar.

Across the street from the Village Gate was a place called the Bitter End that mostly featured folk music, but I worked there with the very good Kansas City singer, Marylin Maye, and pianist Jimmy Jones. Woody Allen and Dick Cavett worked there on some of the same occasions.

All this work was going on in the early and mid-1960s—so much that I still can't remember all of it, and there was no reason to think it would ever diminish. There were a couple of nights accompanying Barbra Streisand at the Blue Angel, a week or two with Nina Simone, and tours back in Europe and California.

Some jazz musicians were moving into studio-recording work, playing on pop records and on advertising jingles. Don Elliott and his cousin Dave Lucas were heavily invested in the jingle business; they hired me from time to time and kindly tried to help me get more of that work. But I couldn't concentrate on what was needed to be fully informed in that business and still have time and energy left to pursue my jazz interests. Besides, it didn't seem necessary. There were still plenty of jazz jobs.

There was a long run at the Five Spot, which had moved a few blocks uptown to Astor Place, near Cooper Union, and was now run by the warm-hearted Canterino family from the Half Note. It was a bigger, more comfortable club, and I worked a couple of months there opposite Charles Mingus, who was always talking about music and bass playing with me, and Thelonious Monk, who never said a word.

I was the house bass player with trios that played between the featured band sets, first with Bobby Timmons and then with Roland Hanna. There were two drummers, Albert "Tootie" Heath and Ben Riley.

Mingus was interested in how I felt about playing with each of those guys. He had his point of view and preferences and wanted to know if I was experiencing from the inside what he was hearing as a listener.

This can be a delicate question for musicians. A listener's impression of how musical relationships are going within the band can differ considerably from how the players feel. Since we all anticipate the possibility of playing with each other at one time or another, it's important to share the inside information. Bass players, being especially vulnerable, are particularly interested in how it might feel to play with different drummers.

Charles was interested in Tootie and Ben and thought that he'd find a particular affinity with Ben's playing. We talked about it a lot, how Tootie's style had a certain stability that came from not being quite as responsive to the surroundings and how Ben's flexibility demanded more stability from the bass part but offered more musical variety. I often have strong preferences in this department. Fortunately, in this case, I liked them both.

Charles also used to come in early before his set and listen to me play. He'd say, "Don't be afraid of the bass. Play strong!" I told him he was a big guy and could overpower the instrument, while my size required doing my best to outsmart it.

Charles's admonishments did get me to play stronger, though. Later, in the early 1970s, when I was working at Bradley's with pianist John Bunch, Charles would come in for dinner and decide it was time to play. He liked my bass; rather than ask to sit in, he'd walk over, stand next to me, take the bass out of my hands to play something for four measures and hand it back to me for the next four. It was both intimidating and fun and, at the same time, intimate and warm-hearted.

David Berger tells of sitting at Bradley's bar with Charles when the crowd noise was at its usual level—nearly drowning out the music—when Charles let out a loud whistle, silencing all the talkers, and shouted, "Everybody quiet! Chuck's playing a solo." It was all very friendly, and I loved that this bear of a guy, who had a reputation for occasional bouts of aggression, was paternally protective of me.

9

BILL REDUX

In May of 1964, Bill had a few weeks of work at the Trident, an idyllic place in Sausalito, California, across the bay from San Francisco. Larry Bunker was again playing with us, and something changed in the way the trio sets worked.

Bill was living with some friends in nearby San Rafael and going through something of which I was only tangentially aware. I know he was ill two or three nights during that period, and we had to get subs for him. That usually indicated that he was sick from drug withdrawal.

Whatever Bill was going through, a sub for him had to be arranged when he was unable to make the gig. The first time, a local pianist with an exaggerated reputation came in and played a feeble version of what he must have thought we expected to hear. The next time, Larry suggested we call Jimmy Rowles, an outstanding LA musician who'd played in many situations with other great singers and instrumentalists. We didn't think he'd feel so intimidated that it would affect his playing. But he flew in at the last minute, arriving from the San Francisco airport by helicopter, and also played disappointingly.

It was hard for pianists to accept themselves in that position. Bill's playing was not superficially pyrotechnical, though, in fact, he had impressive chops when he wanted to use them. To the general public, it must have been hard to understand what the fuss was about, but pianists knew, and they felt obligated to duplicate feats that were beyond their powers when called upon to sub for Bill. It was a frustrating situation for everyone, and I know Bill felt guilty for imposing it.

In any case, Bill, who was almost always quiet, seemed even more withdrawn than usual. Once or twice, he was late for the first set. Larry and I'd be there waiting, Bill would swoop in, no one said anything, and he'd start playing with unusual intensity.

I thought the intensity must have been intended to make up for having been late. Later on, as applause died down after we'd played something, Bill would sit quietly for some time before starting the next tune. Twenty seconds, thirty seconds—what seemed a long time without any communication with the audience or with Larry and me. I don't remember exactly what I felt during those moments of seeming inertia, or exactly when these extended motionless periods between tunes started, but I thought Bill must have been considering what to play next, and it seemed to be taking longer than usual to come to a decision.

We had a repertoire—maybe thirty pieces we played regularly at any given time in the trio's life, and I knew the melodies of some pieces—usually the standards. So, at one point in one of these still-life friezes, after waiting long enough to begin feeling slight discomfort and moderate impatience for us to resume communication with the listeners, I just started to play the melody of "Stella by Starlight." Without hesitation or any indication of having been the least bit surprised or distracted, Bill accompanied me, and the order of events in the arrangement changed: I played the first solo, and after Bill's solo, he ceded the lead back to me, and I ended the piece.

During the break, no one said anything. Bill may have disappeared, as he often did, so I assumed I'd been helpful. I had a good sense of set-pacing, so as these disquieting (for me) moments of inaction became more frequent, so did my initiation of the next tune.

Even though the sets were rarely in the same order, I had a pretty good idea of what Bill might play next after we finished something, and I could make appropriate choices of what might follow logically. It crossed my mind that perhaps Bill might have been irritated—that I was overstepping unspoken boundaries, but he never complained, and I was left with the conclusion that it must have been okay.

I didn't do it all the time, and there were circumstances in which it wouldn't happen at all—more formal situations that required more planning, or where Bill was quicker and more assertive in retaining the connection with the audience. Nevertheless, it was nice for me to have that control and be able to choose what we'd play next from time to time, and it did expand my sense of belonging in the trio.

The engagement at The Trident lasted a few weeks. Sometimes the public was appreciative, and sometimes they were more interested in the view of the bay. I remember a particular lesson from that job. I'd get off a solo that connected easily with my ideas—one that came out with little apparent effort—to applause that were lukewarm at best. In the same evening, I'd reach for something I couldn't do, something faster than I could play or more complex than I was able to hear and identify, and I'd struggle, not quite accomplishing what I'd intended, and that brought down the house.

The listeners might not understand music, but they understand struggle. That taught me a selective understanding of audience response, and the realization that public sensibilities were moving away from a reliable understanding of jazz.

There were still more good gigs with Bill back at the Village Vanguard in New York, one opposite Mingus's band, when he was playing his arrangements of Ellington pieces. And we had a great gig in Tulsa. Sonny and Susan Grey, both musicians, had a road-house-style club called The Rubiot that was beautifully set up for jazz. And it attracted a substantial audience of interested and responsive listeners.

However, incidents began to expose the extent of Bill's drug dependency. What he couldn't find (or perhaps didn't dare look for) in Tulsa, he bought in LA, flying there in the morning and returning the same day before the gig. Something was happening with the money we all should have been earning.

It would be hard to beat the intensity of the experiences we had later that summer in Stockholm at Gyllene Cirkeln.

Sweden is a country with a particularly egalitarian social system. Effort is made to avoid behavior that smacks of class consciousness, so most people are accessible to one another. Crowds at the club reminded me of the cross-section of city life I used to see when I started playing in New York, except that this audience was heavily populated by some of Sweden's most talented theater people. We stayed with singer/actress Monica Zetterlund at her home in Lidingo. (I don't speak any Swedish, but I memorized her telephone number for its musical sound, and I still remember it.) Monica had recorded a version of Bill's "Waltz for Debby," with Swedish lyrics, and it had become a hit. She performed it nightly in Gula Hund, a revue with a fine cast of actors, singers, and comedians. We played three long sets at the Cirkeln, starting around 9:30, and the packed club drew concentrated performances. The last set started after midnight, and every night, we'd look out and see a crowd fill whatever standing room remained, usually an extra twenty or thirty people—the same twenty or thirty people. The entire Gula Hund cast showed up night after night, and we'd have to play for them again and again, each time digging deeper to come up with something fresh. I'd look out there after the second set, already feeling drained, see those people come in, and think, "My God, they love us, and we have to do it again!"

One night during that gig, Bill got sick, and again a sub had to be called. I thought I knew what to expect and didn't look forward to the evening. But Jan Johansson fooled us. He came in, smiled in the reserved way that Swedes usually show pleasure, and played his own music his way, enjoying every minute of interaction with the rhythm section. This guy had enough self-esteem not to allow comparison with Bill to stop him from enjoying the moment. He was a mensch. He had a great time; we had a great time, and we made good music. Jan also was an excellent composer, and I later got to know some of the ground-breaking work he did with the Swedish Radio Jazz Orchestra. Sadly, he died too young in an automobile accident.

While in Stockholm, we also made a fine album with Monica Zetterlund, *Waltz for Debby*, that included lovely versions of Swedish folk tunes that proved especially adaptable to Bill's reharmonization and sensitive playing.

Back in New York, in September of 1964, after the work with Bill in Europe, I got a call from John Dankworth, a fine British alto saxophonist and arranger, asking if I'd be available for a recording date in early October. There was plenty of activity in the jazz recording scene at that time, and calls for gigs weren't unusual, but this one felt different. When Herbie Hancock had called me to record with him or when Gary Burton had asked me to participate on one of his recordings, it felt normal. These were people I knew—my friends, people I'd played with and with whom I'd spent time hanging out, sharing meals, and talking about music. I'd known of John Dankworth's work but hadn't met him and had no idea he knew I existed, so this call was not only a surprise—the international aspect felt different.

I don't remember much about the date or the music—like when I'd been playing with Billie Holiday six years earlier, I was just too busy handling my responsibilities on the bass to have much room to pay attention to anything else. But one moment stands out from the recording session: I came into the studio and saw Clark Terry, Bob Brookmeyer, Phil Woods, Zoot Sims, and Osie Johnson—a roomful of older, more-established players—each one a formidable musician. Besides the powerful assemblage of brass and saxophone-playing jazz soloists, Osie Johnson had been the drummer of choice for so many jazz and jazz-related recordings at that time that you got the impression he never left the studio. Osie, and one of two towering bassists, Milt Hinton or George Duvivier, had made up the rhythm section team for hundreds of recordings.

I took in my surroundings and blurted out to John, "What am *I* doing here?" John's quick response was, "We wanted the best." I was flattered, but what I mostly felt was challenged.

In March of 1965, Bill's trio had a few remarkable weeks at Ronnie Scott's in London; the club was packed every night. I renewed friendships with British musicians I had made a few years earlier when I'd been there with Ballets U.S.A. and made some new ones.

Dudley Moore, the actor, comedian, and jazz pianist, was there most of the time. Sometimes I'd spend time during the day at the BBC in Shepherd's Bush watching Dudley and Peter Cook carry on hilariously in rehearsals and tapings of their TV show, *Not Only . . . But Also*. We also did a TV broadcast hosted by Humphrey Littleton, which you can now see on YouTube.

The next gig was in Copenhagen's Tivoli Gardens, and it was the occasion of the only harsh words Bill ever spoke to me, and the memory of that conversation created a wedge like a nagging splinter that gave me my first thoughts of leaving the trio.

Bill was shy, and people were reluctant to approach him. Besides, they often thought he was some sort of a god, or at least superhuman. They had no such illusions about me, and I was generally more outgoing and accessible, so when there was business to do with the trio, I was usually approached.

While we were in Stockholm, I'd negotiated an extra gig for us at a concert in Bad Holmen. We only had to play for about half an hour, and the pay wasn't much, but it was enough to make it worthwhile. When we got to Copenhagen, I asked Bill about the money for the concert, and he gave me 4 percent of the figure I'd negotiated. I'd expected 25 percent (half for Bill and a quarter each for Larry and me). I remember being in a state of shock walking across Rathus Square as Bill told me he was the one people paid to hear, not me, that I had no idea what his expenses and responsibilities were, and if I wasn't prepared to take what was offered, I was free to quit. I didn't. I took the money—but a wedge had been driven that eventually helped me to break the bond. It forced me to become a more independent musician. It just took another year or so.

We came home to more gigs at the Vanguard, including one disaster opposite the Clancy Brothers and Tommy Makem. Bill must have needed money badly to take it. The house was full of Irish music fans who didn't give a tinker's damn for anything we were doing and were uninhibited in letting us know. People who might have been interested in our music stayed away from that booking. It was an unmistakably hostile atmosphere and the only job I ever had with Bill that felt like drudgery.

More work came up in Europe, and we had a good tour of the Netherlands, culminating at the Concertgebouw in Amsterdam, and an exciting concert in Paris. The French Radio and Television concert hall has a 2,000-seat hall on Avenue du President Kennedy with an inviting physical and acoustic environment. Every place in the hall was filled, and the atmosphere was electric. This was our first appearance in France.

The deteriorating relationship between the public and jazz that was beginning at home had not yet taken hold in Europe. The silence of the audience bordered on breathlessness in anticipation of the first sounds, and after each piece, there was a volcanic eruption of applause. The trio became intoxicated by the audience's response, driving us into deeper concentration. Under those heady circumstances, the music was transcendent.

Back in New York after the tour, we worked at the Café Au Go Go, where I'd been working with Stan a year earlier. During that job, Larry Bunker had to leave. His father-in-law had taken ill, and Larry's wife, Lee, needed him at home in California. Jim Hall came in to replace Larry with guitar instead of drums for a week or two.

I had played the guitar and grown up listening to The King Cole trio. That was as much a part of my personal history of jazz sounds as anything could be. I touch strings, and strings touch me.

As a set of instruments, piano, bass, and guitar are more than okay. If the piano is being played by Bill Evans and the guitar by Jim Hall, better than okay doesn't come close to doing it justice. It defies description.

The final take of "My Funny Valentine," on the record Jim and Bill made together in 1962, *Undercurrent* (they recorded another duet record in 1966, *Intermodulation*), stands as a pinnacle of chamber music achievement. Every time I hear it, it has as profound an effect as any five minutes and twenty seconds of music I know—Beethoven, Bartok, and Stravinsky included. Without this music that Jim and Bill created together, my musical life would be considerably poorer. It speaks volumes in a language that has personal meaning.

I can't remember a thing about how it sounded with my bass playing added. Not a thing! There's no recording to jog my memory, but I'd give plenty to be able to recall the music. I want a sound picture to come up in my mind, and nothing comes. Where did it go? I must have been too occupied within the music to leave a part of myself free to remember the experience. I know I was in heaven, and I can't even prove it to myself with my own musical recollection. I have no idea why the trio didn't continue in this form, but Bill was soon looking for a drummer.

Work for the trio was sporadic, and I got a call in the spring of 1965 from folk singer, Judy Collins, asking me to sign on as her music director for some work that included a tour that took us to Los Angeles.

So there I was in Los Angeles, working with Judy, a lovely person and friend of our family, happy to have work but frustrated by the limitations of her music—no rhythmic interest, no syncopation, only the simplest harmony, certainly no technical challenge. Most of the musical elements that brought joy and fulfillment to my role in Bill's trio were conspicuously absent. The only powerful possibility in the music was the possibility of drawing drama from the meaning of the words, and I couldn't direct Judy's attention to what I thought would bring out that artistic element.

I was glad to be working but forced by the requirements of the situation to abandon thoughts and feelings about jazz so I could try to figure out how to contribute while working within a much more limited musical palette.

It wasn't an easy relationship, and I was troubled and a little depressed about conflicts with Judy and my inability to communicate about what I thought might be helpful to her. Judy has an extraordinary voice. While both she and her listeners basked in its beauty, I was listening for emotional variety and drama and not hearing any. And I was unable to convince Judy that it might have been missing, or that there was value in trying to do something about it. She just wasn't hearing things the way I was. Judy and her audience were satisfied as things were, and I got nowhere suggesting what I thought would be improvements.

My role seemed to be simply to play and be responsible for arranging the accompaniments. I wasn't enjoying what might otherwise have been a rewarding time fulfilling a limited but functional role for a friend and earning some money.

But while I was in LA, Lester Koenig, the owner of Contemporary Records, found out I was in town and quickly set up a recording with his friend, pianist Hampton Hawes, and the remarkable drummer Donald Bailey, who'd left an indelible impression when I'd heard him years earlier playing with organist Jimmy Smith's trio in Boston. Lester and Hamp were interested in exploring the juxtaposition of styles that would result from combining the way I played with Bill Evans, and Hamp's normally more-conventional trio style. Donald Bailey seemed to be a perfect choice to fill the drum chair. Suddenly, I was back in jazz reality. It was both a relief and a shock, and the necessary speed of the re-orientation left me feeling both grateful and disoriented.

Hamp was interested in Bill's music and wanted to take advantage of the experience I'd gained from playing with him, so we played "What Kind of Fool Am I" with the harmonies I'd learned from Bill, and Hamp encouraged me to engage in the same kind of rhythmic freedom and interplay that characterized the accompanying textures in Bill's trio. We made some good music together, but I'm not sure it gelled as well as it might have, had I played simpler bass lines and blended better with Hamp's style. Besides, Donald Bailey's endlessly creative percussion embellishment was already enough, and the sense of timing interplay with Hamp wasn't the same as it was with Bill. There wasn't as much space between phrases, and my playing sounded a little too busy for the best textural balance.

I had a good sense of what Bill's timings were—where a phrase was likely to end and how much time there might be before the start of the next one. And if I interjected complimentary activity, Bill heard it and accommodated it, leaving space, and responded to how long it might last. It was dialog largely led by Bill's playing but sensitive to commentary from the rhythm section. I don't think the trio with Hamp and Donald quite got there. I didn't get the balance quite right. Nevertheless,

I played good jazz with two exceptional musicians, and it began a long friendship with Donald Bailey, who turned out to be as interesting and good a friend as he was a uniquely creative and sensitive drummer. If he'd been in New York when I returned and Bill was looking for Larry Bunker's replacement, Donald might have been a good candidate.

Back in New York after the tour with Judy, Bill auditioned Joe Chambers, and I thought he sounded right. Also a composer, he played with dynamics and a loose sense of space that seemed to fit. I think I'd have been happy with Joe. Bill said he was looking for a drummer with more experience. I don't know what that meant, but I suggested my old friend Arnie Wise.

Bill liked his playing right away. It was smooth as melted butter and adhesive as glue. He rarely instigated anything in the musical texture, but he'd respond to whatever anyone else created, fitting a complementary drum part like a tailor-made glove.

The group became less a trio and more a duo with drum accompaniment. Nobody minded. That was Arnie's musical character. Bill and I had plenty of ways of filling the space, and we weren't aware of missing anything.

At the time, Bill was preparing to record with a symphony orchestra in collaboration with Claus Ogerman, who would write the scores and conduct the dates. The sessions were scheduled through the winter of 1965, and I was looking forward to them.

Producer Creed Taylor hired Grady Tate to play drums. I loved Arnie, but he couldn't be trusted to read music and play with authority the first time. Grady turned out to be a great choice. He did everything required in relation to the orchestra yet was loose and supple in the trio. There wasn't a moment's friction.

I've been lucky with drummers. More than with any other instrument, my associations with drummers have been consistently rewarding. Sure, there are horror stories of miscommunication or being trapped in a situation with someone who was just plain not good, but I fast run out of fingers and toes when I count the joyful relationships. Grady takes a place on that list.

I was disappointed in the sound in the studio. There was little integration of the trio with the orchestra parts. The trio was recorded in isolation booths—for all the communication we had, we could have recorded our parts in dubbing sessions at different times.

The orchestra players had footballs, long notes that weighed down the potential for the music to swing, and no rhythm. We have centuries worth of rhythmically active orchestral music, but this was patterned after Hollywood and TV pop orchestras to smooth out and obscure the jazz elements. Maybe that was the idea, to cover all the grit in Bill's playing, and leave only the pretty elements exposed.

Good music has a balance of rough and smooth elements. A few years earlier, Eddie Sauter wrote some adventurous music for a small string group and recorded it with Stan Getz improvising solo parts. When the recording *Focus* was released in 1961, I thought it was sensationally good, that it stood as a successful example of how to integrate classical string music and jazz. It was head and shoulders above the arrangements we knew from the Charlie Parker with Strings recordings (although Neal Hefti's "Repetition" from that recording had some good, rhythmically active string parts). Part of its success was because the string group was small. Ellington set a higher standard for writing music involving the orchestra in more of the rhythm with "Night Creature," recorded in 1963, but generally, the bigger the string section, the smoother the sound and the less bite.

Most of the repertoire for these orchestra dates was classical pieces with sections inserted for the trio to improvise. That the trio had all the identifiable jazz elements may have been a good decision—strings and woodwinds attempting blues inflections often don't sound convincing, but all the rhythmic elements were in the trio parts. Nothing energized by rhythm was in the orchestra music. There were some classical themes for the orchestra to play but only static, held notes for the orchestra to play along with the trio.

When we got to the last dates and recorded two of Bill's compositions, the music became still more disappointing. Claus's reading of "Time Remembered" turned an essay in unexpected harmonic shifts into a turgid exercise, and "My Bells," a piece Bill played with romantic but unsentimental rubato, plodded in one slow tempo, lead-footed from start to finish. I knew how it should go and wanted to conduct, but I hadn't done anything like that since junior high, and that hardly counted. I didn't have the courage to risk volunteering. Stick your neck out like that, jumping out of your assigned role, and you'd better be sure you're prepared and that your contribution is going to be appreciated. I didn't say anything.

By this time, Helen Keane had been Bill's manager for a while, and I began to see evidence of her influence on his decisions. Helen would later claim responsibility for some of Bill's accomplishments while denying she ever controlled his artistic choices. But I'm not sure either was entirely true.

When you are as dependent as Bill on feeding expensive habits, your life is never your own; you can't conveniently separate the parts you'd like to remain untouched by those unrelenting needs. The illusion that Bill was making all the decisions was based on a pact of mutual deception. Watching from the wings, I thought I could see right through it—mirrors and trap doors exposed.

It was Helen who'd encouraged this project, and she may have been the one to choose Ogerman as arranger/conductor. To me, it represented superficial excess, and the orchestral writing had too little relationship to the trio music, but it was big and, therefore, seemed prestigious. Some jazz critics who probably rarely listened to Bartok or Stravinsky found the music attractive—sweetly romantic. Only Scott Yanow, who had recognized the success of Ellington's orchestral music, listened from a more informed perspective and called it predictably dull and weak. The money spent on this album could have made three better ones.

Creed Taylor's role in this and other projects with Bill was more obvious than Helen's. He was the guy who gift-wrapped every jazz musician who recorded for him with slick productions—maximizing accessibility and selling a lot of records in the process.

His success was symptomatic of profound shifts in the public's relationship with jazz. Creed just sensed it happening and openly went along. It was honest commercialism, and whoever signed on knew what was going to happen. Helen, on the other hand, pretended to only the highest artistic principles, but our idea of what was art and what was commerce differed. She helped Bill become more famous, which did us all a lot of good. But I was wary of some of the decisions she and Bill were making.

I was frustrated by what I saw as the misdirection of creative energy and by my inability to change the situation. But frustration is not always a negative force. I started fantasizing about things I might do differently. Of course, no one was offering me the chance, and I couldn't have accomplished much if they had. I hadn't the necessary tools. But my frustration was building to a point where it would force me into some productive action. If that orchestral project had been better, it might not have left so much of what I saw as an open field.

Things I furtively imagined doing—composing and arranging music, leading a band—were a long way off. I knew that, and I had no experience with patience or discipline. I was still twisted in a ball of inertia, but frustration was the force that started me unraveling it. Would I lose what semblance of self-worth I had managed to paste together from a little nerve and public approbation? Would the part of me that felt I'd acquired real understanding be able to overcome the part that was terrified I might find out I was wrong?

On February 21, 1966, a Town Hall concert was planned for the trio and a big band that was to feature Bill as soloist. I had the enjoyable responsibility of contracting the band. I hired Clark Terry, Ernie Royal, Bill Berry, Bob Brookmeyer, Bill Watrous, Alan Raph, Jerry Dodgion, and Eddie Daniels. In New York in those days, you'd have to make perverse choices not to be able to field five or ten great bands on any given night, so I know it was a good one. This was the first time Bill had been presented in a concert situation in New York; it was an important occasion for us.

The trio played the first part, then Bill played some solo pieces. Most of that is available on Verve Records' *Bill Evans at Town Hall*, more or less as it happened. In the first moments of

Bill Evans, Chuck Israels, and Arnie Wise at Town Hall, February 1966. Donaldson Collection / Contributor / Getty Images

the recording, you can hear us coming out on stage, me checking my tuning, and the trio launching into "I Should Care," as if we'd been playing for the last hour. It was an auspicious start.

When we came into the wings at intermission, the recording engineer, Rudy Van Gelder, opened his arms to me in an embrace of gratitude for catching what we'd done on tape. He was equally grateful for the way the music had gone. People don't think of Rudy as having been a particularly warm guy. He was meticulous about his studio and equipment, always fussing to keep everything clean, and he could get a little overbearing.

But for me, that was a moment of genuine warmth between two people who had participated in an important event and performed their roles to their own and each other's satisfaction. Neither of us said anything, but I remember the intimacy of the moment and how unusual it had been to have experienced the openly spontaneous and emotional expression of Rudy's embrace. A lot of musicians, having experienced Rudy's imperious behavior in his studio, would not have believed it.

After Bill's solos, including the one in memory of his father—one of the most beautiful thirteen minutes of piano music anyone ever played—the band came on and played the arrangements Al Cohn had written. Grady Tate played drums in Arnie's place, Creed's decision again.

I wonder who chose Al Cohn to write the arrangements, Bill or Helen, perhaps, but whoever it was, Bill and Helen decided not to release the recordings of this part. Al was a first-rate musician and an arranger of wide experience. He'd done wonderful things for Gerry Mulligan's Concert Jazz Band and had lots of commercial experience arranging for the Tony Awards show every year. But his arrangements for this concert were not well-suited to Bill's music and didn't get the rehearsal time they needed to have been well-played. The decision not to release those tracks was a good one.

I don't remember why but that concert in February of 1966 turned out to have been a turning point for me. I was being lionized by people who didn't understand what being a functioning musician really entailed, and that made me uncomfortable.

I never wanted to assume the position of bass-playing wunderkind. So I didn't publish collections of solos I'd recorded with Bill or ones I might have created just for the books. I just wanted to participate in the music—to be inside it and to make solo contributions that continued the unbroken thread of the music as Bill so beautifully and compellingly presented it. That had been enough.

I'd felt that way for the entire time I worked in the trio—so much so that when Bill and I had that upsetting conversation in the Rathausplatz in Copenhagen where I confronted him about my $40 share of a $1,000 gig and he told me if I had any complaints I should get my own trio, it didn't occur to me that that might be a possibility.

In retrospect, in terms of the amount of attention being in Bill's trio had gotten me, it might have been. But I didn't think of my bass playing alone as being worthy of enough attention and didn't know another pianist whose playing I could relate to in a way that would create the kind of unified structure and expression that Bill had created. That seemed unique to him. So the idea of going out on my own went into auto-reject—never settled into my thoughts for an instant, and I was stuck swallowing my pride, sucking it up and sticking with the program.

I needed to be able to continue to make the kind of music I'd learned to love, music on which I'd become dependent, music that shaped my very identity as a jazz player, and I needed to do it independently—on my own. For that I'd have to learn to control some of the things Bill controlled: form, harmony, rhythm, texture, dynamics. To be able to continue to live my musical life without Bill, I had to learn to be a composer/arranger, all beyond my power at that point.

I wasn't fully conscious of it at the time, but looking back, it felt as if I had been in a frightening free fall when I quit the trio after the Town Hall concert. I'd jumped from a seductively comfortable position in what I was beginning to see as a limiting relationship. I jumped to save myself, almost blindly, not knowing how I'd land safely.

10

INDEPENDENCE AND STUDY

In March 1966, I knew I had to do something. I needed to integrate thoughts, judgments, feelings, and ambitions pulling me in too many directions to make progress in any one of them.

I told Bill I was going to stay in New York and study. To be able to tolerate my fledgling efforts at composing, I'd have to get away from hearing what he accomplished every night. Bill's music was an example of almost everything I wanted mine to be, and I couldn't produce anything like it. If I continued to play with him and compare my efforts with his, I'd give up and choose his. I had to eliminate that possibility. Bill understood.

I couldn't stay connected to Bill forever, much as I loved his music. Drugs and emotional health problems were affecting Bill's life and music. In indirect but inescapable ways, they were affecting my life too. I was almost thirty and facing the fact that if I was going to flower at all, I was going to be a late bloomer.

Neither courage nor calculated good sense made me decide to leave the trio, just subconscious instinct. I was afraid, yet compelled—the decision seemed to make me rather than the other way around.

Common sense would have suggested hanging on longer. The notoriety that would allow the trio to command more money and attention in the next few years was on the rise. If I stayed, I'd benefit. But the direction was not so clearly upward.

I could feel Bill losing creative energy. You had to be inside to sense this. I don't think it was evident to our listeners, even the most astute of them.

For jazz musicians who wanted help in growing their understanding of music, Hall Overton was a good resource. Hall was a composer and jazz pianist who taught at Juilliard and the Yale School of Music. He was as comfortable with Bud Powell's music as he was with Bartok's, he'd played piano on recordings with Jimmy Raney, Stan Getz, and Teddy Charles, and we all knew the music he'd orchestrated for Monk's Town Hall concert recording. He was just the ticket.

Hall had a loft on 6th Avenue at 28th Street in the wholesale flower district, around the corner from some of our artist friends, Herb Kallem and actor Zero Mostel, who was also an enthusiastic painter. Their lofts had all the light that they needed—in Hall's loft, it was always night.

The first lesson was probably the most important. Hall showed me some simple things to do at the keyboard.

I didn't play the piano and was afraid of it. My coordination is still oriented toward using two hands to accomplish a single sound, as one normally does with string instruments, rather than two hands making multiple, sometimes independent, sounds. But I could see the advantage of connecting the visual information of the keyboard with what my ear had to remember.

I had a good Steinway upright in my one-room apartment, which was, until then, just looking good and taking up space. Now I started practicing what Hall had shown me. I'd never really practiced anything, and now I'd burned my bridges so that I had no recourse. I was cut off from the music I wanted to make unless I could make it myself.

I played the simplest versions of harmonies in pieces where I'd been playing complicated bass parts. The simplicity revealed what some of the other voices were doing—it was a wonder I hadn't understood them already. I certainly wove them in and out of the melodic shapes of my solos, but I didn't know where to find them with any consistency or how it was that they followed predictable conventions. Hall showed me how those conventions held, even under the duress of creativity like Bill's.

I painstakingly traced sevenths moving to thirds and thirds moving to sevenths with my right hand and played the bass notes with my left, as Hall had shown me, morning 'til night. Any one of hundreds of people, including Bill or Larry, could have helped me with these things if I had thought to admit I didn't know them, and simply asked. But it was Hall Overton I'd come to when I was ready, and he had the information prepared and organized. He had a systematic approach to starting all his students.

I was surprised at how quickly I began to enjoy what I was doing, but I didn't dare look too far ahead. If I'd thought about all I didn't know, I'd have been paralyzed by how much time it would take before I'd get to a level I'd been used to from playing with better musicians.

But it wasn't difficult to focus my attention on the page I was on. It felt good to play those three-note shell voicings and hear them move where my ear remembered they should. I played them endlessly, sometimes omitting one voice and singing it instead, or fumbling through the melody while attempting to sing one of the missing parts. There was simple sensuality in the activity, and I looked forward to it with pleasure. The sound of the piano was reinforcing my ear.

There wasn't as much dread or drudgery as I'd expected. Why had it taken me so long to get to this point? All that energy avoiding frustration could have been spent embracing a little of it.

Frustration didn't kill you; it was just the friction that let you know you were moving forward. I was a late starter but not a particularly slow learner. I was getting the point quickly, and I was doing exactly what my college harmony teacher Harold Shapero had said I would: "You'll do it all over for yourself by the time you're thirty." I was twenty-nine.

Soon there were composition lessons. Hall wrote on one page the things that composers did to develop music: repetition, transposition, sequence, inversion, retrograde, retrograde inversion, fragmentation, augmentation and diminution of rhythms and melodic intervals, rhythmic displacement, and on and on.

Then he showed me examples of how this applied to what I'd been playing and hearing and how to get started—how little it took to have an idea.

I was slow at writing, so when Hall gave me exercises and problems to solve, I had to work on them for hours. Once I'd invested all that time, I was damned if I was going to toss away the results, so exercises became more fully developed compositions. Hall didn't mind. That's where we were headed anyway. I didn't work fast, but I caught on fast, and Hall began to show that he liked what I was doing. I heard from some of his other students that he was proud of my progress. Maybe this was going to work out.

Sometimes I'd get stuck, and Hall would show me ways to overcome the impasse. The answer was almost always to take something that was in an earlier part of the piece and use it in a new way to propel the music past the problem. Hall would sketch in a possible solution, and I invariably hated it. It never sounded like anything I would do. But when I went home and applied the same methods Hall had used, I was able to find one of my own I liked.

Not every lesson (taken at two-week intervals) was a good one. Sometimes Hall was so deep in his own musical thoughts that he couldn't get out of them to get into mine, a phenomenon I've come to understand. But the lessons that were good were so important I never felt cheated. This was a good educational relationship.

One of the first results of the attention I was giving to compositional technique and form was that it began to change my perception of Thelonious Monk's music. Hall had done the orchestrations for Monk's big band performances and recordings; he knew the music well. It was a revelation to study it with him. What I'd thought of as bizarre charlatanism was transformed into something that seemed to be the essence of rough-hewn beauty. All I had to do was get some perspective—stop looking for microscopic refinements and, instead, stand back and see the shape. It wasn't Michelangelo . . . it was Giacometti, or Henry Moore, with the playfulness of Paul Klee.

Soon I wanted to hear my work played by other musicians, so, with some trepidation, I assembled a bunch of friends in Hall's loft and tried some of my compositions.
Some things sounded pretty good, and some were not so hot. I'd called people I thought wouldn't mind playing through the work of an unformed composer, and a few of them were in the same place with their playing skills. Hall thought that I couldn't judge the effectiveness of my work until I'd heard it played by better musicians. With my heart in my throat, I called some of the best players I knew. Some of my early rehearsal sessions had Barry Rogers and Garnett Brown on trombone, horn player Willie Ruff, reed players Al Regni and Dave Tofani (both occasionally hired as extra players with the New York Philharmonic), trumpeters Randy Brecker and Jimmy Owens, and my friend from LA, drummer Bill Goodwin, who'd recently moved to New York. Now things started to sound good to me, and I was permanently hooked.

One musician reported that when he'd told a young guitarist acquaintance about playing my music and enjoying it, the response was, "Chuck doesn't know anything about harmony." As far as he knew, he was right because, whenever he had gotten an impression of my musical powers, I'd only half-known the things I needed to know. But when you are halfway there, the second half can come quickly.

I didn't get attention right away. Seven years earlier, I'd gone to Europe looking for myself. Now I was finding myself in New York rehearsal lofts. The world doesn't always take well to people abandoning familiar roles and assuming new ones, but the personal satisfaction I got from hearing my own way of organizing music was almost as good as I'd gotten from sharing in Bill's. The music wasn't as good, but it was satisfying—sometimes thrilling.

There were things about the experience of making music in small jazz groups that I wanted to be able to expand and translate to larger ensembles, with more instrumental colors. I wanted to keep the looseness and freedom I'd experienced in Bill's trio, but there are different big band traditions in jazz, and they don't all follow this direction.

Basie's music depended on one kind of beautiful, but strictly played, dance rhythm. Kenton's bloated world was just what I didn't want. I didn't know Ellington had done just about everything anyone could imagine in his own way, and I could have saved some re-inventions if I'd paid attention to the reverence Herb Pomeroy and Bill Berry had for his music. Mostly, I was interested in Gil Evans's and John Carisi's music, and there was a lot I liked about Gerry Mulligan's Concert Jazz Band.

One thing that I didn't have to struggle with was orchestration. I'd been playing in bands and orchestras all my life, and I had a grasp of this. I loved the tonal palette that the wind instruments provided, especially when you could use French horns and the woodwind doubles most New York saxophonists could play well. Wind instruments breathed a physical manifestation of human life into the music that rhythm players had to create with musical illusions. Form was another story. I had to work on that.

My studies with Hall Overton were moving along. I was getting satisfaction from what I was learning to control, but even though I'd sometimes been annoyed by it, I missed the notoriety of being "Bill's bass player." I wasn't used to the idea that I was just one of dozens of good jazz bass players in New York or that I'd have to compete with all of them for jobs and attention.

I had plenty of second thoughts about having left Bill, and the incremental progress I was making with music didn't result in public recognition. I was probably on the only sane path I could take, but no one was applauding. I spent part of my energy trying to keep myself from bouncing between elusive confidence and tenacious doubt.

With all this internal work occupying my attention, I wasn't always as acutely aware of contemporary cultural shifts as I might have been, even after experiencing the disappearance of the jazz audience in Boston a few years earlier, but occasional glimpses outward revealed that things didn't look so good for a jazz musician.

One unexpected result of studying with Hall—and the Indian Hill experience—was getting to work with Paul Simon.

In the summer of 1967, I was helping my parents at Indian Hill. Paul Simon had rented one of the old estates on Prospect Hill in Stockbridge, just across the street from us. Looking for relief from Indian Hill activities, its teenage community, and the company of my parents, I walked across the road and knocked on Paul's door.

My friends, guitarist Stuart Scharf and pianist/composer Bob James, had worked on recording projects with Paul, and I knew Art Garfunkel's brother Jules. And, of course, I knew some of Paul's music—he was already a pop music icon with a level of fame that put him in social circles far above mine, but this was Stockbridge, where urban people generally drop their city defenses and become more accessible. Besides, how many distractions could you find there during the day? A visit from someone with mutual friends might be welcome. I just ignored Paul's stardom and approached him as if it were perfectly natural to show up uninvited and say, "Hello. I'm a friend of Stu and Bob." Paul invited me in.

His lawyer Mike Tannen and business manager Ian Hoblyn, interesting and friendly guys, were there. I enjoyed being with people who shared professional experiences headier and more powerful than mine but overlapping enough that we felt comfortable with each other. We swam in the pool, shared meals, and talked.

One evening we developed an ice cream "jones," and I suggested we drive seven miles to Lee, where there was a Friendly's ice cream parlor. Paul said he couldn't do that—people wouldn't leave him alone. I didn't understand. I'd been on a date in London with a stunning Swedish movie star. We'd been in public, and no one had bothered us. I pressed the issue with Paul, and he said, "Okay, I'll show you."

We arrived around 10 p.m.—Paul wore a large-brimmed hat to hide his face—to find the place crowded with off-duty teenage camp counselors. We stood unmolested, waiting to be seated, for about a minute. But Paul is easily identified by his small stature, and as soon as someone spotted him, it was a swarm. I don't remember how it was resolved, but we left with take-out orders. It was a demonstration of how celebrity can be a prison as well as a door opener.

Some years later, in 1975, Paul was having difficulty writing songs for a new LP and asked his producer Phil Ramone if he knew anyone who could help with the process. I'd played on a recording Phil had engineered with J.J. Johnson (J.J.'s *Broadway* for Verve, March 1963), and we'd gotten to know each other working in *Promises, Promises*. Phil suggested Bob James and me as possibilities. Paul called. I was thrilled and more than a little flattered that someone as successful as Paul would think I'd be able to contribute to his work. I agreed to teach him some things I'd learned from Hall Overton.

The first lesson was at our apartment in Westbeth. This was Manhattan, where people traveled in inward-looking cocoons of urgency; or if they did notice others, urban mores suggested leaving them alone. Paul could move around relatively unmolested, and he seemed comfortable with us—interested in conversations with Margot and our girls. He was eager, focused, and absorbent, sucking up information like a sponge. In this lesson, and in later ones at his Central Park West apartment, Paul played the guitar and sang beautifully, stopping only at stumbling blocks. His music was lovely, but he'd arrive at places where he wasn't sure how to continue. This was right up my alley—just the kind of problem Hall had shown me how to solve: traditional composition techniques that had worked for centuries.

Paul had a better harmonic vocabulary than his folk-music background suggested, but I could show him things familiar to jazz musicians—like how to arrive at a diminished chord in one key and find exits in others. You could go in one place and come out another, like a traffic roundabout. Changing the key center refreshes music. It's especially helpful in delineating form—making sections sound different. I also showed Paul techniques for continuity—how to hold things together and how to vary them when needed. He was a remarkably quick learner. He wanted and needed the information; it helped him overcome inertia and write more quickly. He was grateful.

Paul has been indefatigable in searching out colorful ensembles and soloists to enrich his palette. African choirs, Brazilian drummers, jazz players, unique instrumentalists—all wonderful additions. But he never sounds better to me than when sitting on his couch accompanying himself with pristine guitar playing and singing with intense emotional commitment. Sometimes the song is at its most powerful in that intimate setting. It's the right size, with nothing to distract from its message.

Paul and Phil Ramone did their best to involve me in their world, clearly enjoying my company as I enjoyed theirs, and wanting to help me make money. I was invited to recording sessions where Paul would play and sing a new song on a rough track—to be discarded later when he'd overdub a final version. Guitarists Joe Beck, Hugh McCracken, and sometimes Hiram Bullock, bassist Tony Levin, drummer Steve Gadd, percussionist Ralph MacDonald, and keyboard player Richard Tee would learn the song by rote and create accompanying parts. This was slow and inefficient compared to the working methods I was used to, where music was written outside the studio and brought in for musicians to sight-read. But it was Paul's way of working and a part of his social life. It was easy company—everyone enjoying the camaraderie, eating fine Chinese food delivered from the Mandarin House, and getting union recording scale for long hours. We learned new music—accepting and rejecting the players' contributions and trying to predict what would make a hit. I never could figure it out, but I was being well paid to try.

As the album project *Still Crazy After All These Years* progressed, Paul asked me to write a string quartet arrangement. I wrote overburdened, overly dissonant, and complicated music that showed a profound misunderstanding of what was required. I had no idea how little you needed to do or how simply you could write to make a useful, attractive, and appropriate sweetening string part. I blew it, and that was the end of access to the one role in that music where I might have been useful. Experience is a hard teacher: first the test, and then the lesson.

Nonetheless, when the recording was released, Paul came to our apartment to visit and asked if he owed me royalties— "points" for any of the songs. He said they were different from what he'd have written without my help. But I hadn't written them; he had. I'd only shared things Hall Overton and Gunther Schuller had shown me, and I'd been well paid for the lessons. I told Paul he didn't owe me anything, but he gave me a thank you on the album, and later a gold record arrived, with another note of gratitude.

Meanwhile, it was getting more difficult to find jazz work that would support me. The changes in audience awareness and lack of support for jazz that I'd experienced during the Berkshire County summers when folk had begun to take over were permeating the urban world, too. Commercial work that used to be directly related to jazz, like playing for dances or backing jazz-oriented singers, was becoming harder to find, and some jazz musicians were moving into the world of advertising music to shore up their incomes.

Benny Golson, a tenor saxophonist and composer from Philadelphia who'd written classic pieces (like "Along Came Betty," "Whisper Not," "Blues March," "Stablemates," and "Fair Weather," mostly for Art Blakey's Jazz Messengers), tried that for a while. Benny's jazz compositions are Bach-like in their unerring sense of harmonic direction. They have satisfying structure and great bass lines, and that aspect of the music appeals to jazz improvisers and serious listeners. But Benny also has a melodic skill set he was then using to write jingles.

Drummer Tony Williams and I turned up in a TV studio at Benny's behest, dressed in white button-down shirts, jeans, and sneakers—trying to look ten years younger than we were, to fit in with the American Bandstand refugees who made up the cast for a soft drink commercial.

None of this was especially harmful if it didn't distract jazz musicians from pursuing their best work—it was a lark for Tony, who was focused on his work with Miles Davis. But if Benny Golson had to write music for "Wink, the sassy one, from Canada Dry," and had no jazz outlet, something was changing.

I couldn't count on any of the jobs I was doing in New York lasting more than a few weeks, so I either had to run from one to another, juggling my schedule and taking anything offered, or I had to find something steady. The only reliable thing I thought I could find was theater work.

There was a weekly cattle call at the musicians' union. Every Wednesday around noon, musicians would show up at the Roseland Ballroom and mill around, socializing and exchanging job leads. Weekend society jobs like weddings and bar mitzvahs were often filled this way, and you could find out a lot about what was going on just by talking with people. I found a lead to Hal Hastings, a conductor who often worked on David Merrick productions, and he hired me to play a couple of shows, *Anya* and *Superman*. It was the beginning of an employment period that would prove reliable—but nearly as depressing as filling mail orders in the back room of Schirmer's in Boston years earlier.

The general misery of Broadway pit work does have some positive aspects, though. It pays well, and it attracts excellent musicians. In *Superman* (orchestrations by Eddie Sauter), I sat behind a horn section of Brooks Tillotson, Ray Alonge, and Dale Clevenger (later principal horn of the Chicago Symphony). That section sounded great, and players who came in to sub—like Richard Berg, Earl Chapin, and Larry Wechsler—were equally good. There were always fine moments—there had to be with the level of musicianship as high as it was in New York—but the automatic, repetitive nature of the work depressed all but the most resolutely optimistic among us. A friend who specialized in playing in and conducting new music ensembles criticized me for giving in to the "gripe culture" of the pit musician and challenged me to learn to live with it or get out. I had to live with it for a while.

The isolation of pit work was another aspect I hadn't experienced. Performers are isolated from the audiences in recording studios too, but there you're creating new music and just storing it so it will have the desired effect when the recording is played. It's possible, even necessary to project, when you're in the studio, so the reality of isolation is replaced by the image of the future audience. But while in a hole in the floor, unable to see either the theater or the stage, where your job is to repeat a rote rendition of what you did the night before while the stage performers garner all the audience communication signals, the feeling of isolation is inescapable, and I depended on an audience as an essential part of musical satisfaction.

The Café Au Go Go, where I'd played with Bill and Stan Getz, booked almost only jazz and good comedians through 1965 and 1966, but by 1967, there wasn't a jazz booking in sight there—only some folk music and a lot of adolescent rock.

What had been a significant part of culture—appreciated by many, discussed in newspapers, appearing on records, and performed in concerts and clubs—was replaced by music made by and for adolescents—music that was discussed and analyzed as the expression of the time and valued as that expression, even as it demonstrated a discontinuity with observable musical values that had endured centuries, and the absence of so much that was meaningful to me that I could find no way of relating to it except as the thing that was destroying my musical world.

I couldn't have put it in that perspective as it was happening, but I knew the fertile ground in which my kind of jazz music had thrived had begun to dry up. It was profoundly disappointing and lonely. Of course, I wasn't entirely alone. I wasn't the only one experiencing the world this way, but there were few of us, and we went from being creators of an important expression of our time to being a largely irrelevant underground. Not an underground of fresh opposition or revered resistance—just an underground of leftovers.

Musicians I knew who had learned some Portuguese and played Brazilian percussion instruments a few years earlier in the heyday of the Bossa Nova were now sporting ponytails and beads and comparing the merits of rock session drummers with Kenny Clarke and Philly Joe Jones. The comparisons were ludicrous enough, but when they came from the lips of former hipsters turned aging flower children, they were exceedingly ridiculous. Musicians, who a few years earlier would have been emulating Wes Montgomery or Jim Hall, were now learning the licks of third-rate musicians with exaggerated reputations (and even bigger incomes).

The philosophies and shifts in values that were blooming in the late 1960s were fertilized in a garden of adolescent excess. Just as I was developing control of a language—jazz—that carried special meaning for me and others who knew it, an explosion of people who did not relate were taking over. It was an inevitable result of market-driven popular culture, where reverence for the market is a governing part of the culture and all that is not central to the market is forced into the margins.

Now, everything not focused on separating teenagers from their money is on the edge of popular culture. That's the world we live in, and it's the downside of the 1960s youth-driven legacy.

I was in the middle of all of this but too deep in my own subculture to adapt. I held on to my musical values and hoped that clarity and mature content would find its audience.

I kept writing, looking inward toward understanding a personal world, and building on the background of jazz and classical music that was my foundation. I imagined that if I didn't acknowledge the significance of the revolution, it couldn't shake my foundation. In retrospect, my behavior looks less ignorant than purposefully exclusive, but at the time, it just felt obsessively like me.

11

Name That Tune

I can think of few historical periods when popular art has risen to the highest standards of durable expression, like the period of thriving Elizabethan theater and the fertile period of American popular music from the late nineteenth through the mid-twentieth century. I don't know what conditions provided enough support to produce Shakespeare's masterpieces, but I have some idea of what supported the best of American popular music and jazz.

In the nineteenth century, a piano in the parlor played the same role as a radio or phonograph in the twentieth. If someone wanted to hear new music at home, it had to be played on the piano.

In the 1840s, Stephen Foster wrote purposely simple but intelligent music, to be sold in printed form, and playable by ordinary people. Of course, those people had to read music and develop facility on the piano keyboard—a level of literacy and skill not required of radio and phonograph listeners. If you could read and play music (and that was a fairly normal middle-class skill), you were more deeply inside the music. You had a richer understanding of it, and more knowledge of its makeup, than those who merely listened. People who created music had every reason to expect a knowledgable public.

So Foster, the first American popular musician to make a living from selling sheet music, had a literate audience. His songs were well-crafted, and while not yet showing much of the African influence that would later identify music as more typically American, they had strong aesthetic balances inherited from centuries of European music. In the mid-nineteenth century, America knew his songs. Almost 200 years later, we still know "Swanee River," "Oh! Susanna," "Camptown Races," "Beautiful Dreamer," "My Old Kentucky Home," and "Jeannie with the Light Brown Hair." It's a long list.

Later, in the 1880s, concert bands were popular, playing in park bandstands in towns all over the country. Marches, like "The Stars and Stripes Forever" and "American Patrol," stirred people's souls and stimulated awareness of musical form. John Philip Sousa was a star, and the quality of his rousing music was extraordinary, full of intriguing variety and sophisticated counterpoint. And the influence of African music was beginning to be felt. Ragtime composers superimposed syncopated rhythms on European harmonies and forms. Jelly Roll Morton and Scott Joplin fashioned their music after the forms John Philip Sousa had perfected. No one calculated the idea. It just happened in the American melting pot—mostly in the South.

Beginning in the next century, Jelly Roll Morton, Louis Armstrong, and the musicians of New Orleans would become harbingers of the even more radical transformation that would emerge as jazz. And hundreds of educated composers—European immigrants and African Americans—wrote songs, movie scores, and shows designed to communicate to a public that was experienced in listening to literate, intelligent, well-executed music. That was the culture I grew up in. It expanded by leaps and bounds, with nothing to restrain it. There was a popular appetite for music that maintained continuity with centuries of European development, even as it accepted African influence.

Everyone knew music written by Irving Berlin, George Gershwin, Harold Arlen, Cole Porter, Jerome Kern, Harry Warren, Fats Waller, and Duke Ellington. Theirs was everyday vernacular, and you heard it everywhere—on the radio, in shows and films, and in dance halls. Of course, there was other good music too—European and American classical, simple but solidly conceived country songs, some good folk music, and the blues—but it was this popular music in what had developed into a tradition of standard, American AABA and ABAC song forms that surrounded everyone.

The various styles of jazz that grew out of this background were more complex and embellished versions of this same popular music. Jazz listeners were as familiar with the popular music underpinnings of jazz as the musicians themselves were. We all knew the tunes, so when Louis Armstrong sang a scat chorus or Charlie Parker hung a harmonically and rhythmically sophisticated new melody on the framework of a popular song, we heard the song and its creative embellishment as one thing. In jazz, the melody wasn't being played during the improvisations, but that doesn't mean it went unheard. Both musician and listener played it internally as subconscious counterpoint to creative fantasy. The songs everyone knew anchored our understanding.

A powerful indication of this common ground was the popularity of Coleman Hawkins's 1939 recording of Johnny Green's popular ballad "Body and Soul." Thrown together at the last minute by request of a producer at the Camden, New Jersey, recording studio, Hawkins responded with a two-chorus masterpiece of improvisational creativity and dramatic control without once referring to the melody.

There was no statement of the tune, and yet the recording became a phenomenal hit. It was on jukeboxes everywhere—collecting nickel after nickel as it was played by people who may not have considered themselves jazz aficionados. For that to have happened, listeners had to have been so familiar with that song's melody that they had internalized it: They could hear it subconsciously while they rationalized and reconciled Hawk's improvisation with the silent melody playing in their heads. And that's how a jazz improvisation became a substantial hit for all of America.

These popular songs were so universally familiar across cultural and economic lines that radio and television shows (*Stop the Music* and *Name That Tune*) were devoted to song recognition contests. After two notes were played, contestants were challenged to identify the song, and sometimes two notes were enough. If the first two didn't elicit a correct answer, notes would be added in succession until someone got it. "You are (the promised kiss of springtime)" quickly identified Kern's "All the Things You Are." All you had to hear were two half notes—the second an octave higher than the first—to recognize Arlen's "Somewhere (over the rainbow)." Some songs took longer. It might take five notes to get "How High the Moon" ("Some-where there's mu-sic. . ."). But the point is that this was both literate and sophisticated music *and* common cultural ground.

But sometime in the late 1960s, as baby boomers reached adolescence, things changed. The cultural landscape reverted to a new youth-oriented version of the culture.

The baby boom was big enough to support its own views. Teenagers thought of themselves and each other as free-thinking, free-loving individuals. Yet so many of them dressed alike, danced alike, opposed war alike, promoted peace alike, took drugs alike, and rejected the previous generation's inconvenient conventions—conventions that invite consideration and understanding, conventions only acquired through mindful periods of continued exposure. I lived in especially fertile times, but that was no longer the common experience.

And so, thoughtful solutions to complex issues out, slogans in. Complex classical music and jazz out, simple-minded folk-based music in. Music written by educated composers for literate listeners out, music aimed at kids, and written by kids who only knew three or four grips on the guitar and had little experience with melody or rhythm, in. The market follows the money, and adolescent money is easy money—earned by hardworking parents and blithely spent by their children.

Many jazz musicians gravitated toward the prevailing public taste—improvising over rock beats and limiting the harmonic palette, playing on one chord for four, eight, sixteen measures or more, simple-minded formal repetition sometimes lasting ten or twenty minutes. Electric keyboards, basses, and solid-body electric guitars further ratcheted up the loudness—not to mention amplification allowing four or five musicians to perform for crowds of thousands. Dynamic nuance—gone, obliterated.

Some favor the premise that the "jazz-rock fusion" music of the 1970s was a natural development of jazz. The concept certainly attracted the attention of many gifted musicians and changed their practices. And it continued the idea that jazz was historically a more complex way of playing popular music: If Jelly Roll Morton built his music on the forms and techniques of Sousa's marches, Armstrong built music on the blues and characteristics of contemporary popular songs, and Ellington, in turn, largely on the popular music of his time, wouldn't it be logical to find jazz styles changing as popular music styles changed?

The logic is irrefutable. The argument that this change always represents aesthetic progress is what's questionable.

When popular music is *literate*—written and consumed by people with a reasonable level of adult sophistication—using it as the basis for a more detailed and developed jazz interpretation produces durable results. "I Got Rhythm," already indelible, is a solid foundation for "Lester Leaps In," "Cottontail," "Anthropology," "Moose the Mooche," and dozens of other jazz tunes. When the literacy level of popular music deteriorates and the music loses character, jazz pieces taking on that impoverished aesthetic suffer proportionally. What looks superficially like a parallel case isn't really: Jazz rhythms welcome syncopation, displacement, and subtlety, while rock rhythms remain relentlessly on the beat; jazz accommodates dynamic nuance, while rock is loud; jazz melody welcomes development, while rock melodies are more repetitive than developed.

Then there was the Coltrane phenomenon—ecstatic jazz, some stunningly passionate and beautiful, even in its excess, and then, some music for whirling dervishes.

Coltrane's later trance music had a direct connection to his era's attraction to psychedelic drugs. It's filled with short but complex repeated patterns overlaid with kaleidoscopic pyrotechnics, pounding, and whirling, with little relief—unrelentingly loud and perfect for a self-involved state of consciousness.

Exotic and fantastic but often so repetitive as to be mind-numbing. The music of the time for the drug of the time.

The only reason formless free jazz is worth discussion is to try to figure out why people are taken in by it and accept its unrelenting boredom. It's nearly always doomed. You can't create dramatic surprise without first establishing expectation—expectation that arises out of a consensual, structured form. "Free" group improvisation defies attempts at coherent communication and controlled drama. It's typically impossible to tell where you are in a free jazz improvisation. Except for experiencing the usually hesitant start and a typical chaotic climax, everything tends to be the same, meandering from one minimally connected idea to another. There's a sameness in its incoherence that prevents the listener from experiencing a dramatic arc. If no one is adhering to a formal structure (a structure that is possible to bend, even while accepting some of its constraints), a musician is unable to sense, with any degree of predictability, what another participant might choose to do next. So you are either always waiting to respond to something someone else is doing or plunging ahead with your own ideas and gestures that only a clairvoyant could be prepared to respond to in a wholly rational and supportive way. It's either frustratingly hesitant or individually assertive. As a group artistic effort occurring in real time, it's hopeless. Most of what passes for "free jazz" is about as surprising as a typical child's fingerpainting. It's another version of hippie freedom: the freedom to act like a two-year-old and pretend that's useful social expression. If there's any value in this kind of thing at the moment (and I argue that the value is profoundly egocentric, if there's any at all), none of it lasts beyond the moment. The things I value in the moment always contain the elements that assure durability.

I'm not sure what Scotty LaFaro was thinking when he played with Ornette—maybe the same things I thought and felt when I was roped into similar activities in Europe with musicians who thought that was advancing the music, that they were fooling themselves and their audience, but I participated a few times before rejecting the activity as a hopeless charade. Yes, Scotty's playing (and mine, and probably most bass players, as a result of the range and typical role of the bass) was grounding—maybe it was all that seemed to hold the music together. I watched part of a video of Cecil Taylor and an improvising percussionist a couple of days ago before giving up in despair at the pretentiousness of the formless drivel. There was no way to experience where you were in the sounds. Anything could have been anywhere—the beginning, middle, or ending.

Successful jazz improvisations are always about something more specific than simply what might occur to a musician to play at a given moment. They are about spontaneous response to a chosen structure—structure that supplies the predictable element essential to creating recognizable form.

Imagine attempting an improvised play without guidelines. Take trained actors who've all had improvisation experience, put them on stage, and instruct them to improvise a coherent drama. If it's been tried, I know of no documented success. The idea of possible coherence beyond a few serendipitous moments, under those circumstances, is patently illogical. Nothing in our experience suggests it. Yet there are musicians who espouse this method in philosophy and practice. What they produce invariably sounds the same: boring, meandering noodling, and almost always loud. Those who do a little better—remembering to occasionally change dynamics, range, or texture—can stumble upon rare, minimally coordinated moments. But batting five out of 1,000 doesn't put you on a winning team.

Ellington, Bill Evans, Erroll Garner, Monk, Charles Mingus, and plenty of others kept to the path they were on, if not content to be on the margins of popular attention, at least realistically accepting of it and unwilling to lose their integrity to reach more people.

I don't blame musicians for wanting an audience. Without that, where does your music go? What's the point? But changing the essentials of your language to communicate with those who lack that language is a bridge too far. We are all drawn to activities that bring attention and success, and that response is not necessarily calculating or cynical, but seeking more applause by responding with what may be the superficial details that elicit that applause can quickly unbalance profound communication.

12

SURVIVAL

So where did this leave me?

Jazz jobs were harder to find, and I was getting more dependent on theater work. Sometime in 1968, I got a call from Arthur Rubinstein—not *the* Arthur Rubinstein, but a friend who had played horn in my band a few times. He was the conductor for *Promises, Promises*, a Broadway show based on Neil Simon's film *The Apartment*. Jonathan Tunick, whom I'd known since he was Pete La Roca's schoolmate at Music & Art, was now a successful orchestrator and working on Burt Bacharach's music for the show. Burt and Jonathan wanted a good rhythm section, and they'd hired Bobby Thomas, the drummer who had done the Ballets U.S.A. tour, and pianist Harold Wheeler. Would I be interested? It sounded like a good job.

There were a few rehearsals in New York before we left for tryouts in Boston and Washington. Burt and Jonathan had decided the dancers on stage could not move as much as they had to and still satisfy their idea of how the music should sound, so there were four women singing with the orchestra from the pit. The lead singer was Margot Hanson, one of the people I'd gotten to know in the cast of the Off-Broadway show *Now Is the Time for All Good Men* when I'd subbed in the show's band a year earlier.

I found myself enjoying Margot's company more and more. We were on the road, and despite grueling rehearsal schedules, there was still a lot of downtime. Boston had been my territory in college, and I showed Margot around. She talked about her daughter, Sarah, then three years old, and her marriage, which was about to end, and we became increasingly good friends. I realized I loved her, and the feeling was not going away. All this came as a shock. I had always believed that when I finally got tired of chasing women who weren't interested, and I got lonely enough, I'd finally marry one of the nice Jewish girls my mother had picked for me and be bored for the rest of my life. It didn't turn out that way.

I don't remember asking Margot to marry me or how it was decided. I know we did decide and that I was confident things would work out. When I introduced her to my father, he took to Margot immediately and was straightforward and supportive. It's the best memory I have of him.

Even if *Promises, Promises* had been better, it would have been difficult to stay interested, what with my new adventure with Margot. Phil Ramone, the well-known sound engineer and record producer whom I'd continue to know later in his role with Paul Simon, had been brought in to design the sound for the show. He covered two-thirds of the pit with deadening material so the orchestra could be miked and the sound controlled through mixers and amplifiers. It was the first attempt to mimic the kind of sound people were used to on recordings in a theater. Much time, money, and effort were spent by talented and well-intentioned people, but the sound was still worse than it would have been if they'd uncovered the pit, let the orchestra balance itself with the conductor's help, and simply amplified the quartet of women's voices.

The impact on musicians in the *Promises, Promises* pit was that the minuscule possible audience contact we were able to enjoy was further reduced by playing into acoustic padding.

I rarely see an orchestra pit full of happy people, despite the resilient spirit that keeps most musicians at their work, but this situation was worse than most. One solution was to ignore any relationship the job had to making music and treat it as a mechanical activity. But because this takes an ability to distance yourself from the emotional connections you develop to communicate through the music, most musicians have trouble with that approach. Another solution was to find as many other jobs as possible and sub out the pit work. The people who managed that were lucky. The rest of us fought the boredom by reading and doing crossword puzzles.

When Harold Wheeler, who had been conducting, left for greener pastures, I was in line for associate conductor. I gladly took the gig and looked forward to the chance to conduct a Broadway show.

The first time was the *only* time it was fun. Everyone watched to see how I'd do and if I had control of the music. Trumpeter Alan Rubin had some useful suggestions, especially "drop your shoulders," but once the piece was started, it was on automatic pilot until the end, and the only ones who watched me were the subs in the orchestra. That was the job: starting, stopping, and cueing the subs.

I was writing more and more, partly to replace the incessant strains of Bacharach's tunes in my head with something more interesting. I took a sketch to Hall Overton that combined some of the things I'd learned.

The music was highly personal, and I had no idea if he'd understand what I intended. I'd taken elements of a tune I'd played hundreds of times with Bill Evans and exploded them vertically and horizontally. The sounds were different but still related to the original tune. Certain key elements remained recognizable, and I liked the security of being able to hear this new musical vocabulary as merely a stretched arrangement of a familiar piece. It sounded like bebop Bartok and made perfect sense to me, but I was afraid that it would turn out to be as subjective as a dream—and no more interesting to an objective listener. Hall surprised me. He liked it and said, "This is your music. You keep writing this."

There was no effort to be new and original—I just had to let myself hear and imagine things rolling around in my head from different sources that had intuitively combined themselves. The hard part was remembering it long enough to notate it intelligibly. I couldn't play this at the piano with any semblance of steady rhythm, so I had to settle for checking individual sounds and trying to string them together with melodic logic. I used some serial techniques in the melodies and upper voices to keep the music moving forward, but the bass line hewed to the time-honored path of functional harmony. I kicked rhythms around in ways that were interesting to me and had fun with the orchestration, but the foundation of the music was still a familiar jazz standard. I hoped the players might hear into the music as Hall had. Margot listened to me searching for sounds, using the piano to find pitches the way a blind man uses a cane. She thought she'd married a far-out nut.

At the first rehearsal, I discovered the second or third minute of the piece was so climactic that I had nowhere to go. I loved the sounds, but things were in the wrong order.

Experience is what you get when you don't get what you want. After a few revisions, things made sense to the players and me; they were able to improvise effectively by superimposing references to the thematic motives of the piece on the familiar chord changes of the song that underpinned the composition.

I'd created something I liked that no one else could have written and that other musicians could understand and appreciate. It had taken me about three years, from starting work with Hall in 1966 until now—sometime in 1969—to accomplish that much, and it had happened more quickly than a typical school curriculum would have allowed.

Of course, my band had no way of creating a commercial existence for itself. The music was demanding, and the musicians were only in it for the pleasure of playing with each other and the chance to be heard by colleagues. The money amounted to an inconsequential part of anyone's income. But I was gaining confidence in my decisions.

Soon after that, I received a composition fellowship at Tanglewood's Berkshire Music Center, largely based on the results of my recent work under Hall Overton's supervision. This was the summer of 1971, and Margot was pregnant—due in September. We stayed in a caretaker cottage behind the beautiful home my parents had bought in Stockbridge, next to Indian Hill. It was cool there, and the camp had a pool.

I spent a few days each week at Hawthorne Cottage at Tanglewood in composition seminars, led by Bruno Maderna, with fifteen or twenty other composers. I had come hoping to learn more about form and development in the works of composers like Stravinsky and Bartok—but found the seminars focused on an area where I already had a lot of experience: exploring improvisational technique.

Maderna would have each of us create recognizable form by restricting individual roles to a particular rhythm, texture, dynamic, pitch range, or otherwise limited group of notes. Suggestions were made for timing of entrances and exits, according to what else might occur in the progress of improvisation, but it was always chaos. Not much changed over several weeks.

Some composers there wrote beautiful works in the general tradition established by George Crumb. But when it came to participating in a group creation in real time, nobody would shut up except for cellist Robert Kogan and me. Everybody else played all the time, regardless of Maderna's instructions. The big lesson of careful control and distribution of musical gesture possibilities—the main point of the exercise—was not happening. It all sounded the same. Again, group improvisation with no rules. Maderna instituted rules, but they weren't being followed. The rules must have seemed impractical or overly restricting. It wasn't fun or enlightening for the participants.

But the experience in that class did heighten my awareness of why good jazz improvisation works as it does. In the first place, it is severely restricted, and the restrictions come about through consensus—not imposed by any one authority.

Further exploration, gleaned from observing dancers improvising choreography to simultaneously improvised music, revealed it's practical to have only one free element at a time. Otherwise, the desire to make elements relate invariably leads to a hesitant series of dominance exchanges where no element can proceed with authority: "After you, Alphonse!" "No, after you, Gaston!"

The balance between predictability and chaos slides down a slippery slope into an abyss of formless meandering. Jazz musicians solve this problem by assigning each player's role to specific regions of freedom and discipline. The borders between these regions are often usefully bent but rarely broken.

I began to think seriously about finding a teaching job.

University music departments that had ignored the existence of jazz for years were just beginning to recognize the advantage of those courses. This was happening at hundreds of universities and colleges, just at the time young audiences were increasingly attracted to folk-based rock music with generic, guitar-grip harmonies and none of jazz's rhythmic character. Only the expanding general population of college students, and specifically those who would pursue jazz anyway, made these new programs viable.

While university courses are often quickly added to keep up with superficial cultural trends, response to actual changing needs is accomplished slowly. The academic world, in its conservative response to reality, was fifteen to twenty years behind in recognizing the justification and need for jazz education.

Most university and conservatory music administrators had backgrounds in music other than jazz and had no established path to finding trained candidates as teachers; they didn't know where to find them.

Often a graduate student in the regular music program either legitimately had jazz experience or, sometimes, they just claimed that they were hip with no real bona fides. Since that person was already in the system, it was relatively easy to promote him or her to a faculty position.

It was a nearly universal tacit assumption that to find a teacher, you had to look within the school system. The problem with this narrow approach was that the qualifications for university positions in jazz were being advertised as requiring advanced degrees. I had only a Bachelor of Arts from Brandeis and no time or inclination to pursue further formal education in an institution. If I wanted to teach, I had to find another way.

Dorothy Klotzman, who had taught composition at Indian Hill, was chairman of the Brooklyn College music department. I went to her in the fall of 1973 for advice on how to find my way into college teaching. Dorothy was friendly about the idea but suggested these things didn't happen quickly.

About two weeks later, she called and asked if I could come to talk with a music faculty committee. The members expressed interest, but Dorothy again suggested that faculty positions didn't materialize overnight.

A few weeks later, she called to offer me a job. Brooklyn College would have a jazz program, and I'd run it. I'd have a band and teach history and improvisation. And I'd do my best to live up to the standards of university classical music programs.

I've never seen searches for similar positions take fewer than several months, usually almost a year. Looking back on the speed and apparent simplicity of these events, it's pretty clear things had to have been politically instigated. The night before each faculty meeting, I got a call from another faculty member who was close to the chairman. She wouldn't dream of suggesting how I should vote, but these were the issues, and this is how she (and the chairman) saw them. No matter, I was delighted to get out of the pit and make a living doing a job where I didn't have to listen to and perform the same music as an automaton eight times a week.

My Brooklyn College responsibilities were only a little more time-consuming than a Broadway theater job, and the drain on my morale was much less. Now, again, I could begin to think about finding a creative outlet.

13

The National Jazz Ensemble

I couldn't expect subsidy for a project so personal as a band that played only my music. But if I could model a jazz band after a symphony orchestra, maybe I could go after the same kind of support.

Symphony orchestras functioned as repertory companies, with the same players, performing programs that included material as diverse as Bach and Stockhausen. Jazz ensembles played a more limited repertoire, often exclusively compositions and arrangements of their leaders or band members. In some cases, Ellington, Monk, Horace Silver, and a few others—this was not such a bad thing and provided enough variety for an evening's listening.

But more often than not, a concert presentation of one ensemble didn't hold enough interest. The Modern Jazz Quartet, for all of John Lewis's careful planning, could begin to sound stilted and prissy after more than a set. My stepfather said, "You've heard of semi-classical? This is semi-jazz."

I had to agree that one of the most endearing effects of an MJQ set was how it made you long for the free-wheeling blues that would come at the end. John Lewis had a lot of things figured out, but for my taste, the meal had too many hors d'oeuvres. A whole evening of Count Basie or Woody Herman was great if you were dancing or otherwise distracted from concentrated listening, but in a concert setting, even a big band could wear thin. There might be variety among the soloists, but the repertoire was usually designed around an identifiable sound that limited compositional variety.

At a normal symphony concert, you might hear Mozart, Schumann, and Bartok performed by the same players. It didn't take a great leap of imagination to see parallel programming possibilities in the jazz band repertoire, if traditional historic boundaries could be breached. What about a program of Fletcher Henderson, Neal Hefti, Billy Strayhorn, Jelly Roll Morton, Bob Brookmeyer, and Thelonious Monk? The more I thought about the possibilities, the more I was attracted to the idea.

This might be eligible for the funding support long established in classical music. Also, by looking a few years back at the history of jazz repertoire, I could identify compositions that merited the continued appreciation a classical symphony enjoyed. The fickle need for a new item of cultural fashion would have reduced power. Things could be both more interesting and more stable. It was worth a try.

If this venture was to be fundable, it would need a board of directors and official not-for-profit status. Then it had to exist for at least a year before consideration by the two public agencies that might fund it, the New York State Council on the Arts and the National Endowment for the Arts.

But a friend of the family who was in charge of the Wolf Trap Foundation outside of DC offered a $15,000 grant, in return for the ensemble's first performance. I had no idea how much or how little that money was, but I simply spent it all on the services of a lawyer, music, musicians, and transportation.

The first performance was inauspicious. Sarah Vaughan, who shared our bill at Wolf Trap Park, refused to perform with us after hearing our sound check. The band wasn't nearly as good as it would later be. We hadn't yet found enough appropriate musicians for this unusually broad repertoire, and the rehearsal was a little unstable. Nevertheless, the National Jazz Ensemble was born.

The Wolf Trap concert program had the kind of variety I thought would be interesting to a jazz audience, but I had the feeling its lack of easy categorization would make it escape the appreciation of most listeners. Nonetheless, I continued to press forward with the concept of assembling programs that interested me, assuming my tastes were not so esoteric that others would also not learn to like the same things.

It was hard work. The music had to be transcribed from records because, unlike classical music, the scores and parts of jazz ensemble pieces were not published. There was no market for them. The only jazz band music you could buy were third-rate compositions or arrangements aimed at the high school and college market and maybe some good Thad Jones and Bob Brookmeyer charts that Thad's band was performing better than we could.

But many people helped. Bass trombonist Pete Phillips transcribed Ellington's "Rockin' in Rhythm," John Carisi shared his scores for "Moon Taj" and "Angkor Wat," Hall Overton gave copies of the Monk pieces he'd orchestrated for the famous Town Hall concerts and recordings, and Gil Evans provided a couple of sketch scores from which I could orchestrate faithful arrangements.

Some guys from my rehearsal band played in the Jazz Ensemble for a while, but it soon became evident that it took a different personality to enjoy jumping from Jelly Roll Morton to Thelonious Monk to a brand-new piece and back again to Fletcher Henderson. Benny Aronov continued to like playing piano in the band, and Joe Hunt, as well as Bill Goodwin, were good drummers for it. There were a few bassists. Buster Williams was a real asset during a two-week rehearsal period, then sent a sub for the Tully Hall performance we'd scheduled with Herbie Hancock as the soloist after Wolf Trap and before we started the New School series.

Pat Martino played guitar at the beginning, sometimes sitting silently at the first rehearsal and then showing up at the next one with his part faultlessly memorized.

Herbie Hancock was one of the first guest soloists. He wrote wonderful arrangements of his "Maiden Voyage" and "Dolphin

Dance" that I edited unnecessarily. Herbie let me do it, thinking I knew something about orchestration he didn't, but I'm not sure he was right. I managed not to ruin them.

As I started forming the idea of the National Jazz Ensemble, I talked with my friend, pianist Dick Katz, about how much responsibility was involved in organizing each performance. I needed some help, and Dick suggested that I get in touch with David Berger, a trumpet player and arranger with an abiding interest in Ellington's music. I had played in David's rehearsal band some weeks earlier and enjoyed it so much I agreed to play at the next rehearsal the following week but uncharacteristically had blanked out about the obligation and didn't show up. I was so embarrassed I didn't want to return David's message asking what happened. How was I going to explain that I'd simply forgotten something I knew was important to him? Now Dick Katz was suggesting I call and ask for his help. It's a testament to David's character that he pursued me until he made contact. He was not only understanding about my transgression but also eager to help. We worked out a great relationship, and he gave me the help I needed to expand the repertoire and form a stable band.

Applying extraordinary skills, David supplied a large part of our library—transcribing compositions and arrangements by Ellington, Strayhorn, and Fletcher Henderson and offering several of his own compositions, including "The Gentle Lion," a three-movement suite he'd written while in Ellington's band. David recommended his trumpet teacher, Jimmy Maxwell, for the lead trumpet chair.

Jimmy was a great player in the Louis Armstrong tradition, with an enormous sound and fine musicianship. He used to claim that since he'd played in the NBC Symphony, Ellington's band, Basie's band, Benny Goodman's band, and *The Tonight Show* under Doc Severinsen, he obviously couldn't keep a job. He stabilized the trumpet section and, thereby, the whole band. He also understood and loved Bill Goodwin's drum playing, an enthusiasm not equally shared by all the wind players. A few felt the traditional style of big band drumming was required to create a single rhythmic center for a band this size. To me, that style seemed unnecessarily obvious and lacked subtlety needed for the dynamics of the music to breathe. I counted on each musician to assume his own rhythmic center and to adjust that to a consensus. Bill's style was more than specific enough for me and Jimmy, who found he could place his rhythms where he wanted them and they'd line right up with Bill's.

Bill was our drummer most of the time, but Keith Copeland, Joe Hunt, and Joe LaBarbera each played a few performances. We went through several bass players, finally settling on Steve Gilmore until the band got tired of my conducting and insisted that I play. I had to admit they were right, but I was hesitant to relinquish my position as non-playing conductor. It gave me a perspective I'd lose as soon as I had to pay attention to playing my own part. The band was adamant, though. They wanted not only to understand my tempos by feeling them directly through my playing but also to be responsible for nuances and balances in their own parts, without me hovering over them. I'd be useful in the rhythm section—and I was out of the way.

The leadership vacuum that decision created was immediately filled by the cooperative effort of the band members. They took responsibility for those things I would otherwise have been monitoring from the front. My playing was more helpful than waving my hands in the air, and the band preferred listening for cues and nuances than to watching for them. It didn't take long to realize the players' instincts had been right, and this was a better use of everyone's abilities.

Lots of thought went into our choice of material, and there was no end of advice from well-wishers. Gunther Schuller recommended a practical approach that included ideas like Glenn Miller's familiar music to ensure an audience. But I wasn't about to play "In the Mood" or even "American Patrol." Those were played in supermarkets, and I didn't have the nerve to ask serious jazz musicians to play tunes that held little interest to me. In practical terms, Gunther was right, but I still couldn't swallow it.

Trumpet player Jimmy Owens, in a generous effort to be helpful, suggested a kind of 1970s pop-jazz with the repetitive funk rhythms that had served Herbie Hancock well in his search for a wider audience. But that wasn't the audience I was seeking, and most of that music went beyond boring and, to my mind, crossed a line into offensive pandering. At least the music Gunther suggested had established a claim to quality by withstanding the test of time. People are still listening to "In the Mood."

14

SIMPLE ISN'T EASY

As a response to the diminishing number of educated jazz listeners, jazz musicians' efforts to modify their music during this period held some merit. If audiences were no longer familiar with the popular tunes and harmonic patterns that formed the underpinnings of jazz, then something had to replace that connection to maintain the connection between player and listener.

Many classic jazz performances are propelled by the composition. A reasonably good jazz improviser can create a creditable work by embellishing the outline of a Cole Porter song because the melody and its harmonic structure are already complete and satisfying. When Charlie Parker improvises on Cole Porter, astute listeners recognize the majesty of the result because they know the song and can appreciate what Parker has added. Take away familiarity with Porter and the audience has fewer signposts to anticipate and understand the directions of Parker's fantasies. If the listener doesn't already know half the story, the story must be simplified so it explains itself.

Musicians used two basic approaches to try to solve this problem. A year after Miles Davis recorded an outstanding version of "Love for Sale," he recorded "So What" as part of what was intended as a "one-off" experiment in the use of minimal form as a basis for jazz composition/improvisation, and it changed the world.

"So What" is from the sessions that created the *Kind of Blue* album, arguably the most popular jazz album of all time. It is by far the most influential piece on the recording and, not coincidentally, the track with the least structure: sixteen measures of one mode, eight measures of the same mode a half-step higher, and then eight measures back at the original pitch. Anything remotely interesting had to be superimposed on that nearly blank form by players who'd spent years learning how to develop coherent melodies by having been guided in their improvisations by the necessity of negotiating the harmonic forms in compositions with more detailed chord patterns. They'd skied at speed through so many slalom gates that you could remove the gates and they'd still ski graceful, beautiful patterns.

A highly accomplished musician can take a simple form and use its open character as a foundation on which to superimpose an effective and communicative artistic structure. Bill Evans used the simplest tonic/dominant ostinato as the basis for "Peace Piece" and achieved a remarkable result that created a beautiful emotional and formal arch, starting with the simplest of melodic motives closely related to the harmony, gradually moving further and further from the tonal center and increasing melodic and rhythmic complexity until the fabric of the piece was stretched to what threatened to be a breaking point, and then moving back incrementally to the original simplicity of melody and harmony. It's a masterpiece of improvisation that demonstrates deep understanding and control of the elements of musical form. And perhaps it is both more remarkable and more accessible because it is anchored by the simplest musical background—just a pattern of two bass notes followed by two chords repeated from the beginning to the end of the piece. It is a monumental accomplishment worthy of comparison to some of the best examples of twentieth-century composition. But similar examples of profound improvisations based on this kind of simple premise are rare, and ponderously pretentious and boring examples, often lauded by critics and accepted by undiscerning listeners, abound.

As a result of the success of *Kind of Blue*, new listeners arrived in droves, in turn attracting hordes of musicians to use the same simplified approach. It was a revolution, and like the other revolutions of the 1960s, it brought attention to some overlooked, or under-appreciated, things. But in eliminating the complexities of sophisticated musical forms, it also lost many useful qualities that improve the chances for coherent and meaningful musical communication.

After "So What," the "rules of the game" were now so simplified that little preparation or existing listening experience was needed. The changing elements and variety embedded in sophisticated jazz forms were eliminated. For some listeners, this represented freedom from prerequisites.

The musicians in Miles' *Kind of Blue* band (including Bill Evans) were all capable of negotiating the slalom-like twists and turns of complex musical form while still maintaining the freedom to create beautiful and emotionally engaging improvisations. They were not constricted by form; they were grounded in it and guided by it. So when the forms were simplified to the point of near absence, they'd been trained by their experience with the guidance of more complex forms to create strong improvisations containing internal formal elements that gave their music integrity and coherence.

Removing the underpinnings of the formal details of a piece like "Love for Sale" still left them with a sense of the necessity of including formal integrity, variety, and development in their improvisations. Those formal elements, released from attachment to a detailed harmonic form, now had to relate to melodic and motivic elements inherent only in the improvised melodies. Seasoned professionals made it seem easy.

While understanding the refinements of any game deepens appreciation of how it is being played, it takes far less preparation to understand checkers rather than chess. So new listeners were attracted, and appreciation of the work of jazz musicians grew in quantity, if perhaps not in sophistication.

Many young jazz musicians who were in the difficult process of learning to improvise while negotiating complex forms perceived a shortcut. A less than well-developed musician could easily fill in "So What" with melodic meandering or unfettered repetition while remaining true to its simple form. That musician didn't need to learn to understand and find pathways through "Love for Sale" to improvise in what had now (thanks to Miles' example) become accepted as professional conditions. Sure, it was far easier. But here's the rub: Both musician and listener lost the advantages of more complex and complete forms in guiding the structure of improvisation and the guiding of the coherent understanding of the listener.

Blues form developed by consensus as a foundational vessel for countless pieces of music. No one person (as far as we know) wrote it, but thousands have used it as the basis for personal expression.

The only other form that has proven so universally useful to so many is the form of "I Got Rhythm," and Gershwin, one man, wrote that. Gershwin was a genius. "Five" is Bill Evans' extrapolation of "I Got Rhythm," and I recognized that easily when I heard it. I wasn't conscious of all that was going on—coming at "I Got Rhythm" from different angles, I just knew it was always "I Got Rhythm," and I could hang on to that while it stretched me away from the song, twisted and massaged my brain so that every moment was new, and still allowed me to follow Gershwin's plot. It was stretched close to breaking, but it didn't break. It explained its logic to me as it progressed, in real time, teased me with the threat of losing its connection but never did. If you're not close to the edge, you're taking up too much room. I loved the thrill.

But there were changes afoot that, while they didn't necessarily immediately diminish the quality of the music, began to adjust it and make it accessible to less-educated ears. And some of those changes moved the music away from practices that suited my sensibilities and skills.

There'd been a slow movement away from jazz musicians playing standard songs and basing compositions on them, and that seemed to accelerate. There were more original jazz pieces being played and recorded. Horace Silver moved toward basing his pieces on repetitive ostinatos instead of using the forms of standard tunes, and that simple repetitive element made the pieces quickly popular and easy to follow for listeners who weren't familiar with American standards. They were good pieces but less interesting to me than compositions that welcomed changing bass parts and bass lines that were more closely aligned with the principles of Bach. Besides the reliance on repetitive bass figures, unlike Bill Evans' "Peace Piece," where the monotony of the droning left-hand figure is played softly—providing a cloud-like cushion for the intensifying right-hand fantasy—Horace's ostinatos are played with maximum force, intruding relentlessly into the listener's consciousness—diminishing listening space for creative melodic improvisation. Like rock music, repetitive, hammering bass and drum parts overwhelm syncopation, subtlety, and melodic invention. It's a different proportional aesthetic that emphasizes primal rhythm over other expressive details.

Some jazz musicians who were well-versed in playing creative versions of standards ignored the foundational integrity of standard forms as models for their own compositions. Many played beautifully but wrote pieces that were less well-developed than the improvisations they could play based on standard tunes or established jazz compositions. The economic practicalities of owning copyrights and publishing licenses encouraged writing their own tunes rather than recording the compositions of others, even if their own pieces weren't as good. Many of those pieces were based on "So What" or similar minimalistic forms.

For the musicians on *Kind of Blue*, the simplicity of the forms wasn't a problem. It was liberating—even challenging—in how it required them to invent good melodies in the face of such minimal structure. The problem was, for less well-prepared musicians, the simplicity of the form appeared to remove challenges. They thought it made jazz easier. All too often, the results were formless noodling. And some listeners, unable to recognize the difference, supported not only *Kind of Blue* but also its lesser followers.

It became not only acceptable but also fashionable to write jazz pieces designed to support improvisation without functional harmonic progression—just one sound played for a while and then a move to another sound, not necessarily related, at what might seem to have been an arbitrary time. Fill in this area.

Okay, that's enough. Now fill in the next area. It all seemed vague to me and hard to keep track of. I played with Herbie Hancock and Bobby McFerrin in a club in San Francisco, and they decided to play "Maiden Voyage," a fine piece of Herbie's that had that kind of static harmony. Herbie knew it well, of course. So did Bobby. I embarrassed myself by getting lost, not knowing the timing of the harmonic changes. If I'd known the tune better and had been able to keep the melody in mind, it might have guided me. But I didn't—and trying to catch the changes of chords that sounded pretty similar to me left me struggling and contributing only confusion. Truly embarrassing, and I haven't been asked to play with either of them since.

The formal underpinnings of jazz were already changing from the foundation of the blues and American popular song, even before the culmination of the 1960s revolution and the overtaking of American music by adolescent rock and roll. For someone steeped in the tradition of harmonic form that itself stood on the functional traditions of Bach, even as it admitted the more colorful textures of impressionism and modern dissonance, things were not looking up.

The audience was being inundated with music that didn't ask them to know much of anything that had come before, and the result was that it untrained them to listen for a lot of the things that held music together—things that made it coherent and communicative at an educated level of literacy. Kids wrote songs harmonized by whatever chord grip on the guitar happened to have the melody note in it, regardless of whether that chord followed the previous one or led to the next with any independent logic, and there were so many other kids who bought that music that it inundated the world and marginalized more demanding and fulfilling music—music that had continuity with the preceding hundreds of years.

Some jazz musicians, laboring under the mistaken idea that since the history of their music had been built on the foundation of the popular music of its time, looked to the newer popular music as a basis for their jazz efforts, although the newer popular style was too weak to support coherent music. Even worse, weak, uninformed, childish posturing was taken seriously, analyzed and written about as if it expressed important things in insightful ways.

I talked about Bill Evans' "Peace Piece," a meditative improvisation anchored by the simplest kind of tonic/dominant ostinato, an instantaneous composition that related to my body by synching with my breathing. The left-hand ostinato connected with my lungs, keeping me calmly breathing, while the right-hand improvisation drew challenging fantasies that stimulated thought—made me follow Bill's ideas as he started the melody with a simple inversion of the interval of the fifth in the bass notes and developed it through ever-more-adventurous tumbling shapes that pulled further and further from the underpinning of the ostinato anchor and finally came back down to land in a controlled glide path. It was a simple concept wedded to the most sophisticated invention, and everything about it engaged my mind and related to my visceral experience—what it feels like to be human and conscious.

Over many years, I've learned to listen for certain things, and those things have become increasingly absent in popular music, theater music, film music, contemporary classical music—almost everywhere. The stasis of "So What" has even influenced the classical music world with pieces that go on for hours with minimal change, intentionally obscuring those changes when they do occur.

A parallel approach to the minimalism of "So What" was to limit the material to forms that could be absorbed and understood in one or two choruses, but more folk-like, or incorporating traditional gospel call-and-response.

This works well for some, but the source runs dry quickly, and things start to sound overly similar. Then there's an added problem—without an interesting enough form for the ears of performer and musician to attach to, improvisations can quickly lose their way. Developing recognizable motives then becomes a critical technique, holding the attention of both listener and improviser to the same subject.

Monk and Sonny Rollins were adept at weaving this technique into their improvisations, even in the demanding context of their sophisticated repertoire. Musicians with lesser skill and creative understanding depended heavily on repetition for their audience hook. This left music's rhythmic foundation, which used to have propulsion of more varied decorative surface elements as its main purpose, without a suitably interesting surface to propel. If bebop had become too obscure and complicated for audience understanding, the anti-bebop created to solve the problem was too often over-simplified.

Experienced musicians who had developed in an environment of deep audience connection cared for that connection and wanted desperately to keep it.

Some younger jazz musicians did not know that experience in relation to jazz but could see the contemporary audience's instant connection to rock. Wanting some of that attention too, those musicians bent the forms and traditions of jazz in an attempt to make it intelligible to an audience that didn't speak its language. It all boiled down to this: desperate attempts to communicate with an increasingly illiterate audience, with no interest in going beyond the monosyllabic musical utterances of rock.

It was all too dumb; there had to be a better way.

Gunther Schuller wanted the National Jazz Ensemble to survive the process of audience educating and building, so he recommended heavier doses of the familiar and nostalgic. Others suggested pandering to fashion, then moving listeners toward more sophisticated material a little at a time. I was convinced success with superficial material would only trap us into maintaining that success by repeating superficial music. I rejected it without a second thought.

Finally, Jimmy Maxwell gave me a piece of advice I was prepared to take. He said the programs we'd selected so far had a particular stamp: They were all about music I liked. He thought that was the way I could pursue my goals honestly, which satisfied him and most of the other musicians, and it was the only way I could operate. I didn't think my taste was so obscure an audience couldn't be found to agree with it. However, if the jazz repertory concert truly was an idea whose time had come, it was also an idea whose audience had yet to be developed.

Our typical National Jazz Ensemble programs included two or three pieces from the Ellington/Strayhorn repertoire. They weren't available in print, so we had to transcribe them from recordings, and we chose pieces interesting enough to warrant the time that would take, usually many hours spread over several days.

I'd never heard Ellington's band live. Once, out of ignorance and unpropitious timing, I turned down a chance to play with him. Joe Benjamin, Duke's bass player at the time, was told by his doctor to take a few months off from the rigors of the road (the Ellington band traveled incessantly), and he called to ask if I'd like to sub for him, assuring me Ellington would take his recommendation. I was recently married, had two daughters, and, even though we were struggling economically, I didn't consider the possibility that being on the road away from my family was going to be a good solution.

The first revelation was how different Ellington's music sounded when I stood in front of the Ensemble at rehearsals and heard it played live. Things that had sounded corny and exaggerated when I'd heard them on records now sounded sublime. It bowled me over. We transcribed "Harlem Air Shaft," "Koko," "Concerto for Cootie," and "Main Stem." I was converted.

Someone suggested Jaxon Stock would be an ideal person to write a new arrangement of Jelly Roll Morton's "Black Bottom Stomp." Everything else we'd been doing in its original form, but he sent a revised version of that piece that not only did justice to the original but made it more colorful without spoiling any of its character.

The banjo part in the original was ingeniously re-scored for two soprano saxophones in voice-crossing counterpoint, and the rest was done in a zany style that owed something to the music of Bob Crosby and the Bobcats. On the few occasions the Ensemble played for new audiences outside of our regular concerts in New York, we programmed that piece with the assurance it would be the kind of hit we enjoyed playing. It opened people's ears (including ours) to the depth of Morton's contributions to the New Orleans style.

Herb Pomeroy accepted a commission for a new piece and wrote "Jolly Chocolate," and Bob Freedman did a Ray Charles-style version of Nat Adderly's "Sweet Emma." I transcribed J.J. Johnson's arrangement of Thad Jones's "Swing Spring" (right up my alley), and Sy Johnson contributed a couple of Mingus arrangements he'd done. Art Farmer sent some Oliver Nelson charts commissioned for European radio bands that would otherwise lie unplayed after their first performance. Then we began adding new music. David Berger and I both wrote for the band (David brought in Sy Oliver's "For Dancers Only"), and Rod Levitt expanded five or six of our favorite things from his octet book.

We had Hall Overton's arrangements of Monk's music, things by John Carisi and Gil Evans, transcriptions of compositions by Mulligan from the *Birth of the Cool* session, classic Basie pieces like "Every Tub" and "Jive at Five," and unison arrangements of Louis Armstrong solos to remind us of the source for all this. It was glorious to my ears, and many musicians began to appreciate the varied musical diet.

The repertory company notion flew in the face of jazz convention. We had to modify the idea that a jazz musician identifies with one style, and that was disturbing to some. Things we held sacred had to be abandoned for us to function in this way, and it took time to get used to the idea. Most of the time, the sheer fun of musical variety overcame our doubts, and we discovered it didn't overly impinge on our personal styles to bend them a little to fit pieces from different eras.

Bob James wrote an arrangement of Coltrane's "Giant Steps," and Tom Pierson wrote a phased version of Wayne Shorter's "Nefertiti." The band accepted all this music with an increasing appreciation for the repertoire's scope. Only one piece caused a problem. Someone produced a copy of the score to George Russell's "All About Rosie." I thought it would be a good idea to program this historic piece, but the band revolted. Greg Herbert called it "fake blues" and "pretentious posturing . . . the only thing we've come up with that doesn't sound real." Otherwise, the band was happy with the repertoire, and I was learning more every day.

One result of daily exposure to the wide variety in the jazz repertoire was recognizing that things I liked were often simpler than I'd imagined them to be. They started with easy musical material and developed it in ways that seemed unforced. I also understood this apparent effortlessness was an illusion ... an important one—but an illusion, nonetheless. This quality was one I wanted in my own music, and it led to simplifying materials and techniques in my work.

While you learn to play, you also must learn to listen. After growing up with Louis Armstrong, Bix Beiderbecke, and Benny Goodman records, in 1954, I fell in love with a Dave Brubeck recording, *Jazz Goes to College*. I played it incessantly in my dorm room at MIT every day. At that moment, it represented some things I found important, things that seemed progressive—advancing and expanding the breadth and vocabulary of the music I'd been hearing. It doesn't sound good to me now. I've heard so much music that draws me in more completely since then, more engaging and more meaningful music, that I find elements I used to like in that recording have turned distracting, distancing, and irritating.

Now that I've heard a lot of music that reaches me deeply, on levels I hadn't experienced at the time I was enamored of the Brubeck recording, I hear it differently. After Bud Powell, Brubeck's piano playing sounds galumphing—rhythmically, harmonically, and melodically unsophisticated. And I now perceive a posture of pretension and self-importance in that music of which I'd been unaware, an element that, in its absence, adds to my involvement rather than detracts from it. A few swinging, judicious, well-placed notes by Basie connect with me in ways that Brubeck's music doesn't. I'm no longer that person.

How do we grow and change as listeners? Expanded exposure helps, and repeated exposure either deepens or diminishes the power of how music affects us. It didn't take long to become susceptible to Charlie Parker, and nothing has diminished its effect in more than half a century of exposure. His music strikes me as complete, modern, and timely now as it ever was. If I arrive at my destination and a Charlie Parker recording is on the car radio (not a common occurrence), I can't turn it off and leave the car. I'm riveted, compelled to listen. The music is tenacious. It relates to so much of my musical character, my humanity, my Americanness, the way my brain works, and the way my body feels, that it grips me and fulfills something I don't even know is missing until I hear it, and then I can't let go. There's something so important that I must absorb it while I can.

I can point to most of the elements in Parker's music that make me respond that way, but I can't say for sure why they work the way they do. It must have something to do with existential validation. It's a cushion against loneliness. I belong in a world in which Parker's music exists.

My new interest in that simpler quality and increasing ability to realize it in my own work was a direct result of what, by now, was constant exposure to Ellington and Strayhorn's music. I was also intrigued by the way Monk's music was full of personal quirks while retaining humor and meaning for others. I saw right away that he left notes out of his harmonies so dissonances would be exposed and scream a little. The resulting sounds weren't tortured, just pinched and prodded. The music would proceed smoothly until it veered drunkenly off its track for a moment, producing a passing sensation of flying off into space only to find its feet again and make me laugh at my momentary disorientation. Monk did this by surrounding those trick passages with stark simplicity and artfully timing them for maximum surprise. That could work only if the context of these effects was sufficiently calm and predictable to lull the listener into expecting the calm to continue. If the musical texture became overloaded with the unexpected, it would cease to have the desired impact. Monk looked for chances to bend his music in personally expressive and funny ways, but his proportions stay natural in that the chaos is balanced by enough easy predictability to keep the apparent disorder in line.

As long as I was so focused on the nuances of Bill's music and the world of what I considered to be sophisticated bebop that surrounded it, the unrelentingly loud and direct sound of Monk's playing seemed unnecessarily crude. I didn't want to hear things that way, and I blocked all the elements of brilliant structure, studiously pared-down texture, carefully controlled, purposeful timing, and glorious rough-hewn craft in his music. I just didn't hear it. It was too far from lots of things I liked that had some of those same elements. Things I loved in Horace Silver's music, Sonny Rollins' expressive roughening of his tone, the power of Bud Powell's endlessly inventive and almost as unrelentingly loud way of playing, and the direct drive of Art Blakey's drumming were all essential parts of what made what I thought of as my music—the stuff that, if it hadn't been there, I wouldn't have felt like myself. Those things were as essential to the way I experienced music as the impression Schubert's Trout Quintet left on me when I'd played it as a young cellist. So it wasn't that I only liked the wonderfully dynamic and rhythmic nuances in the playing of people like Johnny Hodges, Charlie Parker, Miles Davis, Jim Hall, Tommy Flanagan, and Bill. It was just that, for a long time, Monk was a bridge too far in another direction.

I'm not sure at what point Monk's music revealed itself to me—when I opened my ears to it—but I know I worked opposite his quartet at the Five Spot for many weeks, enjoying playing with Bobby Timmons, another wonderful musician. I heard the quartet night after night and hardly paid attention to Monk—didn't let his music in, even as I liked the rest of the band—Larry Gales, Ben Riley, and Charlie Rouse.

Monk behaved in ways that exceeded anything I considered normal. He might get up from the piano and seem to wander aimlessly while Charlie and the rhythm section played. Sometimes he did a kind of private, lurching, flat-footed shuffle dance—not unlike the rhythms in his playing, apparently unconcerned about how it might look to the listeners. I found it distracting and bizarre and beyond any kind of behavior I would have expected from other musicians or that I might have allowed myself. It made me unnecessarily afraid of him and contributed to my blocking out his music. What a loss for me!

Years later, I've been able to bring students to an immediate appreciation of Monk's music by describing its aesthetic boundaries before they hear it—telling them to imagine Michelangelo sculpting the *David* in marble with chisels and fine abrasives until every surface is perfect. Then imagine another sculptor with equally ambitious artistic impulses who has only felled logs, a chainsaw, and ropes to lash together the shapes he's able to create. You'd have to stand back from such a sculptor's work, look at the big picture and not be distracted by a lack of fine surfaces. With that introduction, the understanding is immediate and almost universal.

Another thing that allowed me to miss the value of Monk's music, and some other things that also took time for me to develop appreciation for, was the proliferation of available good jazz—not necessarily *great* jazz but an overwhelming quantity of good jazz. Jazz masterpieces emerge from an atmosphere of generally good jazz received by an audience that appreciates and understands it.

The world of music today is not even remotely comparable to what surrounded me for the formative part of my life. Machinery and mechanical contraptions have made the creation of sound recordings available to people with no musical training or experience, and the results resemble the machines that make them more than they represent anything that relates to my experience as a living person—or even the humanity of the people manipulating the machines. Now musicians and dancers often sound and look more like machines than people.

Charlie Parker's vocabulary was still at the root of my music, but that language was being leavened by my exposure to the breadth of jazz repertoire. I wasn't forgetting Bartok or Bud, but I was paying more attention to Ellington, Strayhorn, and Monk and making a conscious effort to keep my music sounding natural.

The National Jazz Ensemble found a concert space in Greenwich Village. Alan Austill, Dean of the New School, offered their 500-seat auditorium as a regular venue for our New York performances. Hank O'Neal, owner of Chiaroscuro Records, supplied various support, including almost unlimited use of rehearsal and recording time in his studio on Christopher Street. We made two recordings for Chiaroscuro that documented the band in its early stages.

It was always a problem getting the jazz audience to focus on the piece instead of the personalities. I don't know where I got the idea that I was going to change jazz audience habits, but I kept trying.

We hired well-known soloists at each New York concert—paralleling the design of most symphony programs. They played in the second half, and we enjoyed picking out good pieces for them—sometimes writing pieces for them or arranging something for our band that they'd written.

Some brought music they thought would fit our needs and had the kindness to leave copies in our library. The band loved playing with the soloists, and we had a bunch of incredible ones. Bill Evans, Gerry Mulligan, Tommy Flanagan, Hank Jones, Barry Harris, Roy Eldridge, Mike Brecker, Budd Johnson, Carrie Smith, Bob James, Herbie Hancock, Lee Konitz, Jim Hall, Pat Martino, Slide Hampton, Art Farmer, and Phil Woods were all guests.

Roy Eldridge was particularly affected by the response the band showed him. Everyone loved him and his music, and Roy was taken by surprise at the depth of appreciation he found. There were moments when he was in tears, and we, in turn, were moved by this great artist's open emotional response to our interest in him. We felt we were giving back something to Roy and all he represented. Those chances don't come often enough.

But there were frustrations too. We never did figure out a way to focus attention on the repertoire itself. How were we going to keep this music alive if no one recognized its importance?

15

THE JAZZ EDUCATION INDUSTRIAL COMPLEX

We got no help from the jazz education system, which was becoming an industry with its own marketing rules.

Big 3 Music published four of our Ellington transcriptions and four other compositions and arrangements from our library in an attempt to crack the high school and college jazz band market. But the schools were as inundated with garbage as the world of popular music, and there was a lot of financial investment in the status quo.

We approached the National Association of Jazz Educators for help, only to find people either ignorant of musical values that were meaningful to us or committed to serving the system from which they were deriving benefits. David Berger and I started attending their yearly conventions. We were trying to win converts for a repertoire we could defend as having the quality that's existed for centuries in the tradition of classical music education.

School music publishers and jazz educators are locked in a commercial embrace as vulgar and pandering as anything in the world of pop-music marketing. Except for a handful of schools whose programs are directed by enlightened musicians, what's played in school jazz programs bears no resemblance to what attracted me when I was a young musician. If I'd heard what was played in most of those schools when I was first exposed to jazz, I'd have run back to Beethoven and Mozart without a second thought.

Jazz teachers, attempting to reach their students, use cheap arrangements of even cheaper TV themes, or pop hits, to avoid having to introduce young people to new musical experiences. Yet all the while, they claim that's what is necessary to get them to accept jazz.

Whatever the kids are accepting, perhaps it would be better if they did not.

Consider a high school drama teacher suggesting a TV sitcom script for a student production because it's accessible to young people who don't know Thornton Wilder or Shakespeare. That's the same premise on which the school Jazz Ensemble system is based.

In a standard school jazz repertoire, the rhythmic complexities that produce swing are minimized, and what remains are almost always written in concerted passages for the whole band. There's little Ellingtonian polyphony, not much from the New Orleans tradition. Slow pieces most often move in turgid harmonic plodding, over which a soloist is supposed to create inspired melody. Rhythm in slow-tempo pieces is restricted to the rhythm section, as if subdivisions smaller than half notes were beyond the understanding of young wind players.

Count Basie's wonderful, already simple, dance music style is purveyed by school music publishers in a further simplified form that ought to insult the intelligence of a bright high school musician. Other pieces sound like bad marching band music with rock rhythm section parts.

Typically, when an art becomes institutionalized, it acquires partial protection from the vagaries of commerce, and its practices stiffen. By the time I began looking for a teaching job in the early 1970s, university music departments were adding jazz programs, and both those things were happening.

Methods of teaching classical music developed over hundreds of years, and in most institutions, they are repertory-based. After learning the basics—how to negotiate an instrument and play simple ditties—students are introduced to accepted classic pieces. They are given earlier, usually less technically demanding works, then they are gradually moved through the history of music, getting exposed to more contemporary music as they acquire experience, technique, and understanding.

The effective results of this method are resoundingly established, and there should be no theoretical reason for jazz departments to choose a different model. But the difficulty in finding published versions of jazz repertoire was largely responsible for forcing jazz schools to adopt a theory-based system instead.

Bach and Mozart are in the public domain. Their music is readily available in well-researched and beautiful editions. In the jazz world, professional jazz compositions are still under copyright protection, owned by publishing companies that collect royalties but have no economic reason to actually print music. The market for published scores and parts of worthy professional jazz compositions is too small to justify the expense of preparation and distribution by publishers who do print music for schools. They'd have to pay substantial fees to publishers that own the rights; the financial incentive is not there.

So, instead of publishing real Jazz Ensemble music—Ellington, Basie, or any number of other sources of material written for professional musicians—school music publishers created a glutted market of watered-down arrangements made easy (unchallenging technically and musically). Most are void of the very details that make the originals come alive.

That was bad enough, but publishers could sell still more music if they commissioned school jazz band arrangements of TV themes and vapid pop tunes. The school jazz publishing industry filled institutions with these pieces and poorly conceived original compositions designed to appeal to adolescent sensibility. Jazz departments were inundated with publications but not good music. No such condition exists for students in other fields. English students read beyond children's books; theater students perform in adult plays.

Of course, young classical musicians played music specifically written for students but soon graduated to easily accessible pieces from the classic repertoire. In junior high school, we played "The January February March," a charming enough piece written for student orchestra by the fine composer Don

Gillis, and moved on to Dvorak's "New World Symphony." Our orchestra director understood that the intellectual and spiritual benefits of real-world music outweighed the struggle with its technical challenges. No one seemed to think we'd be unprepared to understand and be rewarded by the music, or that its difficulties were beyond us. (Nothing against well-written music for students. Henry Purcell's "Dido and Aeneas," written to be performed by a girls' school at the end of the seventeenth century, remains a masterpiece.)

This paucity of respectable material was a significant factor in directing the tenets of jazz education away from *repertoire*-driven to *theory*-driven. So students who had never learned to play "When the Saints Go Marching In" were taught the two scales that relate to the modal harmony of "So What" and told to improvise on them. Yet they hadn't played enough music to acquire a vocabulary of phrases and figures.

Since jazz was being taught with more emphasis on theoretical elements, which conveniently succumb to being written and cataloged, than on listening and remembering, many things became over-simplified. Swing all eighth notes. Play them as if they were a quarter-note triplet followed by an eighth-note triplet. Never mind that real jazz eighth notes are as varied as the pronunciation of "o" in English: frog, for, look, old, food, women. . .!

Schools are mostly designed for the institution's convenience and efficiency and only coincidently in the students' best interests. Nevertheless, classical music education has managed to turn out musicians who know a broad range of music, while that's not the case for most jazz schools.

If the people who run jazz programs want to gain the respect they believe their classical music education counterparts enjoy, the very least they must do is something equally respectable. They may never gain the respect they want in this society, but what they are now doing is aesthetically indefensible and educationally questionable.

Still, even with young musicians being open to learning from the experience of someone who's been in circumstances they might admire, the situations they confront have changed enough that decisions I might have made earlier may not fully apply. Nevertheless, there are things I'd like to be able to share that are not so easy to express in ways that don't have a shading of disapproval, even though I understand that younger musicians are necessarily influenced by their contemporary surroundings in ways that were not there when I was in similar stages of growth.

And I understand the pressure to adjust to changing musical tastes. Some of the problematic pressures encountered by young jazz musicians is that, for reasons both of fashion and financial considerations, musicians well-equipped to perform established pieces are encouraged to write their own material, and some are less well-prepared to do a good job of that. Those pressures are there for instrumentalists and singers alike, and they're not easy to resist. There are producers waiting to discover and exploit the next Joni Mitchell.

When I started playing jazz, one of the most attractive characteristics of the music was the way it was presented with neither excessive decoration nor over-simplification. My first experiences playing with other people were with the trio with Steve Kuhn and Arnie Wise and in various groups put together for gigs in clubs or informal concerts around Boston. Then there was the recording session for Tom Wilson with Cecil Taylor and John Coltrane, gigs in Europe with Bud Powell and others, and my entry into the New York scene in George Russell's sextet. In all those bands, the music was presented undiluted, with no sense that it needed smoothing or anything that might make it easier to digest.

And that situation prevailed in Bill's trio in the beginning while we played clubs and recorded for Orrin Keepnews at Riverside Records. Helen Keane became Bill's manager sometime in 1963 and signed him to a contract with Creed Taylor at Verve Records, certainly for more money than he could have been making at Riverside, and the first thing that happened was a trio recording with Gary Peacock in the bass chair I'd been filling for about two years. That happened with no notice to me—not from Helen, not from Bill. I learned of it when the record was released as *Trio 64*. I was back in the trio soon after,

Paul Motian left, Larry Bunker filled the drum chair, and we were back in the studio to record *Trio '65* under Helen and Creed's direction.

Orrin Keepnews' role as producer, as far as I could tell, was to organize the logistics of the sessions, book the engineer and studio, and perhaps discuss some elements of the repertoire with Bill. After that, we recorded the music, and Orrin and Bill selected the best takes and released the recordings. I wasn't aware of much more participation on Helen and Creed's part until *Trio '65* was released with my bass solo cut from the released version of "Who Can I Turn To?"

I never wanted for solo space in the trio, and there are plenty of bass solos on that recording. But every so often, you think you've hit your mark as a musician and played your best. In the studio playback of the chosen take of "Who Can I Turn To?", I thought I'd done that—taken the music from the point Bill handed it to me and carried it, unbroken and with added beauty and invention, to the point where he again took over. It was disappointing, not because I hadn't enough solo space but instead because that had been one take with which I'd been particularly satisfied. Maybe I'd played something that might stand in comparison with an Oscar Pettiford or Red Mitchell bass solo. That was my first experience with producers making decisions that interfered with musicians.

Of course, that wasn't the first time it had happened, but it was the first time it affected me. No one would have considered that kind of editing of anything I'd participated in before. Looking back on it, the moment seems to have been a precursor to other ways that Helen, Creed, and some other jazz producers were thinking—thinking about how to frame jazz differently, to smooth some of the rough edges and present it more like the popular music from which it had developed and expanded.

There were record companies that didn't do this: Prestige, Blue Note, Riverside, and Savoy were among them. And even some recordings on major labels like Columbia and RCA were still being released as undiluted jazz performances. But Creed Taylor, because he understood changing public taste, had a big influence on the companies he worked for—Verve and Impulse—and he soon had CTI, a company of his own. Creed's CTI productions took jazz musicians who'd developed their music in unadorned small groups and recorded them as soloists with large ensembles. Of course, it wasn't the first time that had been done; Charlie Parker with strings was well known. It was something Parker had wanted to do, and he played as well as he ever did on those recordings. But Creed turned what had seemed to be a special condition in which to hear jazz improvisation in the context of an arranged background into common commercial practice. And it sold records.

Jazz musicians with good reputations and careers as small group players grew larger audiences and made more money, even as the ensemble interplay of small group jazz was replaced by arranged backgrounds for large bands—sometimes good (Lalo Schifrin, Oliver Nelson), and sometimes, to my ears, less good. Creed Taylor wasn't a villain. He'd done a lot of good for a lot of fine musicians and produced many excellent jazz recordings. This was simply a packaging that responded to a public less prepared to hear and appreciate the subtle jazz rhythm section/soloist interplay than it was to hear jazz solos backed by a bigger but often less-detailed and less-distracting cushion of orchestral sound. Good as that might have been for a lot of fine jazz soloists, as a small-group bassist, it wasn't so good for me.

There's plenty of history of memorable jazz solos played against the background of written arrangements played by larger groups. Ellington soloists were often featured in concerto-like arrangements, and Miles Davis' collaborations with Gil Evans, produced by George Avakian with profits from Columbia's pop projects, turned out to be masterpieces. The difference between these things and the run-of-the-mill Creed Taylor productions was the level of development in the writing for the band and the space for rhythm section interplay to emerge.

More often today, everyone, especially young singers, is in danger of letting what starts out as personal style become a caricature as they respond to audience approval of decorative flourishes, by doing more of them than a focused performance of a song can handle—embellishment beyond the call of beauty.

16

PANNING FOR GOLD

There are two largely opposing views about what's been happening in jazz over the last forty or fifty years.

Most schools, journalists, broadcasters, recording companies (those that still exist), and commercial interests think any music containing improvisation over the background of a steady beat can be called jazz. This broad category includes all kinds of music lacking rhythmic subtlety and lilt, harmonic interest, and any relationship with Louis Armstrong, Charlie Parker, or Ellington. Some are simply crassly commercial, and some are driven by a desire to incorporate more European musical elements—not in itself necessarily a bad thing. Ellington, Strayhorn, John Lewis, Bill Evans, and Gil Evans have successfully integrated a greater proportion of European elements into music that was Afro-European fusion to begin with. But attempting to improvise music lacking key rhythmic, stylistic, and formal elements is misguided.

Using a paintbrush to carve a marble statue produces neither a painting nor a statue. Using jazz methods and techniques to create European music yields similar results. It fails both as jazz and non-jazz. Improvised music superimposed over mundane rock beats and dominating bass parts fares no better in connecting with core jazz elements but is included under its rubric among jazz generalists. Our local "jazz" radio station proudly announces its programming as "Jazz Without Borders," which makes as much sense as countries without borders. Anything with improvisation counts. Rhythmic subtlety, as well as melodic, harmonic, and textural contrasts and dramatic development, are rendered inconsequential to this definition of jazz. Improvisation is the only remaining common element. I don't hear it that way.

Jazz improvisation methods and practices are uniquely successful in creating a particular kind of music, with other key elements strongly represented: a satisfying and predetermined formal framework; a compelling rhythmic palette; a harmonic language that balances dramatic tension and resolution; and recognizable patterns of development both predetermined and spontaneous. Without these elements, the elements that created this Afro-European art form, improvisatory methods fall short of producing satisfying results. If the goal is good music with an essentially non-jazz, European aesthetic, the best approach is to use the methods of composers who've created durable music in that world.

Jazz at Lincoln Center stands in bold contrast to this view. The institution represents connection and continuity. Its artistic director, Wynton Marsalis, grew up in New Orleans, surrounded and influenced by both jazz culture and the contemporary popular music of his youth. If you can't find threads leading back to Armstrong, Morton, and Ellington, it's peripheral to JALC's interest. Over its thirty-year history, this organization has renewed interest in the significant repertoire of classic jazz compositions and commissioned new works that expand it without abandoning its values. The program has been an invaluable antidote to the prevailing jazz education system.

In addition, Lincoln Center Jazz Orchestra has maintained an international audience and employed a full-time big band of creative jazz musicians. But like every art institution, it has stifled certain advantageous expressive and free-wheeling elements of the art.

When the band was formed, Wynton had to learn to organize and run it from a then more experienced leader, David Berger, my former Jazz Ensemble partner. Under their joint leadership, a group of fully formed, experienced musicians gave the band a sophisticated, personal ensemble sound and well-developed solo personalities. But there was a price to pay: The musicians had different ideas of how things should go and were not shy in expressing them.

Wynton was unprepared to corral those disparate points of view. And he had the prescience to know that people would be unimpressed by older musicians in suits playing high-level jazz, even with consummate authority, while younger players speaking the musical language of previous generations would attract attention. So all but one of the experienced musicians—baritone sax player Joe Temperley—were let go and replaced with gifted young virtuoso players with little experience.

Joe Temperley's exceptionally expressive musical qualities and his reticence about expressing artistic disagreements kept him in his job for years. He sometimes complained to friends about shortcomings in the band but never did so to Wynton or his bandmates. And his musical contributions were unforgettable. No one since Harry Carney had played the baritone with such passionate beauty, and there were expressive elements of Joe's playing that even exceeded Carney's monumental achievements. Joe was a more fluent and spontaneous soloist and stood head and shoulders above all the younger players (except Wynton) in leaving an indelible impression every time he played. Joe was a master.

Now the band plays with stunning precision and deceptive ease. Demanding pyrotechnical ensembles come off without a hitch and everything's in tune and in time.

Yet neither ensemble passages nor solos have the expressive personality the older players brought. The younger players have repressed individuality in favor of uniformity. Some solos are more athletic than integral. Wynton is such a virtuoso and high-level improviser that he can exhibit nearly superhuman trumpet playing while developing coherently integrated solos. The other guys are uniformly good, just not as memorable.

JALC and the orchestra are maintaining continuity with what I see as the stream of quality jazz development. The problem is they are monolithic. They own most of the territory, and only those under their aegis get a chance to be heard.

By the time Jazz at Lincoln Center had become an official part of that organization in 1991, under Wynton Marsalis's leadership, there were helpful counterbalances to the discouraging condition of jazz education. To expand and broaden its reach, Lincoln Center gave Wynton the administrative and financial foundation necessary to support a permanent jazz repertory band with big public relations and education resources. Our National Jazz Ensemble had published four Ellington transcriptions almost twenty years before but were overwhelmingly outsold by jazz school music that sounded like a marching band with a rock rhythm section—they went largely unnoticed. Wynton cunningly circumvented the deeply entrenched culture of the mostly university-level jazz educator organizations and concentrated on high schools. He set up a well-organized and publicized yearly band competition and supplied the schools with free copies of Ellington's music. It was a brilliant idea. This has undone some of the earlier damage by raising thousands of high school students' awareness of good music and sending them on to university programs with a background in repertoire sometimes exceeding their teachers'.

So things have improved somewhat. And there have always been scattered pockets of quality education—informed teachers often overcoming less-informed administrations to maintain jazz integrity. While institutionalization of what was created as a consensual, popular art form has drawbacks, when there's no longer enough popular interest to support that art, institutions become its protectors.

Other small pockets of quality jazz creativity surely exist, but they're always nearly quashed by either the aesthetically impoverished commercial marketplace or by Wynton's overwhelming monopoly. He's devoted his life to creating and maintaining jazz culture to the benefit of the music and society. It just has left no room for competition.

I don't know how much more life there is left in natural-born, creative jazz—jazz outside of institutions—but the human spirit is impossible to subdue, and something inspired will pop up again somewhere, somehow, in some other way. If the era of most creative jazz is over, something else will have to take its place.

Nothing is more important to the way I hear and play music than playing syncopated cross-rhythms against a steady, underlying pulse. It's not anything I think about except in retrospect—figuring out how I arrived at this aspect of my musical character. It's just the way my internal music developed. I'm sure appreciation for a study pulse started with playing for square dances when I was twelve and, a few years later, hearing the bluegrass of Flatt and Scruggs, the strong folk music of the Weavers, Leadbelly, Sonny Terry and Brownie McGhee, The Duke of Iron and Josh White, and the pulse of the early jazz records I heard at home.

Then, without consciousness that it was happening, the freer juxtaposition of American speech patterns over the steady, dancing pulse that Louis Armstrong demonstrated in everything he played or sang became my rhythmic language. And my personal, quirky way of expressing those rhythms is the only sure thing that identifies my playing and my written music. (And it's much harder to write than it is to play. All written language is an impoverished version of language as it's spoken and heard.)

This background, and an appreciation of classical music rhythms, from Bach and Handel through Mozart, Beethoven, Brahms, Chopin, Verdi, Bizet, and on through Stravinsky and Bartok, is what led to what musical rhythm means to me, and a big part of why I was so perfectly prepared to be convinced, even bewitched, by Bill Evans's rhythmic language. I heard in Bill's playing many things that resonated with my background: always at least a hint of blues inflection; micro-dynamic variety more than matching the greatest classical pianists; harmony informed by twentieth-century French and Spanish composers; and lines with the bebop bite of Bud Powell, the grace of Charlie Parker, and a composer's developmental logic. All of that had to have had a subliminal effect on how I heard Bill's music and what magnetized me to it. But it was the rhythm above all that I intuitively understood and loved.

And none of this was a part of the fusion music that had emerged in the late 1960s and early 1970s—claiming to be jazz's new direction. I'd been part of, if not the avant-garde, at least in the forefront of jazz in the public's attention for a few years. Now there was no place for me in what many of my friends were doing.

Rock had marginalized music I loved, nearly to the point of obliterating it, and many talented, well-trained jazz musicians accepted it as simply another style of popular music to provide fodder for jazz exploration and embellishment. I don't believe it's an easy thing to live in a world in which one is ensnared in a web of lies, and I know good jazz musicians for whom embracing rock music and incorporating it into their work was not in the least troublesome. So it seemed unlikely that their motivation was an entirely venal one of attention-getting and financial survival—they still must find what they're doing not only acceptable but also interesting and musically rewarding.

I think that's likely to be true for enormously gifted people like Bob James and Herbie Hancock. And Quincy Jones has been able to embrace a broad expanse of popular and commercial music genres. All of them seem like honest people, and all of them are highly accomplished jazz musicians. But what worked for them didn't work for me. So much of what I value in the jazz that I grew to love is specifically excluded from the inclusion of pop rock into jazz that it results in what, to me, is an exclusion of essential qualities.

Most of the bass gigs in recording studios became Fender electric bass guitar gigs. The instrument is loud, relatively easy to play, and can be easily and consistently recorded. The style of overbearing and mostly repetitive Fender bass parts prevailed in popular music. There wasn't much use for the subtleties you could draw from a bass violin, and it was much harder to get a good recording of the quieter acoustic instrument. I took a few Fender bass gigs—somewhere I was required to come up with coherent bass parts for incoherent music created in the studio by untrained kids ignorant of anything about music.

Producers operated under the illusion that, since the Beatles were successful, they could take almost any teenager who thought of himself or herself as a potential songwriter and make a star. (Actually, all too often, they could.) I was an alien in that environment—exploited for my musical knowledge and ability and paid decent union scale but with no share of any potential profit, even though I was being asked to make substantial creative contributions beyond just playing my part. It was insulting. Bass players were still needed, but not bass players who did what I'd been focused on doing. There was no place for me.

It was easier for other instrumentalists to make the shift away from the rhythmic interplay of soloist against the matrix of rhythm section form and pulse. Horn players, pianists, and guitarists had fewer things to change than I'd have had to change in order for their parts to fit into the more rigid rhythmic mold of fusion style. In order to play fusion bass parts, whether on the electric bass or on the bass violin, I'd have had to abandon all the hard-won development of rhythmic vocabulary I'd acquired and limited my playing to repetitive patterns that might have felt good for a few measures but ultimately felt boring, restrictive, and unlike the graceful physical movements that I hoped my rhythms inspired. It didn't relate to my mind or to my body.

I remember making an overture to a fine jazz player who'd formed a commercially successful fusion band, perhaps not openly asking for inclusion but implying that I'd like to have some work. His reply was not unfriendly but clearly told me he didn't think this was for me. And, of course, I knew it and needn't have asked. I was just feeling left out—left out of something that had little musical meaning for me but was getting attention. It wasn't that I wanted the music—just some attention, and that didn't justify my inclusion. Sometimes we're driven by impulses that are not in our best interest.

Over time, little of that music has endured. I don't hear young jazz musicians playing fusion compositions, and I don't remember any of them except Joe Zawinul's Birdland.

What remains of that trend is the continued impoverishment of popular music form and rhythm.

Fusion ideas are fashionable, and I've been involved in a few projects that have been designed around the contrived pasting of one musical language on another. Claude Bolling, a good jazz pianist and composer, wrote a suite for flute and jazz piano trio for the French flute virtuoso Jean-Pierre Rampal. When Bill Goodwin and I played the drum and bass parts with them at a concert in Carnegie Hall sometime in the late 1970s, the recording of the piece had already become so popular the hall was not only filled to capacity but there were also listeners seated in chairs on stage filling it to within a few feet of us. The piece remained popular for longer than I expected and spawned another similar piece Bolling wrote for cellist Yo-Yo Ma. But when I listen to the piece now, it strikes me as it did then, as a pastiche of inauthentic baroque (how would it be possible to write with full commitment and authenticity in that style with twentieth-century ears?) and overly precious and restricted jazz, alternating back and forth and rarely combining. Both musicians are fine players, but neither is doing what they do best. And the rhythm section parts are superficial. The piece would be missing little in their absence. It still sounds like classical music for those who neither know nor like classical music and jazz for those who don't know or like jazz. There's nothing authentic about that music.

A couple of years ago, here in Portland, I was asked by a good Indian dancer/choreographer to write and play some music with some Indian Carnatic-style musicians she was bringing from India for the performance—another fusion idea. "These two things have some similarities. Let's mix them together and see what we can produce." Both groups of musicians were excellent, and everyone made the maximum effort to understand the music. The American jazz musicians had a superficial understanding of Carnatic music, and the Indian musicians certainly knew something about how jazz music functioned. No one was ignorant. But the result was two groups of musicians engaged in crosstalk in two languages. There was no fusion, and there could not have been any under the quickly contrived circumstances of a couple of hours of rehearsal. It doesn't work. It takes a long time and continued exposure to become conversant in another language or for two languages to meld and become one.

Jazz is a prime example of a real and successful fusion—one that took a century or two to develop; a fusion that no one contrived and that happened despite strenuous efforts to prevent it. It's a result of the insidious intrusion of West African culture into European music and the equally stealthy influence of European music into the ears of the West Africans in America. Nothing is recognizable as American absent the influence of West African culture. Anything culturally American is a fusion—a natural one resulting inevitably from the cohabitation of at least two powerful sources. Contrived fusions remain contrived.

I remember someone's description of Beethoven's music as being full of surprises that become inevitable in retrospect. The best jazz strikes me the same way. I hear Charlie Parker start to play, and I can't not listen. I'm compelled to follow, gripped by the succession of sounds. Another human is opening his mind to anyone who understands the language and will listen, exposing thoughts and feelings I understand—that are meaningful to me. There's a logic—structural and emotional—that insists I follow. One event happens and the next one continues the thought, creating a pattern that carries me. I'm bewitched by a story I want to hear to completion. I become totally engaged in sharing the experience of another human being.

The best composers accomplish this. Enduring masterpieces of Western music have this effect. There are countless examples—from Handel and Purcell through Stravinsky and Bartok. The best jazz does the same, and I want that experience as often as I can afford to give myself to it—to abandon self-awareness and lose myself in the immediacy of music. And jazz does this for me in a most personal way. It speaks to my experience with all I know of European classical form and developmental logic, and the rhythms and inflections of what I know of America, its idioms of speech, its humor— even its body language.

When music is being performed effectively, on the most essential level, it doesn't matter if it's been written in advance. A valid performance convinces you it's being created in real time. That's the art of believable performance, and its characteristics supersede style. A fine string quartet "invents" a convincing version of Beethoven or Bartok, and Thelonious Monk plays Crepuscule with Nellie—the same chorus, played twice, in his calculated, hesitant, stumbling, lurching timing—and you hear him invent it in real time. You are captivated, even though you've heard him play it almost the same way before. It takes a good piece and a convincing dose of emotional spontaneity to do that. And it's thrilling.

But if you add to that formula a degree of controlled improvisation, an element of new music with one phrase following the previous one, exposing insight into the logic of the improviser, and continue that in the moment, extending it—unbroken, as long as the mood can hold—and you do it with impeccable, riveting jazz rhythm, that's as exciting as it gets.

It takes balance of planning, prepared vocabulary, and spontaneous impulse to accomplish this. It's a high-wire act at warp speed, knowing where the wire is, staying on it, and choreographing a dance across it that convinces the observer that he or she could do it, that it would fit their body, if they only had the control. It's high-level human endeavor that thrills and enthralls understanding humans with vicarious participation.

The past only supplies subconscious underpinning, and there's no room to imagine the future beyond what's leading to the next musical moment. You have to be overwhelmingly enveloped by "now"—unaware of, and undistracted by, anything else.

Epilogue

The Last Gig with Bill

In August 1977, Bill Evans called to ask if I'd sub for Eddie Gomez, the bass player who'd been playing with him since I'd left the trio. Eddie had to reschedule some things and couldn't play a concert booked at the Eastman School of Music. I agreed and met Bill and drummer Elliot Zigmund at the airport for the flight to Rochester. Bill had added some new material, and there were a few things I'd forgotten, so he sketched them out on airline stationery. We played a successful concert that was later broadcast by the local public television station. It was wonderful to play with Bill again.

Since leaving the trio, I'd seen Bill only once before this. I went to hear him play at the Village Gate, where we had a friendly conversation between sets. He was momentarily clean. I told him his extraordinary skills meant he could write symphonic music, an opera, or a show. Bill responded that it was beyond him, saying it was all he could do to hold his life together.

My playing had become an important part of the National Jazz Ensemble sound after I'd abandoned my conducting role, but the power of twelve wind players can do a lot to obscure the effects of bass nuances.

My creative life as a bass player didn't stop, but that channel for expression was considerably narrowed. So when Bill called again in the next year and asked me to play with him and drummer Philly Joe Jones at the Village Vanguard, I was eager to do it.

I've had luck with drummers and rewarding musical relationships with dozens of them. I've played with almost every drummer I admired in one situation or another. It's easier to say that I never played with Art Blakey and only once with Elvin Jones (when he was drunk and not up to his usual standards) than to go through the long list of gratifying collaborations that did happen, but I'd never played with Philly Joe.

He was as high on my list of admired musicians as anyone. Joe had a unique drive in his playing and a special way of using the form of the piece to create opportunities for variety and change of texture. He was smart about timbre, too, and played solos saving the cymbal sound for the return of the accompanying texture and gaining variety by leaving something out. Besides that, he left rests in his solos, making the percussive sounds mark the beginnings and ends of silences that became as important as the sounds themselves. He was a swinger, and he was smart. I wanted some of that.

Eddie Gomez had recently left the trio after an eleven-year tenure, and Bill was looking for a replacement. Other bassists, including the excellent Mike Moore, had been playing with him at the Village Vanguard a night or two at a time. But a new problem had surfaced in the music. Bill and Philly Joe, both notoriously heroin users, had switched drug allegiances and were now intravenously injecting harrowing amounts of cocaine—stimulating them to the point that the music was always rushing. The changes in metabolism affected their perception, and they unwittingly, and constantly, plunged forward. The music didn't usually lurch; it just tipped forward off its center of metric gravity and got a little faster all the time. Besides this, Bill was starting the pieces at faster tempos than he was used to, so that by the end of the tune it got quite unreasonable. The speeding up was mostly gradual, and the music was otherwise as superb as I expected it to be. It wasn't ugly or erratic, just accelerating in a way that degraded part of its rhythmic power by cheating the notes of their full metric value. This drove the other bass players nuts, but I can be as mulishly resistant to rushing on the bass as Mel Lewis could be at the drums; I took it as a challenge.

I dug in my heels and held my ground, anchoring the music as well as I could, but I always had to think about it. I could never let down my guard and relax or the tempo would just take off; Bill and Joe couldn't control it. The only time the tempo would surge out of range from my control was at the beginning of bass solos when I'd stop playing time or accompanying figures, and there'd be a moment's rest in the bass part. Then Joe would leap ahead and increase the tempo a couple of notches. I could mitigate that by starting each bass solo with a clear, emphatic rhythmic figure. Joe would respond and drop back to a place close enough to where we had been that I could tolerate it.

If this sounds difficult or disturbing, it was a little. But it was also challenging fun to try to make things come out the way they should. Everything about the music was exquisite except for this one characteristic, and even as ever-present as it was, it couldn't ruin the rest.

Bill was despairing of finding someone to take the job and had concerts and a TV broadcast coming up in The Netherlands in a week or so. He needed someone he could rely on and asked if I'd rejoin the trio.

I didn't know what to do. I knew it was a career move that would restore public visibility, but the price would be relegating The National Jazz Ensemble activities to times between gigs with Bill; I didn't see how it would survive under those circumstances. Bill's schedule had become much more active since I'd left, and downtimes were short and unpredictable. I was torn.

I knew there was one more bass player Bill wanted to hear. A young man trained in the North Texas State jazz program who'd been playing with Woody Herman's band was flying in at his own expense to audition for Bill. Marc Johnson turned out to be a terrific musician, and the die was cast. I had told Bill I'd bail him out if he needed me but needed to continue the other things I was doing if he found someone suitable. Now, even if I'd wanted to change my mind, Marc's appearance at the right time, with the right skills, made it too late. Soon after that, Joe LaBarbera replaced Philly Joe.

A little more than two years later, on September 15, 1980, Bill succumbed to the physical toll of his addictions and died.

We are more than a little created by our surroundings, and sometimes, for some people, as our surroundings change, so do we—sometimes out of convenience, sometimes out of necessity. Popular music deteriorated sometime roughly in the mid-1960s. Some would say it simply changed. And many creative musicians, those who could, and those for whom the previous aesthetic world held no overpowering control, changed with it. We are all subject to the necessity for adaptive change. It's part of the human condition, and it's happened to me in innumerable ways, but you can't shake my belief in what remains musically meaningful. You can't make me believe the popular music environment of the early twenty-first century, including its theater music and film music, contains much of anything that reaches as deeply or remains as durable as Louis Armstrong, Fats Waller, Duke Ellington, Berlin, Gershwin, Arlen, Frank Loesser, Charlie Parker, Monk, Mingus, Ray Charles, or Bill Evans. And I'm not convinced that the circumstances of contemporary "classical" music are all that much better. The fact that so much attention is paid to what amounts to musical finger painting, and that such juvenilia is so popular, and makes so much money, that it's written about with credulity in otherwise respectable journals, doesn't make the comparison any less ludicrous.

In art, as in love, durability is what counts.

INDEX

Acoustic Research, 64
Adderly, Nat, 192
aesthetics, 52, 71–72
Africa, 58
Aks, Harold, 16
alcohol, 103
"All About Rosie," 192
Allen, Woody, 123, 124, 127
"All Set," 38
"All the Things You Are," 164
Alonge, Ray, 157
American Federation of Musicians, 70
"American Patrol," 162, 181
"Angkor Wat," 179
"Anthropology," 165
Anya and Superman (Broadway show), 157
Arenal, Electa, 20
Arlen, Harold, 27, 162, 164
Armstrong, Louis, 10, 162, 163, 165, 180, 193, 211
Aronov, Benny, 179
arrogance, 96
Arvanitas, George, 57

Austill, Alan, 196
Avakian, George, 205

Babbitt, Milton, 38
baby boomers, 164
Bacharach, Burt, 169, 171
Bad Holmen, 136
Baez, Joan, 65
Bailey, Donald, 29;
  trio with, 139–40
Baker, Chet, 4, 60
Baker, Dave, 68
Ballet, Whitney, 71–72
Ballets U.S.A., 1
Bancroft, Anne, 46
Bangkok, 115
banjo, 9–10
Barber, Phil, 46
Barber, Stephanie, 46
Bardot, Brigitte, 58
Barrow, George, 90
Bartok, 173, 215
Basie, Count, 13, 177–78, 180, 192
bass lines, 105, 107–8

222 / INDEX

Bauman, Mordecai, 9, 12, 14–15, 15–16, 17
the Beatles, 212–13
"Beautiful Dreamer," 162
bebop, 195–96
Beck, Joe, 155
Becker, Lee, 91
Behrman, S. N., 16
Beiderbecke, Bix, 10, 193
Belafonte, Harry, 111
Belle Moskowitz (Israels, E.), 7
Benjamin, Ben, 59, 85
Benjamin, Joe, 38, 76–77, 89, 191
Bennett, Lou, 57
Benny, Jack, 77
Berg, Richard, 157
Berger, David, 128–29, 180, 199, 208–9
Berhman, David, 16
Berkshire Music Center, 45, 47; fellowship at, 171–73
Berlin, Irving, 8, 13, 27, 92
Bernhardt, Warren, 119
Bernstein, Leonard, 46
Berry, Bill, 143
Big 3 Music, 199
Bill Evans at Town Hall, 143–44
Birdland, 213
birth, 7
Birth of the Cool, 85
Bishop, Walter, Jr., 125
"Black Bottom Stomp," 191
Blakey, Art, 28, 63, 156, 195, 218
Bley, Carla, 68, 74
Blitzstein, Marc, 10, 14, 55
Blue Angel, 127
bluegrass, 211
"Blue in Green," 4
Blue Note (club), 57, 59, 73, 87
Blue Note Record, 204
blues, 186

Bob Crosby and the Bobcats, 191
"Body and Soul," 163
Bolling, Claude, 213–14
Bossa Nova, 158
Boston, jazz scene in, 24–27
Bourbon, Jean-Pierre, 58–59
Brandeis Festival of the Arts, 39
Brandeis University, 33, *35*, *36*, 37–38, 92
Brazilian music, 158
Brecker, Mike, 197
Brookline, 40
Brooklyn College, 174–75
Brookmeyer, Bob, 47, 112, 135, 143
Brown, Clifford, 29, 30, 63
Brown, Garnett, 151
Brown, Lucy, 89
Brown, Oscar, Jr., 127
Brown, Patti, 57
Brown, Ray, 110
Brubeck, Dave, 94, 193
Bruce, Lenny, 126
Buffington, Jimmy, 38
Bullock, Hiram, 155
Bunch, John, 76, 128
Bunker, Larry, 103, 120–21, 137, 204
Burnett, Carol, 111
Burrell, Kenny, 51, 76–77
Burton, Gary, 112–13, 114, 125, 135
Byard, Jaki, 26
Byas, Don, 58
Byrd, Donald, 28, 125

Café Au Go Go, 127, 137, 158
Calder, Alexander, 90
Cameron, Jay, 119
"Camptown Races," 162
Canterino, Sonny, 126

Caribbean music, 124
Carisi, John, 100, 152, 179
Carlin, George, 113
Carnatic music, 214
Carney, Harry, 209
Catlett, Buddy, 57
Cavett, Dick, 127
cello, 11
Chaloff, Margaret, 39–40
Chaloff, Serge, 29, 39–40
Chambers, Joe, 140
Chambers, Paul, 110
Chapin, Earl, 157
Chares, Teddy, 38
Charles, Ray, 192
Charles, Teddy, 148
Chazin, Gigi, 20, 33–34
"Chega de Saudade," 60
Chevalier, Simone, 59–60
Chiaroscuro Records, 196
Childers, Buddy, 76
Chittison, Herman, 27–28
Chopin, Frédéric, 8–9, 88, 93
chord roots, 3–4
Clancy Brothers, 136
Clark, Sonny, 4, 88
Clarke, Kenny, 54, 158
classical music education, 201–2
Cleveland Heights, 9–12
Cleveland Institute, 12–13
Cleveland Institute of Music, 9
Cleveland Orchestra, 12–13
Clevenger, Dale, 157
Clooney, Rosemary, 51
Cohan, George M., 12
Cohn, Al, arrangements of, 145
Cole, Nat, 13, 137
Coleman, Ornette, 5, 60, 74;
  LaFaro and, 166–67;
  press recognition of, 69–71

Collins, Judy, relationship with, 138–39
Coltrane, John, 42, 43, 45, 192, 203;
  in popular culture, 165–66
"Coltrane Time," 45
Columbia Records, 65, 204
Commanday, Betty (grandmother), 7–8
Commanday, Frank (grandfather), 7–8
Commanday, Irma (mother), 7–9, 15–16
Commanday, Robert (uncle), 8–9
communication, of musicians, 43
composition, 171–72;
  of Evans, B., 94–95, 171, 184, 186–87, 194–95;
  improvisation and, 183–84;
  in jazz, 183;
  of Monk, 194
"Concerto for Cootie," 191
Contemporary Records, 139
Cook, Peter, 136
Cooper, Clarence, 123
Copeland, Keith, 181
Copenhagen, 92, 136, 146
Copland, Aaron, 46
Copley Square, 26
"The Copper Kettle," 65
"Corn Cob," 9–10
Cosby, 124
"Cottontail," 165
Cowell, Henry, 16
Crosby, Bing, 27, 51
Crosby, Bob, 191
Crosby, Israel, 2, 3–4, 88
"The Cruel Mother," 65
Crumb, George, 173
CTI, 205
Cuban music, 49–50, 124

Daniels, Eddie, 143
Dankworth, John, 135
Davis, Miles, 4, 57, 63, 85, 156, 195;
  Evans, B., and, 98–99;
  improvisation of, 183–84
Dawson, Alan, 49
Decca, 74
Dehner, Dorothy, 16
de Kooning, Bill, 72–73
Deliverance (film), 124
Deloget, Marcel, 62
DePriest, Jimmy, 49
"Desafinado," 60
Dickens, Hugo, 49
"Dido and Aeneas," 202
Diehl, Eddie, 49–50
DiStasio, Gene, 26
"Django," 47
D'Lugoff, Art, 127
Dodgion, Dottie, 75, 76
Dodgion, Jerry, 143
"Dolphin Dance," 179–80
Dolphy, Eric, 92
"Don't Fence Me In," 13
Dorham, Kenny, 28, 42–43
Dorough, Bob, 47
"Double Clutching," 45
Driscoll, Phil, 33–34
drummers, 140–41
Duvivier, George, 135
Dvorak, Antonin, 12–13, 202

Eastman School of Music, 217
education: classical music, 201–2; jazz, 199–202, 210
Edwards, Buttercup, 55
Eldridge, Roy, 197
Ellington, Duke, 27, 101, 142, 162, 165, 167, 177, 194, 208;
  Israels, C., on, 179–80, 191;
  transcriptions of, 210
Elliott, Don, 40–41
Ellis, Don, 74–75
Evans, Bill, 2, 38, 69, *144*, 167, 197, 208;
  as composer, 94–95, 171, 184, 186–87, 194–95;
  Davis, M., and, 98–99;
  death of, 220;
  drug use of, 97, 102–3, 133–34;
  harmonic system of, 99–100, 106–7;
  LaFaro and, 4, 106;
  last gig with, 217–20;
  Motian and, 108;
  in New York, 143–44;
  personality of, 98;
  play style of, 87–90, 99;
  quitting trio with, 146;
  relationship with, 41, 103, 122–23, 136, 145–48;
  reputation of, 4–5, 131–32;
  in Sweden, 134–36;
  at the Trident, 131–32;
  Wise and, 140;
  working with, 92–96, 98–99, 101–2, 119–20, 203–4
Evans, Gil, 152, 179, 205, 208
"Every Tub," 192

family, 191
Farmer, Art, 38, 51, 112, 197
Feinberg, Nina, 124
Fender electric bass guitar, 212
Fischer, Clare, 120
"Five," 94, 96, 186
Five Spot, 5, 67, 69, 73, 125, 127, 195
Flanagan, Tommy, 4, 88, 195, 197
Flatt, Lester, 124
Flatt and Scruggs, 211

Fol, Raymond, 57
folk music, 10
Fontana, Carl, 76
Foss, Lukas, 46
Foster, Stephen, 161
Franco, Francisco, 61
Freedman, Bob, 192
free jazz:
  critique of, 166;
  improvisation in, 166–67
Freidman, Don, 87
fusion, 165, 212;
  Israels, C., on, 213–14

Gadd, Steve, 155
Galbraith, Barry, 38
Gales, Larry, 195
Gardner, Ava, 61
Garfunkel, Art, 153
Garland, Red, 4, 40
Garner, Errol, 87–88, 167
Garrison, Jimmy, 49
Garvey, John, 47
Gaudry, Michel, 56
Gebler, Jean-Pierre, 59–60
"The Gentle Lion," 180
Gentry, Eve, 16, 21
George Russell Sextet, 74
Germany, 116
Gershwin, George, 8, 13, 162, 186
Gershwin, Ira, 8, 13, 64
Getz, Pamela, 112, 137
Getz, Stan, 40–41, 112, 137, 141, 148;
  relationship with, 113–15, 115–18
"Giant Steps," 192
Gilberto, João, 60
Gillis, Don, 201–2
Gilmore, Steve, 181
Giuffre, Jimmy, 38, 47

Golson, Benny, 112, 156
Gomez, Eddie, 217, 218
Goodman, Benny, 10, 75–76, 87, 193
Goodwin, Bill, 151, 179, 180–81, 214
Gordon, Joe, 29, 42
Gossett, Lou, Jr., 46
Gould, Morton, 9–10
Grant, Rodgers, 49–50
Green, Johnny, 163
Greenhouse, Bernard, 9
Green Street Bar, 51
Greenwich Village, 196
Grey, Sonny, 133
Grey, Susan, 133
Guérin, Roger, 56
guitar, 9–10, 11–12
Gyllene Cirkeln, 134

Haden, Charlie, 110, 112
Half Note Club, 126
Hall, Jim, 29, 47, 125, 137, 158, 195, 197;
  as guitarist, 63, 110
Hall, Trully, 179
Halliday, Lin, 51
Hammond, John, 119
Hampton, Slide, 197
Hancock, Herbie, 125, 135, 179–82, 188, 197, 212
Handel, George Frideric, 215
Hanna, Jake, 51
Hanna, Roland, 128
Hanson, Margot, 154;
  marriage to, 169–70;
  pregnancy of, 172
Harburg, Yip, 64
Hard Driving Jazz, 45
Harewood, Al, 76–77, 112
Haritounian, Vartan, 26

"Harlem Air Shaft," 191
Harris, Barry, 4, 126, 197
Harris, Joe, 57
Hart, Lorenz, 64
Harth, Sidney, 15, 16
Harth, Teresa, 16
Hastings, Hal, 157
Hawes, Hampton, 29;
    trio with, 139–40
Hawkins, Coleman, 163
Hayes, Louis, 42–43
Haynes, Roy, 115, 125
Heath, Albert "Tootie," 128
Heath, Percy, 110
Hebrew Immigration Aid
    Society, 7
Hefti, Neal, 141, 178
Henderson, Fletcher, 178,
    179, 180
Herbert, Greg, 192
Herman, Woody, 177–78
heroin, 97, 102–4
Hickory House, 103
high school, 11
High School of Performing Arts,
    19–20, 22, 28, 34, 42–43
Hines, Gregory, 50
Hinton, Milt, 135
Hispanic-American music, 124
Hoblyn, Ian, 153
Hodges, Johnny, 195
Hogan, G. T., 55, 58
Holiday, Billie, 46, 67–68, 135
Holladay, Marv, 76
Holland America Line, 53
Hollywood, 120
Hot Five, 10
Hot Seven, 10
"How High the Moon," 164
Humair, Daniel, 56
Hunt, Joe, 75, 112, 179, 181

"I Got Rhythm," 96, 165, 186
improvisation, 3–4;
    composition and, 183–84;
    of Davis, 183–84;
    in free jazz, 166–67;
    on *Kind of Blue*, 184–85;
    of Parker, 183;
    successful, 167
Impulse, 205
Indian Hill summer camp, 16, 19,
    21, 22, 112, 124, 174–75
institutionalization of art,
    199–201
Intermodulation, 137
"In the Mood," 181–82
Ireland, 53–54
"I Should Care," 144
"Israel," 100
Israels, Carlos Lindner (father), 7
Israels, Chuck, *48, 109, 144*. See
    also specific topics
Israels, Elizabeth (sister), 7, 22, 46
Ives, Charles, 12

JALC. See Jazz at Lincoln Center
Jamal, Ahmad, 2, 3–4, 88
James, Bob, 153, 192, 197, 212
jazz, 10;
    in Boston, 24–27;
    composition in, 183;
    contemporary developments in,
    207–8;
    education, 199–201, 210;
    European music and, 208–9;
    formal underpinnings of,
    185, 188;
    harmonic progressions in, 105;
    historical development of,
    162–63, 214–15;
    misconceptions about, 104–5;
    in New York, 74;

in 1970s, 165;
in popular culture, 158–59, 163, 188–89, 204–5, 210–11;
public reception of, 137;
record label practices, 204–5;
rock music and, 189–90, 212;
slowdown in bookings, 156–58, 169;
standards, 186–87;
styles of, 163;
as surprise, 71–72;
symphony orchestras and, 177;
syncretic nature of, 214–15;
transcription of, 179;
in university departments, 174
Jazz at Lincoln Center (JALC), 208–10
jazz ensembles, 177–78
Jazz Goes to College, 193
"Jazz Me Blues," 10
Jazz Messengers, 156
Jazz Without Borders, 207–8
Jazz Workshop, 26–27
"Jeannie with the Light Brown Hair," 162
Jenkins, Artie, 49–50
"Jive at Five," 192
Jobim, Antônio Carlos, 60
Joffe, Charles, 124
Johansson, Jan, 134
Johnson, Budd, 197
Johnson, J. J., 154;
 recording with, 125–26
Johnson, Lyndon, 114, 116
Johnson, Marc, 219
Johnson, Michael, 50
Johnson, Osie, 135
Joio, Norman Dello, 10
"Jolly Chocolate," 192
Jones, Elvin, 218
Jones, Hank, 4, 88, 197, 212

Jones, Isham, 8, 13
Jones, Jimmy, 127
Jones, Philly Joe, 55, 158;
 Israels, C., playing with, 218–19
Jones, Quincy, 57
Jones, Thad, 192
Jordan, Louis, 13
Jordan, Michael, 50
Juilliard, 1, 31, 123

Kagan, Lenore, 11
Kahn, Gus, 8, 13
Kalina, Joyce, 48
Kallem, Herb, 148
Kapuscinski, Richard, 10
Karpe, Kenny, 50–51
Katz, Dick, 47, 180
Keane, Helen, 111, 142, 203–4
Keepnews, Orrin, 74, 96;
 as producer, 203–4
Kelly, Paula, 48
Kern, Jerome, 27, 162
Kiger, Alan, 68, 74
Kind of Blue, 4, 187;
 improvisation on, 184–85;
 success of, 184–85
Klotzman, Dorothy, 174–75
Knepper, Jimmy, 38
Koenig, Lester, 139
Kogan, Robert, 173
"Koko," 191
Konitz, Lee, 197
Kresge Auditorium, 24
Kruger, Joe, 14–15
Kuhn, Steve, 27, 38–40, 42, 48, 63, 203

LaBarbera, Joe, 181, 219
LaFaro, Scotty, 47, 87, 112;
 Coleman and, 166–67;
 death of, 1–3;

Evans, B., and, 4, 106;
friendship with, 88–89;
Israels, C., on replacing, 105–6
Land, Harold, 30
La Porta, John, 38
Laredo, Jaime, 21–22
Laredo, Ruth, 16
La Roca, Pete, 50, 169
Latin music, 49–50
Laws, Hubert, 46
Leadbelly, 13, 15, 211
Ledbetter, Huddie. *See* Leadbelly
left-wing activism, 14
Lenox School of Jazz, 47
"Lester Leaps In," 165
Levin, Tony, 155
Levitt, Rod, 192
Lewis, John, 47, 67–68, 177, 208
Lewis, Mel, 219
Lexington Hotel, 75
Lincoln Center Jazz Orchestra, 208–9
Lionni, Leo, 54
Lionni, Nora, 54
Lionni, Paolo, 54
Lipkin, Seymour, 10, 16
Littleton, Humphrey, 136
Loesser, Arthur, 10
Loesser, Frank, 64
Los Angeles, 138
"Love for Sale," 183, 185
Lucas, Dave, 127
Lucier, Alvin, 53
Lydian scale, 68–69

Ma, Yo-Yo, 214
MacDonald, Ralph, 155
Mackay, Dave, 126
Maderna, Bruno, 173
Madrid, 60–62
"Maiden Voyage," 179–80, 188

"Main Stem," 191
Makem, Tommy, 136
Mariano, Charlie, 29
marijuana, 103
Marlboro Festival, 47
Marsalis, Wynton, 208–9
Mars Club, 57
Marshall, Maria, 76
Martinelli, Bruno, 91
Martino, Pat, 179–80, 197
Max Roach's Quintet, 47
Maxwell, Jimmy, 180, 190
Maye, Marilyn, 127
Mayer, Jon, 57–58, 62
McCarthyism, 14
McCracken, Hugh, 155
McEwan, Vinnie, 49
McFerrin, Bobby, 188
McGhee, Brownie, 13, 211
McGhee, Howard, 40–41
McKusick, Hal, 38
McLean, Don, 123
Meckler, Ruth, 21–22
Menotti, Gian Carlo, 90
Merrick, David, 157
Mers El Kébir, Algeria, 58
Mester, Jorge, 1, 90
Michelot, Pierre, 57
Migliori, Jay, 51
Miles Davis Quintet, 42
Mills, Fred, 90
Mingus, Charles, 2, 4, 25, 38, 90, 92, 167;
friendship with, 127–29
MIT, 23–24, 27, 28, 30–31, 193
Mitchell, Red, 29, 61, 63, 120, 204
Mobley, Hank, 28
Modern Jazz Quartet, 47, 97, 177
Monk, Thelonious, 124, 127, 150, 167, 177, 189–90, 215–16;
compositional style of, 194;

Israels, C., on, 194–95
Monteverdi, Claudio, 38
Montgomery, Wes, 90, 158
Montoliu, Tete, 61–62
Montrose, J. R., 51
"Moon Taj," 179
Moore, Dudley, 136
Moore, Mike, 218
"Moose the Mooche," 165
Mordente, Tony, 20
Morgenstern, Dan, 46–47
Morosco, Vic, 90
Morton, Jelly Roll, 162, 165, 191
Moseholm, Eric, 92
Moskowitz, Belle Lindner (grandmother), 7
Mostel, Zero, 148
Motian, Paul, 87, 95, 105, 119, 203–4;
 Evans, B., and, 108;
 play style of, 108
Mount Auburn, 47, 48–49, 63–64, 65
Mount Vernon, 7
Mucci, Louis, 38
Mulligan, Gerry, 25, 28, 71, 145, 197
Murray, Ed, 16
music theory, 37–38
Mussulli, Boots, 29, 40–41
"My Bells," 142
"My Funny Valentine," 137
"My Old Kentucky Home," 162

National Association of Jazz Educators, 199
National Endowment for the Arts, 178
National Jazz Ensemble, 180, 217–18, 219;
 audience development for, 190–91;
 conceptual formation of, 178–80;
 in Greenwich Village, 196;
 repertoire of, 192–93;
 transcriptions published by, 210
"Nefertiti," 192
Nelson, Oliver, 4, 90
nervousness, 44
Netherlands, 136–37
Neves, John, 25, 26
The New Blues Quartet, 59
Newhart, Bob, 20–21
New Orleans, 208
The New School, 196
Newsum, Phil, 50
New World Symphony, 12
"New World Symphony," 202
New York:
 Evans, B., in, 143–44;
 jazz scene in, 74
New York State Council on the Arts, 178
"Night Creature," 141
nineteenth century, 161–62
North Texas State, 219
Norvo, Red, 76
Now Is the Time . . . (Broadway show), 169
Nureyev, Rudolf, 91

O'Brien, Hod, 47
Ogerman, Claus, 140–42
"Oh! Susanna," 162
O'Neal, Hank, 196
"On Green Mountain," 38
orchestration, 152
Orfuss, Irv, 20
Ormandy, Eugene, 77
Otto's, 51

Overton, Hall, 152, 155–56, 171, 172–73, 179;
  arrangements of, 192;
  learning from, 148–50
Owens, Jimmy, 181–82

Panzéra, Charles, 17
Paris, 54;
  Powell in, 54–56
Parker, Charlie, 63, 68, 124, 141, 163, 205;
  improvisation of, 183;
  Israels, C., on, 193–96;
  press recognition of, 69–71
"Peace Piece," 93, 184, 187, 189
Peacock, Gary, 111, 114, 203–4
Perowsky, Frank, 90
personal growth, 193–94
Petrillo, James, 70
Pettiford, Oscar, 2, 50–51, 63, 110, 204
Phillips, Pete, 179
piano, 148, 161–62
Pierson, Tom, 192
pit musicians, 157, 169–70
Pleshette, Suzanne, 20
"Polka Dots and Moonbeams," 101
Pomeroy, Herb, 25, 26, 152, 192
Pope, Odean, 49
Popular Concert Attractions, 15
popular culture:
  baby boomers and, 164;
  Coltrane in, 165–66;
  critique of, 220;
  deterioration of popular music, 220;
  jazz in, 163, 188–89, 204–5, 210–11;
  music in, 161–62
Porgy and Bess (opera), 13

Porter, Cole, 13, 27, 64, 162, 183
Portland, 214
Possell, Jacques, 10
Powell, Bud, 3–4, 25, 93–94, 148, 193, 195, 203;
  in Paris, 54–56
Powell, Richie, 30
practice, 16–17
Prestige, 204
Prince, Bob, 1, 91
Promises, Promises (Broadway show), 169
Proskauer, Joseph, 34
Pryor, Richard, 113
public domain, 201
Purcell, Henry, 202, 215

radio, 162–63
Ramone, Phil, 154, 155
Rampal, Jean-Pierre, 214
Raney, Jimmy, 112, 148
Raph, Alan, 143
Ray, Nick, 61, 62
"Ray's Idea," 25
RCA, 204
Redd, Freddie, 51
Red Lion Inn, 46
Red Norvo Trio, 25–26
"Re: Person I Knew," 100
"Repetition," 141
Rhein, Bill, 21–22, 24
rhythm sections, 3;
  importance of, 93;
  in rock music, 164–65;
  syncopation, 211
Richardson, Jerome, 57
Riley, Ben, 119, 128, 195
Ripley, Robert, 9
"Riverboat Shuffle," 10
Riverside Records, 4, 203
Roach, Max, 29, 47

Robbins, Jerome, 1, 5, 14, 17
Robeson, Paul, 10, 13
Robinson, Perry, 58–59
Robison, Paula, 1, 2, 5, 89, 91
"Rockin' in Rhythm," 179
rock music:
  jazz and, 189–90, 212;
  rhythm sections in, 164–65
Rogers, Barry, 151
Roker, Mickey, 125
Rollins, Jack, 124
Rollins, Sonny, 189–90, 195
Ronell, Ann, 107
Roosevelt, Eleanor, 37
Roseland Ballroom, 157
Rosen, Jerry, 16, 21–22
Rosenblith, Walter, 23, 31
Rouse, Charlie, 195
Rovère, Paul, 56, 57
Rowles, Jimmy, 131
Royal, Ernie, 143
Rubenstein, Harry, 64
Rubin, Alan, 171
Rubinstein, Arthur, 169
The Rubiot, 133
Ruff, Willie, 151
Rushing, Jimmy, 76
Russell, George, 4, 5, 38, 47, 85, 112, 192;
  working with, 67–69, 77, 203

Salter, Bill, 20, 49, 50
Sangarro, Louis, 59–60
Sankey, Stuart, 123
San Rafael, 131
Santisi, Ray, 26
Sauter, Eddie, 141
Savoy, 204
Scharf, Stuart, 153
Schoolhouse Rock! (cartoon), 47
Schubert, Franz, 12–13

Schuller, Gunther, 38, 47, 67–68, 155–56, 181, 190;
  relationship with, 85
Schultz, Ellaine, 97, 102–3
Scott, Ronnie, 135–36
Scriabin, Alexander, 88, 93
Scruggs, Earl, 124
SEATO. *See* Southeast Asia Treaty Organization
Seeger, Pete, 10, 11, 13, 17
session musicians, 158
Severance Hall, 13
Severinsen, Doc, 180
Shahn, Ben, 90
Shapero, Harold, 38, 148
Sheen, Mickey, 76
sheet music, 161–62
Shelly's Manne-Hole, 119–20
"Shifting Down," 45
Shihab, Sahib, 57
Shorter, Wayne, 192
Shure, Leonard, 11
Silver, Horace, 63, 87–88, 177, 186–87
Sim, Pierre, 91–92
Simmons, Art, 57
Simon, Carly, 123
Simon, Lucy, 123
Simon, Neil, 169
Simon, Paul, 152;
  meeting with, 153;
  working with, 154–55
Simone, Nina, 127
Simon Sisters, 123, 125
simplicity, 183–84
Sims, Zoot, 76, 116, 135
"Sippin' at Bells," 68
Smith, Al, 7, 37
Smith, Carrie, 197
Smith, C. Ruggles, 33
Smith, Jimmy, 139

Solal, Martial, 56, 58, 91–92
"Somewhere (over the rainbow)," 164
Sousa, John Philip, 162
Southeast Asia Treaty Organization (SEATO), 115
"So What," 183–84, 185–86, 189
spirituals, 13
Spoleto, 1, 91
The Stable, 48–49
"The Stars and Stripes Forever," 162
"Stella by Starlight," 132
Stern, Isaac, 77
Still Crazy After All These Years, 155
Stinson, Albert, 110
Stock, Jaxon, 191–92
Stockbridge, 123, 153
Stockholm, 136
Storyville, 26–27
"Stratusphunk," 68
Strauss, Richard, 1
Stravinsky, Igor, 91, 173, 215
Strayhorn, Billy, 178, 180, 194, 208
Streisand, Barbra, 127
Stroyberg, Annette, 54
"Suite En Ré Bemol," 56–57
"Summertime," 14
Sunday at the Village Vanguard, 89
Swallow, Steve, 93, 110, 112, 116
"Swanee River," 162
Sweden, 134–35;
  Evans, B., in, 134–36
"Sweet Emma," 192
swing, 52
"Swing Spring," 192
symphony orchestras, 177
syncopation, 211

"Take Five," 94
Tanglewood, 45–46, 47
Tannenbaum, Mike, 153
The Tarriers, 123, 125
Tate, Grady, 140, 145
Taylor, Cecil, 53, 68, 142–43, 167, 203;
  recording with, 42–43, 45
Taylor, Creed, 111;
  as producer, 204–5
teaching, 174–75
Tee, Richard, 155
Teenage Jazz Club, 29–30
Temperley, Joe, 209
Terry, Clark, 135, 143
Terry, Sonny, 13, 211
Tetley, Glen, 91
Thomas, Bobby, 90, 169
Thomas, Michael Tilson, 46
Thomas, Rene, 51
Thompson, Lucky, 58
Tillotson, Brooks, 157
"Time Remembered," 141–42
Timmons, Bobby, 128, 195
Tivoli Gardens, 136
Tofani, Dave, 151
The Tonight Show, 180
Torkanowsky, Werner, 90
Town Hall concert, 144, 146
transcriptions:
  of Ellington, 210;
  of jazz, 179;
  by National Jazz Ensemble, 210
Transition Records, 41
Triangle Shirtwaist Factory fire, 7
the Trident, 131–32
Trio 64, 112, 203–4
Trio '65, 204
Tristano, Lennie, 3, 126
Trout Quintet, 195
Tulsa, 133

Tunick, Jonathan, 169
Turrentine, Stanley, 57
Twardzik, Dick, 29

Undercurrent, 137
Unfinished Symphony, 12
Urtreger, Rene, 57

Vadim, Roger, 54
Van Gelder, Rudy, 144–45
Vanguard Records, 65
Vaughan, Sarah, 178
Verrett, Shirley, 90
Verve Records, 111, 143–44, 204–5
Vicenzio, Fernando, 62
Village Gate, 217
Village Vanguard, 2, 74, 97, 126
Villchur, Ed, 64
violin, 110

Waldron, Mal, 46
Waller, Fats, 13, 27, 162
Waltz for Debby, 135
"Waltz for Debby," 134
Warren, Harry, 27, 162
Watkins, Doug, 28
Watrous, Bill, 143
Weavers, 10, 14, 211
Wechsler, Larry, 157
Wein, George, 26–27, 29
Weissberg, Eric, 123–24
Weston, Randy, 46
"What Kind of Fool Am I," 139
Wheeler, Harold, 169, 171

"When the Saints Go Marching In," 202
Whiskey Jazz Club, 59
White, Josh, 211
Whitsell, Dick, 119
"Who Can I Turn To?," 204
Wilder, Thornton, 200
Wilen, Barney, 57
Williams, Buster, 179
Williams, Martin, 47
Williams, Tommy, 112
Williams, Tony, 49, 156
"Willow Weep for Me," 107
Wilson, Tom, 28, 45, 203;
  friendship with, 41–42
Winter, Paul, 119
Wise, Arnie, *48*, 51, 57–58, 126, *144*, 203;
  Evans, B., and, 140;
  playing with, 38–40
Wolf Trap Foundation, 178
Woods, Phil, 57, 135, 197
World War II, 27
Wyble, Jimmy, 76

Yanow, Scott, 142
Young, David, 68
Young, Victor, 27

Zawinul, Joe, 213
Zebra Lounge, 24, 25
Zetterlund, Monica, 134, 135
Zigmund, Elliot, 217
Zitano, Jimmy, 25, 26, 42